Public Interest in Criminal Prosecution in the Modern Era

Public Interest in Criminal Prosecution in the Modern Era

A Comparative Analysis

Edited by Rahime Erbaş

BLOOMSBURY ACADEMIC
NEW YORK • LONDON • OXFORD • NEW DELHI • SYDNEY

BLOOMSBURY ACADEMIC
Bloomsbury Publishing Inc, 1359 Broadway, New York, NY 10018, USA
Bloomsbury Publishing Plc, 50 Bedford Square, London, WC1B 3DP, UK
Bloomsbury Publishing Ireland, 29 Earlsfort Terrace, Dublin 2, D02 AY28, Ireland

First published in the United States of America 2026

A catalog record for this book is available from the Library of Congress.

ISBN: HB: 979-8-216-38054-2
ePDF: 979-8-216-38056-6
eBook: 979-8-216-38055-9

Typeset by Integra Software Services Pvt. Ltd.

For product safety related questions contact productsafety@bloomsbury.com.

Contents

Cases

Alexandria City Court (Romania), Criminal Sentence 110 of 23 January 2018
Ashif and Ashraf v HM Advocate [2015] HCJAC 100
Bacău City Court (Romania) - Criminal Section, Sentence no. 1262 of 28 September 2016 penal/confirmare-renuntare-urmarire-penala-jurisprudenta-1262-2016
Beggs v HM Advocate [2025] HCJAC 69
Chang Wing-Siu [1985] AC 168
Collins v HM Advocate [2013] HCJAC 167
Constitutional Court of Romania, Decision no. 23 of 2016, published in the Official Gazette no. 240 of 31 March 2016
Constitutional Court of Romania, Decision no. 390 of 2 July 2014, published in the Official Gazette of Romania, Part I, no. 532 of 17 July 2014
Decision of the Constitutional Court of Ukraine (CCU) (Second Senate) of 18 June 2020, No. 5-p(II)/2020
Decision of the CCU of 1 December 2004, No. 18-рп/2004
Decision of the CCU of 16 June 2011, No. 6-рп/2011
Decision of the CCU of 16 July 2019, No. 9-p/2019
Decision of the CCU of 19 October 2009, No. 26-рп/2009
Decision of the CCU of 1 June 2016, No. 2-рп/2016
Decision of the CCU of 8 April 1999, No. 3-рп/1999
Decision of the CCU (Second Senate) of 5 June 2019, No. 4-p(II)/2019
Ferguson v HM Advocate [2008] HCJAC 71
Gordon v HM Advocate [2018] HCJAC 21
Goryaynova v Ukraine, App no 41752/09 (ECHR, 8 October 2020, final 8 January 2021)
Guja v Moldova, App no 14277/04 (ECHR, 12 February 2008)
Hay v HM Advocate 1968 JC 40
High Court of Cassation and Justice of Bucharest (Romania) Decision No. XXXV of 6 November 2006 in File no. 25/2006, Published in the Official Gazette, Part I no. 368 of 30 May 2007
HM Advocate v ARK and AR [2013] HCJAC 107
HM Advocate v Cairns 1967 JC 37
HM Advocate v Cooney [2022] HCJAC 10

HM Advocate v PG and JM [2024] HCJAC 43
Iaşi City Court (Romania), Criminal Sentence no. 534 of 18 May 2017
Jackson v HM Advocate [2017] HCJAC 72
Jogee [2016] UKSC 8; [2017] A.C. 387.
Judgment of the Constitutional Tribunal (Poland) 16 June 1999, P 4/98
Judgment of the Court of Appeal in Szczecin 10 April 2014, case no II AKa 48/14, LEX no 1459031
Judgment of the Supreme Court 6 September 2001, case no V KKN 216/01, OSP No 3 (2002) item 44
King's Advocate v Lord Dunglas (1836) 15 S 314
Kolevi v Bulgaria, App no 1108/02 (ECHR, 5 November 2009)
LB v HM Advocate 2003 JC 94
Lord Advocate's Reference (No. 1 of 2023) [2023] HCJAC 40
MacDonald v HM Advocate [2020] HCJAC 21
McBain v Crichton 1961 JC 25
Miln v Cullen 1967 JC 21
Opuz v Turkey (2010) 50 EHRR 28.
Özkan Kart v Turkey, App no 24241/09 (ECHR, 31 May 2016)
R v Coutts [2006] 1 WLR 2154
R v R [1992] 1 AC 599
Ramos Nunes de Carvalho e Sá v Portugal, Apps nos 55391/13, 57728/13 and 74041/13 (ECHR, 6 November 2018)
Resolution of the Supreme Court of Ukraine, 18 October 2018, Case No 822/3692/17
Resolution of the Supreme Court of Ukraine, 23 July 2020, Case No 925/383/18
Resolution of the Supreme Court of Ukraine, 25 April 2018, Case No 806/1000/17
Resolution of the Supreme Court of Ukraine, 26 June 2019
Resolution of the Supreme Court of Ukraine, 26 July 2018, Case No 926/1111/15
Resolution of the Supreme Court of Ukraine, 31 October 2019, Case No 923/35/19
Ruling of the Supreme Court of Ukraine, 5 April 2021, Case No 420/8512/20
Ruling of the Supreme Court of Ukraine, 5 January 2023, Case No 991/5572/22
SJ v HM Advocate [2020] HCJAC 18
The 34th Batch of Guiding Cases by the Supreme People's Procuratorate: Lang and He Defamation Case (Guiding Case No. 137)

The Second of the Third Batch of Five Typical Cases on Corporate Compliance Reform Involving Enterprises: Wang XX Case of Disclosure of Insider Information and Jin XX Case of Insider Trading

Toal v HM Advocate [2012] HCJAC 123

Van Phan v HM Advocate [2018] HCJAC 7

X v Sweeney 1982 JC 70

Yargıtay, 16.C.D., Date. 29 November 2017, E. 2016/7553, K. 2017/5508 (UYAP, 29 April 2018).

Legislations

Act of 26 July 2024 amending certain acts to improve the operations of the Armed Forces of the Republic of Poland, the Police, and the Border Guard in the event of a threat to state security

Act of 28 January 2016 – Law on the Public Prosecutor's Office

Announcement of the Marshal of the Sejm of the Republic of Poland of 20 February 2024 on the publication of the consolidated text of the Act – Law on the Public Prosecutor's Office

Bail and Release from Custody (Scotland) Act 2023

Circular 1/2015, of 19 June, of the State Attorney General's Office, on guidelines for the exercise of criminal action in relation to minor offences following the criminal reform introduced by Organic Law 1/2015 (FIS-C-2015-00001)

Civil Procedural Code of Ukraine (2004) No 1618-IV [VVR 2004, No 40-41, 42, art 492]

Child Protection Code in 2005 No. 5395

Code on the Establishment, Duties, and Powers of First Instance Courts and Regional Courts of Appeal in 2004 No. 5235

Constitution of the People's Republic of China (2018 Amendment)

Constitution of the Republic of Poland 1997

Constitution of Ukraine (1996) No 254к/96-ВР [VVR 1996, No 30, art 141]

Convention on the Rights of the Child, approved by the United Nations General Assembly on 20 November 1989 (Resolution 44/25)

Coronavirus (Recovery and Reform) (Scotland) Act 2022

Coronavirus (Recovery and Reform) (Scotland) Act 2022 (Extension of Temporary Justice Measures) Regulations 2024 (SSI 2024/322)

Council of Europe Convention on preventing and combating violence against women and domestic violence, done at Istanbul on 11 May 2011

Council of Europe Recommendation No. R (87) 18 on the Simplification of Criminal Justice

Council Framework Decision 2001/220/JHA

Criminal Code of the Republic of Macedonia

Criminal Law of the People's Republic of China (2023 Amendment)

Criminal Procedure Law of the People's Republic of China (2018 Amendment)

Criminal Procedure (Scotland) Act 1995

Criminal Procedural Code of Ukraine (2012) No 4651-VI [VVR 2013, No 9-10, No 11-12, No 13]

Directive 2012/29/EU of the European Parliament and of the Council of 25 October 2012 establishing minimum standards on the rights, support and protection of victims of crime and replacing Council Framework Decision 2001/220/JHA of 15 March 2001 on the standing of victims in criminal proceedings (*Official Journal of the European Union* L 315/57 of 14.11.2012)

Execution and Security Measures Code in 2005 No. 5275

German Penal Procedure Code

Human Rights Act 1998 (UK)

Law 4/2015, of 27 April, on the Statute of the Victim of Crime ("BOE" n. 101, of 28/04/2015)

Law of Ukraine 'On Amendments to the Constitution of Ukraine (regarding justice)' (2016) No 1401-VIII [VVR 2016, No 28]

Law of Ukraine 'On National Security of Ukraine' (2018) No 2469-VIII [VVR 2018, No 31]

Law of Ukraine 'On Protection of Childhood' (2001) No 2402-III [VVR 2001, No 30, p 142]

Law of Ukraine 'On Sanctions' (2014) No 1644-VII [VVR 2014, No 40, art 2018]

Law of Ukraine 'On the Constitutional Court of Ukraine' (2017) No 2136-VIII [VVR 2017, No 35, p 376]

Law of Ukraine 'On the Judiciary and the Status of Judges' (2016) No 1402-VIII [VVR 2016, No 31, art 545]

Law of Ukraine 'On the Prosecutor's Office' (2014) No 1697-VII [VVR 2015, No 2-3, p 12]

Law on Amendments of the Criminal Code, Official Gazette of the Republic of North Macedonia 7/2008

Law on Amendments of the Criminal Code, Official Gazette of the Republic of Macedonia 139/2008

Law on Amending the Law on Criminal Procedure, Official Gazette of the Republic of Macedonia 28/2014

Law on Criminal Procedure, Official Gazette of the Republic of Macedonia 150/10, 100/12, 142/16, 198/18

Law on Execution of Sanctions, Official Gazette of the Republic of North Macedonia 99/19, 220/19, 236/22, 74/24

Law on the Determination of the Type of Sentence and the Determination of the Length of the Sentence, Official Gazette of the Republic of Macedonia 199/2014

Law on Prevention of Corruption and Conflict of interests, Official Gazette of the Republic of Macedonia 12/2019

Mehakim-i Nizamiye'nin Teşkilatı Kanun-ı Muvakkatı (Turkish)

Police and Fire Reform (Scotland) Act 2012

Prosecution of Offences Act 1879

Public Prosecution Service for Northern Ireland, Code for Prosecutors (2023)

Recommendation [85] 2 of 28 June 1985 of the Committee of Ministers of the Council of Europe on the position of the victim in criminal law and criminal procedure

Recommendation [87] 21 of 17 September 1987 of the Committee of Ministers of the Council of Europe on assistance to victims and the prevention of victimization

Recommendation [99] 19 of 15 September 1999 of the Committee of Ministers of the Council of Europe on mediation in criminal matters

Recommendation REC(2000)19 of the Committee of Ministers of the Council of Europe on the Role of the Public Prosecution in the Criminal Justice System (6 October 2000) https://rm.coe.int/16804be55a accessed 9 January 2025

Road Traffic Offenders Act 1988

Scotland Act 1998

Organic Law 6/1985, of 1 July, of the Judiciary ("BOE" n. 157, of 02/07/1985)

Organic Law 10/1995, of 23 November 1995, of the Criminal Code ("BOE" n. 281, of 24/11/1995)

Organic Law 5/2000, of 12 January, regulating the criminal responsibility of minors ("BOE" n. 11, of 13/01/2000)

Organic Law 1/2004, of 28 December, on Comprehensive Protection Measures against Gendered Violence ("BOE" n. 313, of 29/12/2004)

Organic Law 8/2006, of 4 December, which modifies Organic Law 5/2000, of 12 January, Regulating the Criminal Responsibility of Minors ("BOE" n. 290, of 5/12/2006)

Organic Law 1/2015, of 30 March 2015 amending Organic Law 10/1995, of 23 November 1995 on the Criminal Code ("BOE" núm. 77, de 31/03/2015)

Organic Law 10/2022, of 6 September, on the comprehensive guarantee of sexual freedom ("BOE" n. 215, of 07/09/2022)

Organic Law 1/2025, of 2 January, on Measures for the Efficiency of the Public Justice Service ("BOE" n. 3, of 03/01/2025)

Organic Law of the People's Procuratorates of the People's Republic of China (2018 Revision)

Royal Decree of 14 September 1882 approving the Criminal Procedure Act ("Gaceta de Madrid" n. 260, of 17/09/1882)

Swedish Code of Judicial Procedure (1998)

Kanun-i Esasi in 1876 (the first Constitution of the Ottoman Empire)

The Code for Crown Prosecutors (*CPS*,1986)

The Code for Crown Prosecutors (*CPS*, 2004)

The Code for Crown Prosecutors (*CPS*, 2018)

Turkish Constitution (1982)

Turkish Penal Code in 2005, No. 5237

Turkish Penal Procedure Code in 1929 No. 1412 (The former)

Turkish Penal Procedure Code in 2005 No. 5271

Victims and Witnesses (Scotland) Act 2014

Victims, Witnesses, and Justice Reform (Scotland) Bill

Acknowledgements

This edited book project was first conceived during my postdoctoral research at Glasgow Law School in Scotland (2023–2024). I gratefully acknowledge the support of the Scientific and Technological Research Council of Türkiye (TÜBİTAK), whose funding made this research possible. I am also especially thankful to all my colleagues in Criminal Law and Criminal Justice at Glasgow, particularly Prof. Lindsay Farmer and Prof. Fiona Leverick, for their encouragement, insightful discussions and the inspiring academic environment they created.

I would like to extend my heartfelt gratitude to all the contributors of this book. My deepest thanks go to Prof. Dr. Valentina Bonini and Anu Sivaganesan, whose unwavering support and belief in this project meant more than words can express.

I am also profoundly grateful to my family for their unconditional love and support.

Finally, I am deeply grateful to Ryan Dradzynski for his outstanding guidance and assistance during the publishing process.

—Rahime

Foreword

Prosecutors are central actors in all modern criminal justice systems, yet for a long time surprisingly little attention has been paid to how they make decisions. It is common to come across references to prosecutorial discretion, even in systems which supposedly try to eradicate discretion through the principle of legality. But it has become increasingly important to try and understand how that discretion is structured and operates in practice.

Beyond the requirement that there be a sufficiency of evidence, most modern criminal justice systems pay lip service to a principle that (amongst other things) prosecution should be in the public interest, but it is not always clear what this means. One of the great virtues of this book is that it explores this question both from a comparative perspective – looking at a large and intriguing range of jurisdictions – and from a normative or theoretical perspective. This sheds important new light on how the public interest is understood in different jurisdictions, how it is related to the institutional history and legal culture of prosecution in those jurisdictions, and indeed on what different jurisdictions might learn from each other as they engage with the question of what the public interest means in complex modern societies.

A range of important issues emerge from the discussion in the essays in this book. Once the persistence of an irreducible element of discretion has been recognized, the questions are how this discretion should be structured, how the independence of prosecutors can be protected from undue political influence, which factors (or whose interests) should be weighed in prosecutorial decisions, and (of increasing importance) how these decisions should be made both transparent and accountable. And the answers to these questions are then understood as being bound up with the different ways in which we understand the public interest. The public interest is referred to give guidance on what sort of crimes should be prosecuted or when an individual or a form of conduct should not be prosecuted (or prosecution discontinued). The public interest is cited to defend the independence of prosecutors from police or other criminal justice agencies – even where they are presumed to be working in the public interest as well. And the public interest is also cited as a principle which can be used to defend prosecutors from political influence. At the same time, the public interest might be invoked to support the demand that prosecutors act to respond to concerns about crime rates or a rise in particular kinds of anti-social conduct. The public interest might demand that certain individual offenders, or a class of offenders (such as juveniles) be treated differently. And the public interest is increasingly relied on by the victims of crime to argue that their interests be properly recognized, or represented, in prosecutorial decisions. We can see then that the public interest in prosecution can mean many different things in different contexts, and so it is important to understand what it might mean.

There is one last sense in which it is increasingly important to interrogate the idea of the public interest, and that concerns the transparency and accountability of prosecutorial decisions. It is all too easy for prosecutors to use the idea that they acted in the public interest as a shield, to protect their conduct from scrutiny. If a decision was made in good faith in the public interest, how can it be challenged? However, there are increasing moves towards turning this idea on its head and to explore the different ways in which prosecutors might be made accountable to victims and their families, to those who are prosecuted, and to the communities which they serve. The idea of the public interest, in other words can be used to support the demand for transparency and accountability.

These are the significant empirical, political and normative questions that are raised by the fascinating essays in this book and it is to be hoped that collectively this can help to bring the question of the meaning of the public interest in prosecution to the forefront of discussions of contemporary criminal justice.

Lindsay Farmer
University of Glasgow

Introduction

Mapping the role of public interest across legal traditions

Rahime Erbaş

Some concepts in criminal law do not merely resist definition, but they transcend it. They are vast, fluid and elusive, yet they lie at the very heart of legal reasoning. Like the oxygen we breathe, their presence is often unnoticed, but their absence is immediately and deeply felt. Public interest is one such concept. It sustains the life of the criminal justice system silently, shaping outcomes through unspoken values and normative instincts. It is essential without being fully seen, powerful without being precisely pinned down.

Once sufficient evidence has been obtained, it is the public interest that lies at the heart of the decision to prosecute.[1] However, public interest is a broad and vague term, for which no universally accepted definition exists across legal systems or scholarly literature. It remains, indeed, a cornerstone of modern criminal justice, playing a crucial role in both initiating and preventing prosecutions, depending on the jurisdiction's legal framework and understanding. In some jurisdictions, public interest functions as a mandatory criterion requiring prosecution, while in others, it serves as a guiding principle to justify whether a prosecution should proceed. To put it another way, in some cases, public interest serves as a key that opens a set of doors through the prosecution, while in others it serves gatekeeper of criminal prosecutions. Consequently, the authority responsible for determining public interest effectively becomes either the initiator or the gatekeeper of the criminal justice process. As is often said about prosecutors, 'most of the time, they do not even face a challenger'[2] for their decisions (particularly no-prosecution decisions) prior to trial. For example, in Scotland, because of the wide range of powers of the procurator fiscal in weighing public interest, the procurator fiscal is considered as the gatekeeper of the Scottish criminal process.[3] Since the prosecutor's decisions are not public like court rulings, there are concerns regarding the principles of equality, consistency and transparency.[4] Japanese law similarly establishes a gatekeeping function for prosecutors/prosecutorial office within its criminal justice system.[5]

In contrast to the Scottish example, in the criminal justice systems of China, North Macedonia, Romania and Türkiye, the discretion of public prosecutors in weighing public interest is far more restricted, resulting in the majority of cases referred to prosecutors proceeding to prosecution. These remarks represent only the most preliminary insights I have derived from this book.

Taking a more nuanced view of the matter, it may be argued that the degree of prosecutorial discretion in assessing public interest is often shaped by whether a legal system leans towards an adversarial or inquisitorial model. However, contemporary challenges such as the heavy volume of cases handled by the courts, the rise of managerialism and the need for efficiency in the criminal justice system compel jurisdictions of all types in order to reassess the role of public interest in prosecutions. Regardless of the procedural model or jurisdiction, various factors such as the gravity of the offence serve as benchmarks for evaluating public interest in criminal justice. While public interest considerations influence whether prosecutions proceed, the decisions made by those exercising this discretion are often opaque and subject to little scrutiny. In most jurisdictions, prosecutorial decisions regarding whether to prosecute in the public interest are neither published nor made publicly accessible as Colvin has rightly noted that 'prosecutorial discretion is often seen as mysterious and impenetrable'.[6] This lack of transparency raises concerns about prosecutorial independence and accountability; as McManus thus recommended the introduction of *a publicly available marking system* on prosecutor's decisions in the Scottish example.[7] Even when jurisdictions provide mechanisms for victims to challenge prosecutorial decisions or allow private prosecutions, the broader decision-making process remains largely unchecked, posing challenges to the principle of justice and equality before the law.

Unlike the well-established efforts to standardize judicial sentencing, the harmonization of prosecutorial discretion in applying public interest remains an underexplored area. For example, in England and Wales, as a common law jurisdiction, a Sentencing Council provides guidance to judges, whereas in Türkiye, following the Continental European model, the Penal Code prescribes a structured framework for determining and individualizing punishments. Conversely, similar mechanisms for prosecutors are either severely limited in scope or do not exist at all. As a matter of fact, in Turkish law, the prosecutor's authority to evaluate the public interest is often viewed with concern. Rather than granting prosecutors broad discretion, the legal system tends to prescribe alternative measures through detailed conditions and specific procedural sequences, effectively limiting prosecutorial discretion. However, considering that the very nature of prosecution is inherently tied to discretionary decision-making processes,[8] it becomes clear that further engagement with the concept of 'public interest' is essential.

Notably, many scholarly works begin by attempting to clarify the conditions under which the public interest test should be applied such as the gravity of crime which is a commendable effort in itself. This is often noted as 'challenges in framing the discretion to prosecute'.[9] Yet, Chapter 1 by Kajsa Dinesson goes a step further by demonstrating the need for a normative foundation for the concept of public interest within the context of England and Wales, highlighting the increasing significance of this principle in prosecutorial decision-making. The creation of the CPS in England and Wales initiated key discussions around principles and normative frameworks in prosecutorial practice as Chapter 1 depicted. To Dinesson, public prosecutors hold significant responsibility and influence in the justice system, yet there is a clear lack of clarity regarding the purpose of their power in the context of England and Wales.

Chapter 1 provides a particularly valuable case study through its focus on England and Wales, where the public prosecution service – established relatively recently (in 1986) compared to many jurisdictions – offers a revealing lens into the evolution of the modern prosecutorial role. Chapter 1 demonstrates that, despite its institutional youth, the CPS has become a central actor in shaping discretionary decision-making and applying the public interest test. The chapter traces, almost as a legal and conceptual journey, how debates over prosecutorial discretion, institutional identity and normative legitimacy have developed from 1986 to the present. As such, it serves as a compelling narrative of how a prosecution service can grow into a modern legal actor with significant normative responsibilities.

The next chapter turns to Scotland, a jurisdiction with a much older prosecutorial tradition as a national public prosecution service and a *sui generis* approach to criminal procedure within the UK context.[10] Chapter 2 by Pamela R. Ferguson focuses on the historically rooted and well-established structure of the Scottish prosecution service, as well as the broad discretionary powers it exercises in assessing the public interest. These features mark a clear departure in Scotland from the English and Welsh systems. The broad scope of authority exercised by the Scottish prosecutor in public interest assessments makes it a compelling and instructive case study. Ferguson draws attention to the fact that Scotland's prosecution service has a much longer history than those of the other UK jurisdictions. Scottish prosecutors have always held considerable discretion in deciding whether to prosecute a case, a key feature of the Scottish legal system. Historically, the prosecution of crime in Scotland was the responsibility of the victims or their families, a form of 'private prosecution' that still exists for serious crimes, though it is now rare. Ferguson emphasizes the role of the public interest in prosecutions, particularly the appeal court's focus on ensuring that prosecutions are 'efficient and expeditious'. Timely trials and bringing cases to a swift conclusion are seen as essential components of serving the public interest.

Ferguson focuses on the unique role of the public interest test in the Scottish prosecution system, applied even when there is sufficient admissible evidence to proceed. According to the Crown Office and Procurator Fiscal Service (COPFS) Prosecution Code, prosecutors must weigh thirteen public interest considerations before deciding to prosecute. These include the seriousness of the offence, its impact on victims and witnesses, the personal circumstances of both the accused and the victim, the motive for the crime and the risk of reoffending. Additional factors such as mitigating circumstances, the potential consequences of prosecution for the accused, and the availability of civil remedies, also play a role. To Ferguson, this structured yet flexible approach reflects the wide discretionary authority granted to Scottish prosecutors and underscores the system's emphasis on fairness, proportionality and public confidence.

Chapter 3 by Bartłomiej Oręziak and Marcin Wielec analyses the role of the prosecutor in Polish criminal proceedings as both a guardian of the rule of law and an advocate for the public interest. It demonstrates that the rule of law, while lacking a strict legal definition, functions as a dynamic, value-laden principle embedded in Poland's legal system. This principle is closely tied to legality and influences how public interest is perceived and implemented. The chapter emphasizes that the prosecutor operates within a legal framework defined by the Criminal Procedure Code and the Constitution, but their actions also reflect deeper axiological commitments that transcend formal legality. These commitments include values rooted in Polish society and broader European legal culture. As such, the prosecutor's decisions must not only comply with legal norms but also align with the substantive values underpinning the rule of law. The analysis concludes that serving the public interest requires more than legal conformity; it demands a value-conscious interpretation of legal principles, ensuring that both legality and legitimacy are upheld in practice. This reinforces Kajsa Dinesson's call in Chapter 1 for a more principled normative framework, underscoring that prosecutorial legitimacy demands not only formal legal compliance but also a deep engagement with the foundational values of the rule of law.

In line with the foundational values of the rule of law, we now turn to Chapters 4 and 5, which explore how this approach is applied in specific contexts within Spain. Chapter 4 by Adán Carrizo González-Castell explores the circumstances that led to the introduction of the principle of opportunity in juvenile criminal proceedings in Spain, marking a departure from the traditional principles of officiality and legality that characterize the Spanish criminal justice system. Chapter 4 examines the motivations behind this shift, particularly in the context of juvenile justice, where the focus is often on the rehabilitation and best interests of minors. It further investigates the implications of the approval of Organic Law 10/2022, enacted on 6 September, concerning the Comprehensive Guarantee of Sexual Freedom. This law specifically addresses sexual and gender-based violence committed by minors and has had a significant impact on the application of the principle of opportunity. Chapter 4 also evaluates how this new legal framework affects the balance between the protection of minors' rights and the broader public interest in ensuring justice for victims of sexual violence and gendered crimes.

Chapter 5 by Selena Tierno Barrios focuses on the impact of the ongoing crisis in Spain's justice system, particularly in the field of criminal justice, and the growing importance of efficiency-driven reforms. It surveys the longstanding issue of slow and ineffective justice in Spain, particularly within the criminal justice system, where these deficiencies are most pronounced. In this context, Chapter 5 examines the growing trend towards the extension of the opportunity principle within Spanish criminal proceedings. Chapter 5 addresses recent criminal policies aimed at enhancing efficiency, including the regulation of criminal liability for legal persons, the implementation of compliance programmes, and the increased use of Alternative Dispute Resolution (ADR) in the criminal justice system. It further analyses how the opportunity principle and the concept of public interest are applied within these areas, specifically in relation to criminal proceedings involving legal persons.

Chapter 6 by Rahime Erbaş, Hüseyin Şık and Çiğdem Dönmez, traces the historical development and current structure of criminal prosecution in Türkiye. It outlines the emergence of the modern public prosecutor which is conceived as 'the Republic's Prosecutor' and examines the principle of mandatory prosecution as a defining feature of the system. While rooted in the continental European model, the Turkish framework is shown to have evolved distinctively, particularly in its restrictive approach to prosecutorial discretion. The chapter emphasizes that Turkish prosecutors are legally obliged to initiate investigations upon learning of a potential offence, and that the system excludes private prosecution, reflecting Türkiye's inquisitorial tradition. Although certain discretion-limiting reforms (such as prepayment or restorative justice or serial process) have been introduced, these measures remain tightly regulated and do not allow broad application of public interest considerations. As a result, Chapter 6 expresses concern over an increasing reliance on rigid formalism and procedural alternatives, such as prepayment, serial process and restorative justice mechanisms, which are used as functional substitutes for discretionary decision-making. These alternatives, while valuable, remain tightly regulated and do not compensate for the lack of a principled discretion model grounded in public interest in contrast to the Scottish example as addressed in Chapter 2.

Chapter 7 by Mihail Udroiu and Cristian Dumitru Miheş discussed several noteworthy decisions from Romanian courts, highlighting how, through careful and gradual reasoning, these courts have started to develop and apply public interest criteria in prosecutorial and judicial decision-making. Chapter 7 begins by examining Article 7 of the 2014 Romanian Code of Criminal Procedure, which sets out the prosecutor's obligation to initiate and conduct criminal proceedings ex officio. This reflects a strong emphasis on legality and official responsibility in Romanian criminal justice. It then explores how the former Criminal Code (specifically Article 18 index 1) allowed prosecutors and courts to avoid pursuing minor offences that lacked sufficient social danger, offering administrative sanctions as an alternative. Through this lens, Chapter 7 discusses how Romania has historically sought to balance the burden on the criminal justice system by recognizing degrees of harm and social interest.

Moving to the new Code in Romania, Chapter 7 highlights how Article 318 formally introduces the principle of opportunity, allowing prosecutors to dismiss or drop charges under strict and limited conditions when criminal prosecution would not serve the public interest. This reform reflects Romania's gradual shift from a strict legality principle towards a tempered approach that balances efficiency and fairness. Chapter 7 also addresses key controversies, including inconsistent jurisprudence regarding administrative sanctions for concurrent offences and the interaction between the opportunity principle and simplified procedures. Ultimately, it shows that while Romanian prosecutors now hold greater discretion in low-priority cases, this discretion is carefully regulated to maintain transparency and judicial oversight.

Chapter 8 by Aleksandra Gruevska Drakulevski and Aleksandra Deanoska Trendafilova explores how public interest shapes both legislative and judicial approaches to penal policy in the Republic of North Macedonia. They first discuss the officially stated aims of punishment as defined in the country's Criminal Code – namely, deterrence and rehabilitation. Chapter 8 demonstrates that a concise overview is provided of the range of punishments codified by lawmakers, followed by an analysis of the actual sanctions imposed by courts in North Macedonia. This includes categorization by the type and severity of the offence, offering insight into how judicial discretion aligns with legislative intent. To ground their findings, Chapter 8 incorporates an analysis of key phenomenological aspects of crime within the country. This comprehensive approach enables a more accurate evaluation of how penal policy responds to crime trends and whether it effectively serves the public interest. Chapter 8 emphasizes the vital role of penal policy analysis in assessing the efficacy of various forms of punishment. By examining the correlation between sanctions and crime rates, the authors attempt to determine the practical impact and societal value of these measures.

Chapter 9 by Larysa Zhdankina offers a broader perspective on the concept of public interest by situating it within the framework of international law and the jurisprudence of the European Court of Human Rights. It highlights the complex relationship between public interest and state sovereignty, particularly within the Ukrainian context. In the realm of criminal law, the sovereign authority of the state and its exclusive power over the administration of justice are presented as fundamental pillars. What distinguishes this chapter is its detailed analysis of numerous Ukrainian court decisions that engage directly with the notion of public interest. These decisions illustrate how domestic courts in Ukraine, often drawing on ECHR jurisprudence, have begun to integrate public interest considerations into their legal reasoning – especially in cases involving prosecutorial discretion, pre-trial detention, and the protection of victims' and defendants' rights. By showcasing these judgements, Chapter 9 reveals a legal landscape in which Ukrainian courts cautiously but deliberately articulate how public interest can and should guide the state's criminal justice responses, even amid complex political and security challenges. As such, Chapter 9 underscores how the pursuit of public interest in Ukraine is not merely a matter of policy or prosecutorial initiative but a principle gradually being developed through judicial interpretation. It presents criminal justice as a key domain through which sovereign power is both asserted and tested – particularly in a transitional legal system navigating between national imperatives and supranational legal standards.

Chapter 10 by Tang Lanchi examines the evolving role of public interest balancing in China's prosecutorial system, particularly considering the July 2024 suspension of related discretionary practices. The chapter contextualizes this shift within a broader global trend, where public interest is commonly considered in prosecutorial decision-making, from East Asian systems like Japan and South Korea to Western civil and common law jurisdictions. The chapter begins by outlining the structure and distinct features of China's prosecution system to orient unfamiliar readers. It then moves to a theoretical discussion on the legitimacy and necessity of public interest balancing in criminal proceedings. Chapter 10 displays how Chinese prosecution authorities previously applied this concept, especially in two experimental areas: compliance-based non-prosecution of enterprises and the shift from private to public prosecution in defamation cases. It then explores how those initiatives deviated from intended goals. Finally, it calls for a reflective pause rather than a full abandonment of public interest balancing, advocating for reform based on clearer boundaries and a more scientifically grounded approach. The structure reflects continental transitions by showcasing legal traditions in a geographic and systemic flow, from Europe to Eurasia and then to Asia. This progression not only highlights regional variations in prosecutorial approaches and public interest considerations but also allows readers to observe how different legal cultures interpret and implement similar principles across diverse jurisdictions.

This edited book, as such, brings together perspectives from a diverse range of jurisdictions, including China, England and Wales, North Macedonia, Poland, Romania, Scotland, Spain, Türkiye and Ukraine to explore how public interest is understood and applied within criminal justice systems. The overview provided above offers a preliminary glimpse into the core concerns and contributions of each chapter, setting the stage for deeper engagement with the issues they explore. Structured primarily on a geographical basis, the book facilitates comparative insight into different legal traditions, ranging from adversarial to inquisitorial models. Beyond criminal procedure, the book explores the role and impact of the public interest test across wider aspects of the criminal justice system, including punishment, considerations of state interest, and the broader exercise of public interest within prosecutorial functions. By addressing a largely underexplored area in comparative criminal law, the edited book aims to challenge both the over- and underestimation of public interest in prosecution and seeks to contribute to a more coherent framework for its application across jurisdictions.

Notes

1 See Victoria Colvin, 'The Riddle of Prosecutorial Discretion', in Victoria Colvin and Philip Stenning (eds), *The Evolving Role of the Public Prosecutor: Challenges and Innovations* (Routledge, 2019) 139.
2 Rachel Elise Barkow, *Prisoners of Politics: Breaking the Cycle of Mass Incarceration* (The Belknap Press of Harvard University Press, 2019) 154.
3 Peter Young, *Crime and Criminal Justice in Scotland* (1st edn, The Stationery Office, Edinburgh 1997) 3.
4 Dan McManus, *Scotland and the Alternative Disposal: Thinking Differently?* (LLM(R) thesis, University of Glasgow 2021) 46, 51–6 and 91.
5 David T. Johnson, *Japan's Prosecution Review Commission on the Democratic Oversight of Decisions Not to Charge* (Palgrave, 2022).
6 Colvin (n 1) 139.
7 McManus (n 4) 92 ff.
8 Colvin (n 1) 146.
9 Ibid.
10 Gerald H. Gordon, 'Institution of Criminal Proceedings in Scotland' (1968) 19 (3) *Northern Ireland Legal Quarterly* 249; Lindsay Farmer, '"The Genius of Our Law ...": Criminal Law and the Scottish Legal Tradition' (1992) 55 (1) *The Modern Law Review* 25; Lindsay Farmer, *Criminal Law, Tradition and Legal Order: Crime and the Genius of Scots Law, 1747 to the Present* (Cambridge University Press, Cambridge 1996).

1

Prosecuting in the public interest

The CPS and the evolving role of the public prosecutor in England and Wales

Kajsa Dinesson

Introduction

The public prosecutor is an important gate-keeping actor in the justice process, entrusted with impactful discretionary decisions in their task to prosecute in the public interest. This chapter examines the evolving role of the Crown Prosecution Service (CPS) and of the public prosecutor in England and Wales since the establishment of the CPS in 1986.* It outlines how evolutions in the prosecutorial role, in terms of both the role of the CPS as an institution and in the extent of individual prosecutorial power and responsibility, have outpaced the development of guidance and principles to guide that work.

Normative questions have been raised since the early days of the CPS. Andrew Ashworth asked in 1986, a year after the service's creation as it had just become operational, 'On what principles should Crown Prosecutors act?'.[1] I suggest that nearly forty years on, this question remains. Public prosecutors shoulder a great deal of responsibility and influence in the justice system, but we lack a clear sense of what that power is for. Whereas the framework and guidance for discretionary decision-making have markedly expanded over time, a clear sense of the CPS as an institution and of the public prosecutor's role has been lacking, and policy and guidance have remained reactive and haphazard.[2] I further posit that in failing to keep pace, the available guidance falls short of robustly accounting for the extent of prosecutorial role and responsibility and the principles which ought to underpin its exercise. This chapter seeks to highlight two, closely related but separate, failures: that the CPS lacks a robust sense of what it is for and what it should be doing; and that individual prosecutors have a corresponding lack of clarity as to their role in interpreting and developing the law, flowing from the CPS's broader failure. This has implications for the CPS as an institution, and for the work of individual prosecutors as decision-makers.

The chapter begins with an analytical overview of the prosecutorial role, drawing on CPS documents to set out an institutional account of the role of the CPS and of the public prosecutor. It then proceeds to ask and reflect on normative questions about prosecutorial discretion with an emphasis on the public interest: what function the public interest has served and continues to serve in prosecutions, and what role it may serve in the future in the midst of a criminal justice system faced with new challenges and constraints. Here, the evolution of the doctrine of joint enterprise is drawn on as an area of law illustrative of the power of the prosecutor to shape the scope and terms of criminalization in impactful ways, acting as an intermediary between the legislature and the courts. Through this example I offer a more comprehensive analytical account of the role of the public prosecutor and of the CPS in the criminal justice system as an intermediary between the legislature and the courts. In sketching this revised analytical understanding, I also highlight the important normative gap left by a failure to clearly and robustly define the role of the public prosecutor. I call for a more robust normative framework to support prosecutorial discretion that recognizes the growing power and responsibility of the prosecutor in the criminal justice system, and the role of the CPS more widely as more than a safeguard on police power: as a mediator between the legislature, the courts, and the public.

In closing, drawing on a critical discussion of Jonathan Rogers' proposed restructuring of the public interest test, I suggest that returning to the core of the public prosecutor's and the CPS's role – prosecuting in the public interest – offers a promising way forward. Drawing on the work of Rogers, I suggest that the public interest principle may be expanded on as a thicker normative principle to structure and guide the exercise of impactful criminalization-shaping and law-developing discretionary decisions, and that this work needs to account for and support the impactful and important role of prosecutorial discretion in the justice system.

The creation of the CPS – the need for a public prosecution service

A national public system of prosecutions had been considered long before the CPS was established by the Prosecution of Offences Act 1985, becoming operational in 1986. The introduction of the Director of Public Prosecutions (DPP) in 1879 to handle serious prosecutions in the public interest marked a substantial step forward and introduced a degree of centralization,[3] but the system remained muddled. Prosecutions largely remained a police or private matter, but were increasingly being publicly funded.[4] A gap remained however in cases where the public interest required a prosecution, but private means were limited.[5] Recommendations for a public prosecution service to fill this gap reach back at least to the early 1800s, with three Royal Commissions needed to finally bring about the creation of the CPS.[6] The latter of these was the Royal Commission on Criminal Procedure led by Sir Cyril Philips which reported in 1981,[7] established following the Fisher Inquiry which shed light on police misconduct and the need for fundamental changes to the workings of the criminal justice system.[8] Adding to the recommendations of Justice (the British part of the International Commission of Jurists), the Philips Commission successfully recommended the establishment of a public prosecution service.

The Royal Commission's terms of reference were to examine – with regard to the community's interest in bringing offenders to justice, the rights of the accused, and the need for efficient resource management – whether changes were needed in police investigatory powers and responsibilities, the process and allocation of powers of prosecution, and any related criminal procedure and evidence considerations.[9] The Commission's findings highlighted a need for fundamental change and restructuring. The new service was recommended and adopted to address the deficiencies identified which, according to the Commission, called for 'a complete reformulation and restatement of the procedure for bringing a person before the court'.[10] The system was described as haphazard, raising concerns for arbitrary variation between different areas, a lack of openness and accountability in decision to prosecute and risks inherent in the combination of investigatory and prosecutorial responsibility in the hands of the police, and efficiency issues in terms of delays and resource use.[11] Following the Commission's recommendations, the Prosecution of Offences Act 1985 created the CPS and transferred the power and responsibility to prosecute from the police to an independent and legally trained body of staff managed by the DPP. In taking over the power to prosecute, the CPS was tasked with ensuring greater consistency, improving efficiency by reducing the number of weak cases being prosecuted, and crucially with counterbalancing police power.[12]

Twenty-three years later, the House of Commons Justice Committee reviewed the role of the CPS in the justice system. The Committee's report outlined how 'the prosecutor's role seems to be defined by what it takes away from others, rather than having a proactively defined strategic place in the criminal justice system'.[13] Their 2009 report highlights how despite the pivotal nature of CPS decisions, with prosecutors acting as gatekeepers to the justice system, the role of the public prosecutor and of the CPS lacked an overarching vision and direction and had developed in a reactive and piecemeal fashion.[14] This was not the first, nor last, critique of the CPS's lack of a clearly spelt out role.[15] Although progress has been made, as I will proceed to outline herein, the criminal justice system has continued to develop over time, and with it the prosecutor's role and influence have expanded. The robust normative work called for by a chain of reviews, meanwhile, remains to be done.

One way in which we may begin to assess this progress is by tracing developments in the story of the prosecutorial role through institutional narratives, as reflected in policies and principles set out in the Code for Crown Prosecutors (the Code) and related policies and guidance. These offer important insight in shedding light on the story the CPS itself tells of its role and the role of public prosecutors, and how this has evolved over time. This may then be compared to observed practice to assess the extent of the gap alluded to above.

In the public interest

There is a growing body of policy and guidance documents across which allow us to trace an institutional account of the role of the public prosecutor and its evolution over time. These documents shed light on a series of developments intended to guide prosecutors and define the role and realm of the CPS in the criminal justice system. The central guiding document for CPS prosecutors is the Code for Crown Prosecutors. The first edition of the Code was issued in 1986, and the most recent eighth edition was issued in 2018. The Code sets out a two-stage test for prosecution decisions (listed as two questions in the first edition) intended to 'promote efficient and consistent decision-making as to develop and thereafter maintain public confidence' in the service.[16] The Code remains the central public-facing guiding document for the CPS alongside a combination of publicly available and internal guidance on specific issues, offences and procedures.

The first question of evidential sufficiency in the first edition of the Code echoed the familiar 'fifty percent rule' in asking whether the evidence available is sufficient to justify a prosecution, in terms of requiring a 'realistic prospect of conviction'.[17] In the first Code, this was followed by thirteen questions of evidence for the prosecutor to have regard to in evaluating the evidence, including any police misconduct that may impact the admissibility of evidence, the reliability of witnesses, and consideration of the likely public perception of proceeding given the facts of the case.[18] In its present form, the evidential test asks four wider questions to help the prosecutor assess the sufficiency of evidence and the prospect of conviction.[19] These questions task the prosecutor with assessing admissibility, reliability, credibility and whether further evidence may be gathered.[20]

The second question instructed the prosecutor to 'consider whether the public interest requires prosecution'.[21] The first Code outlines that the new service will be guided by the DPP-endorsed approach outlined by former Attorney General Lord Shawcross: that a prosecution ought to proceed 'wherever it appears that the offence or the circumstances of its commission is or are of such a character that a prosecution in respect thereof is required in the public interest'.[22] Considerations of public interest were expanded on in the 1986 Code to include effects on 'public morale and order, and with any other considerations affecting public policy'.[23] Whereas this is outlined to be both case and fact dependent, a broad direction is given that seriousness is a central concern in assessing the public interest.[24] A number of case characteristics generally tending for or against prosecution are then listed, including likely penalty, youth or age, mental illness and an emphasis on the seriousness of sexual offences,[25] as well as the relevance of community attitudes and the prevalence of the offence in question locally and nationally.[26] The emphasis on efficiency, cost-effectiveness and a need to more effectively screen and dispose of weak cases was clearly engrained in the shape of the public interest test from the outset – whether indirectly in prioritizing public funds for serious cases or directly in entitling the Crown Prosecutor to consider cost in their decision-making.[27] The 2018 Code offers a non-exhaustive list of questions to consider, including: seriousness; suspect's level of culpability, age and maturity; the harm and circumstances of the victim; impact on the community; proportionality; and the protection of sources.[28] The Code is the central guiding document for the exercise of prosecutorial discretion, yet it offers little by way of certainty or predictability as these criteria will likely pull in different directions. It expressly disclaims that any one criterion is more important than the rest,[29] but suggests a difference in emphasis with offender youth and seriousness being indicated as primary considerations.[30]

The eighth edition of the Code as issued in 2018, prefaces the test with a list of thirteen general principles. The general principles first appeared in the third edition of the Code, which featured two general principles as well as a statement of purpose and values.[31] This reviewed edition of the Code followed efforts to restructure the CPS following early challenges, which included simplifying and clarifying the Code as a public-facing document. This included listing, for the first time, public interest and evidential factors in a more accessible style and format which remains today.[32] The 3rd Code also listed general principles in the form of duties for the public prosecutor to act fairly, independently and objectively in prosecuting the right persons for the right offences and presenting all relevant facts to the courts. The annual report published in the same year emphasized the important and impactful role of the public prosecutor and the CPS 'in a changing and developing criminal justice system'.[33] The report describes the general principles as being aimed at supporting consistency, fairness and efficiency – if everyone knows the principles that the CPS works to, and police take account of these in their early decisions about a case, then greater fairness and efficiency can be achieved.[34] The list of general principles grew to four in the fourth edition issued in 2000, which primarily involved a change in emphasis,[35] and expanded to five in the fifth edition issued in 2004, which added offering guidance and advice to investigators in the midst of greater emphasis on the CPS's role working with the police, where historically much emphasis had been on separating the two as far as possible.[36]

At the time of writing, the now thirteen general principles do offer a brief account of the role of the prosecutor and the CPS in the justice system. These emphasize prosecutorial independence and impartiality, the role of the prosecutor and the nature of their decisions, and a series of duties for the prosecutor to act in a fair and objective way 'to secure justice for victims, witnesses, suspects, defendants and the public'.[37] They are to do so with regard to legal duties and obligations, including complying with the Code, additional guidance on particular offences and offenders, and the Human Rights Act 1998.[38] The principles serve to clarify and distinguish the role of the prosecutor from both the police and the courts. The general principles mark a positive step towards outlining the principles underpinning the CPS's practical aims in terms of securing justice and what this requires. Whereas the principles outline general commitments and the role of the prosecutor has these have primarily been defined by what lies beyond their remit in comparison to other actors as opposed to through a robust positive sense of the prosecutorial role. This leaves many normative questions around the role of the CPS, and the work of individual decision-makers, unaccounted for or at least underexplored.

The CPS still occupies the space as was envisioned for it by 1985, as an intermediary between police investigations and court proceedings. But the public prosecutor has come to exercise a role which is more substantial and impactful than was perhaps anticipated. The Justice Committee noted in 2009 that the CPS had grown and changed to come to an influential role in relation to charging, pleas, cautioning and through advocacy.[39] In light of these changes, the Committee's report highlighted a need for safeguards, clearer policy and openness and transparency supported by more stakeholder engagement.[40] In particular, the Committee identified inconsistencies in CPS delivery and linked this to the failure to identify a clear role for the prosecutor and guidance for consistent decision-making, bridging local responsiveness and system-wide consistency.[41] A series of steps were taken in response to this report, but each remained focused on specific issues highlighted rather than embarking on a substantial overarching endeavour.[42] The response markedly seemed to lack the overarching 'bold' work recommended to define the role of the CPS and of the individual public prosecutor.

The work to set out an overarching vision and direction for the CPS and carve out a clear role for the prosecutor beyond reactive clarifications is, at the time of writing, yet to take place. As a survey of the Code, guidance documents, and public consultations has highlighted, some progress has been made. There has been a moving away from defining the CPS in terms of practical aims (namely efficiency and counterbalancing police power) towards an outlining of the underpinning principles this serves (securing justice) and what this requires of the public prosecutor (to be fair, independent and objective). But the need for more substantial and proactive work of this nature remains. Although the successive development of guidance, including general principles, has begun to sketch or suggest the shape of a normative account from the institutional perspective, it has failed to robustly account for how this relates to the role of the CPS and of the individual public prosecutor in practice to sufficiently account for (analytically) and guide (normatively) that work. This gap becomes clearer when the institutional account of the role of the CPS and of the public prosecutor is examined alongside observed practice – which I turn to below.

Despite positive moves towards consistency, accessibility and transparency as the CPS has grown into its role over nearly four decades of its work, we still lack an overarching and principled normative framework for the role of the public prosecutor. The significance of this gap was highlighted as early as the CPS's own 1993–1994 annual report, which noted the growing influence and impact of the CPS and its prosecutors in a changing justice system. Since 1986, the CPS has evolved from a safeguard on police power to a powerful actor in their own right with significant influence through an expanding list of powers in relation to charging, pleas, and cautioning. As I proceed to illustrate below, the work of establishing a framework for the exercise of this role, and even an up-to-date understanding and appreciation of the role and its influence, has not kept pace with the speed of change in the criminal justice system and the place of the prosecutor therein. In order to understand the need for and begin to develop a normative framework to guide the public prosecutor in the modern era of English criminal justice, we need to appreciate and account for the power and responsibility of the prosecutor.

The prosecutor and the scope and terms of criminalization – joint enterprise prosecutions

The working context of the CPS and the public prosecutor has changed markedly since 1986. The criminal justice system in England and Wales is increasingly overworked, under-funded, and burdened with a backlog of cases and the implications of overcrowded prisons. The criminal offences that prosecutors are tasked to enforce have also expanded, not only in number but also in scope in the midst of a preventive turn where an increasing number of criminal offences intervene at earlier stages in broader terms.[43] The modern era of criminal justice is one in which the role of the prosecutor is changing and growing and where they are expected to do more with less. For the purposes of this chapter, I will focus on a part of the prosecutorial role which has been under-recognized and under-theorized to date, which is growing, and which highlights the need for renewed conversations about the prosecutor's role: how prosecutors bridge the law-making work of the legislature and the courts and influence the shape and scope of criminalization in doing so in ways that exceed analytical accounts such as the institutional account examined above.

The legislature in England and Wales makes law by statute, and higher courts hold the power to set precedent – both thereby criminalizing in the formal sense. The doctrine of precedent applies equally to interpretations of statutory criminal law as it does to common law offences and doctrines, and both are formally, legally authoritative. This places the legislature and judiciary in the same category overall, as both hold the power to 'create, interpret, and develop the law'.[44] Prosecutors do not, and cannot, engage in criminalization in the formal law-making sense of the activities of the legislature, nor do they make decisions of law in the way courts do in setting precedent. Yet prosecutors do shape criminalization in impactful ways.

Whereas it is widely recognized that the prosecutor enjoys a range of powers, and that prosecutorial practice has direct impacts on criminalization, conventional understanding tends to limit this story of prosecutorial powers to a few distinct powers (e.g. pleas and charging) or to the overall impact of patterns of enforcement over time. We also need to account for landmark cases like *R*, where the CPS brought a case which ought to have had no reasonable prospect for conviction but which led to the criminalization of marital rape.[45] Cases like *R* are, however, quite rare – and debates arise as to whether such cases constitute an overstep. Here I posit that understanding the day-to-day of the prosecutorial role in terms of mere patterns of enforcement, with only rare exceptions of cases like *R*, is an increasingly incomplete account of the prosecutorial role and of the relationship between the prosecutor and criminalization in the modern era of criminal justice.

It is useful to illustrate this through an example from observed practice. The influence of the prosecutor in actively shaping the scope and terms of criminalization has been on display in the doctrine of joint enterprise, which allocates responsibility to accomplices involved in joint criminal ventures. Prosecutorial influence shaping criminalization can be found both before and after the change in law following *Jogee*.[46] Prior to *Jogee*, following the 1985 decision in *Chang Wing-Siu*,[47] the required *mens rea* for secondary parties to a crime – known then as the doctrine of parasitic accessory liability – was being diluted.[48] Under the doctrine of parasitic accessory liability, the required *mens rea* for a secondary was satisfied by association with the principal, requiring mere foresight of the possibility of the offence in issue given that the two shared a common purpose. This held even where the second party was opposed to the crime committed being carried out, or where they merely offered encouragement which went unnoticed by the principal.[49] The mere foresight of the possibility that an armed robbery may go wrong and result in the principal committing murder was therefore sufficient *mens rea* to establish guilt of same for the secondary party.[50] In practice, it came to be that the exchange of phone calls or mere presence at the scene of the crime was sufficient evidence for the inference of the required participation and foresight on behalf of the secondary.[51]

These fact patterns, argued by prosecutors and accepted by courts to meet the requirements of the substantive law, seem far removed from the expectations we may have from the offence requirements as set out in the letter of the law. The power of prosecutors to shape the law in action through interpretation and application is an important step in understanding why and how this came to be the case. As outlined by Green and McGourlay, the standard for secondary party liability that emerged and developed in joint-enterprise prosecutions stemmed not from the law itself, but from the application thereof through prosecutions.[52] By interpreting and applying the law and framing the law in a certain way in relation to a given case before the court, the prosecutor holds significant power to shape the law.[53] In acting as an intermediary between formal criminalization by the legislature and the authoritative precedent-setting interpretations of the courts, the prosecutor enjoys a substantial degree of discretion in relation to charging generally, and in relation to evidence in case-building in particular. Such discretionary decisions stand to shape the scope of criminalization by adding to its content. Whilst this takes place in the context of an existing offence, it shapes the scope and terms of criminalization by shaping what the substantive law requires in terms of fact patterns.

In bringing a given case before the court, the prosecutor invites the court to draw particular authoritative lines of criminalization through their proposition that a given collection of facts on the basis of a particular set of evidence satisfies a given offence. That is, the charging and case-building decisions of the prosecutor frame issues in ways which set up the authoritative law-making of the court. This is a dialogue, in the sense that the court may of course agree or disagree with the prosecution in the given case, but it does so reliant on the terms of prosecution. This dialogue takes place in individual cases, as I focus on here for clarity, but when we widen our scope to chains of cases over time we see that this dialogue extends over the course of many cases where prosecutors will adapt to decisions prior in the cases they bring and on the basis of what evidence. That is, the relationship is not one directional. Yet, importantly, the law-making of the court is in an important sense bound by *what* is brought before it and *how* it is brought, such that the realm of possible outcomes the courts can reach is in some important respects constrained by prosecutors' decisions, because the court rules on what is brought before it. It is of course ultimately for the court to authoritatively interpret and apply the law, but this is not a direct relationship from legislature (enacting statute) to courts (and their authoritative interpretation resulting in common law). The process from statute to interpretation hinges on the prosecutor presenting facts and evidence and claiming that this is prohibited by the offence in question – which the court can either agree with or not.[54]

Returning to joint enterprise, the influence of prosecutorial practice did not end with *Jogee*. In *Jogee*, the decision in *Chang Wing-Siu* was framed as a 'wrong turn' in the law on accessory liability, and the doctrine was abolished.[55] It was instead established that liability is only to be imposed on secondary parties in cases where there is certainty in the participant's knowledge of the principal's crime, alongside encouragement or assistance and the intent to do so.[56] This constitutes, at least on paper, a step away from any mere 'guilt by association' that applied previously.[57] However, although joint enterprise is now just one way in which one may assist or encourage an offence, cases following *Jogee* suggest little change in practice where foresight remains good evidence for intent,[58] and evidencing association and common purpose remains a low bar. Recent research has highlighted how rap and drill music is frequently being used in joint enterprise prosecutions for serious crimes, to establish association as well as intent.[59] This includes cases where joint enterprise is argued on the basis of the accused being involved in the same gang, and where intent to assist and encourage is being inferred on the basis of evidence like rap videos in which some of the defendants featured.[60] Cases like these raise important questions about practice and how prosecutorial case-building stands to shape the scope and terms of criminalization in significant ways – and how the exercise of prosecutorial discretion might be (and may need to be) better guided and structured with this in mind.

This is not to suggest that recent trends in joint enterprise prosecutions stem from ill intent, nor even from prosecutors intentionally shaping criminalization. Rather, it is far more likely that prosecutors who increasingly have less time and resources to dedicate to each case – perhaps especially so in the face of new, unclear or particularly broad or vague legislation – are left with the most viable strategy being to put everything they think may be relevant to the court and seeing what sticks.[61] It is also important to emphasize that a chain of decisions, many of which do not involve the prosecutor, are relevant in this process. This includes what evidence is gathered and passed on by investigators as well as how both evidence and law are engaged with and interpreted in court. That said, we would be amiss not to note the role of the public prosecutor in the evolution of joint enterprise over time and how this may inform our thinking about prosecutorial responsibility.

Prosecutors do, through case-building, propose to the court that certain evidence satisfies elements of the offence. Prosecutors also act as safeguards on policing and enjoy discretion in assessing each case, following the Code and other relevant guidance in doing so. This prompts questions about how the exercise of this growing power and responsibility ought to be structured and guided, and whether long overdue conversations about the public prosecutor's role and place in the criminal justice system need to be revisited with a renewed sense of urgency in light of their growing responsibilities and influence.

Towards a normative framework for the public prosecutor

In closing, I will endeavour to sketch one route along which the conversation about the public prosecutor's role and place in the criminal justice system, and how their growing power and responsibility ought to be structured and guided, may proceed. I posit that a more robust normative framework is needed to guide prosecutor's discretionary decisions of what to bring, and how to bring it, with a clear sense of what acting in the public interest entails in how this shapes criminalization. Frameworks seeking to guide the exercise of this power and responsibility, I argue, ought to draw on the prosecutorial role in furthering, and serving, the public interest. This will require expanding on the principle and the test as held in the Code, informed by questions of what it means to prosecute in the public interest in the modern era of criminal justice. To briefly discuss what this might look like I will draw on one of the rare academic works outlining a revised framework for prosecutors as presented by Rogers.[62]

Rogers proposes that the public interest test may be expanded on and subdivided into two different tests for two different kinds of prosecutions: application and developing.[63] In short, Rogers makes space for two kinds of prosecutions: cases where the prosecutor is applying legislative intent by discerning and applying it to the accused as a justification to punish and prosecute them,[64] and cases where the prosecutor may prosecute to develop the law in the sense of seeking clarification where law and/or legislative intent is unclear such that he may apply the law in the future, with due regard to the harms of prosecution.[65] Rogers offers a promising direction for normative work in that it proposes a restructuring which would clarify the prosecutorial role and expand on the contents of the public interest test with regard to the community norms that underpin it. However, I posit that this restructuring needs some further refining, as this framework seems to constrain prosecutorial power and responsibility too narrowly relative to what public prosecutors are actually doing. That is, the role Rogers has sketched for the public prosecutor is too narrow relative to the realities of the prosecutorial role as we find it in the modern era of criminal justice. Whilst this is not itself an inherent problem – indeed we might think the prosecutor's power and responsibility needs constraining – I suggest that the prosecutor has more of a role to play than merely applying and *asking* about the law. I posit that beyond asking for clarification, the power to *assert* allows the public prosecutor to act in the public interest to secure justice.

Rogers' framework makes some space for prosecutorial work developing the law, but I suggest not enough. To limit the prosecutor's role in developing the law to seeking clarification suggests that the prosecutor ought to be a passive part in this process. This seems far removed from the realities of prosecutions as we find them today, where prosecutors are not asking but asserting claims about facts and offences, which the court then assesses and decides on. If prosecutors were simply asking, they would presumably not be justified in doing so through a prosecution which exposes the accused to the harms not only of prosecution but also potentially of conviction and imprisonment.[66] That is, prosecutors seem through prosecutions to genuinely present what they assess to be a faithful interpretation and application of the law to a particular set of facts, and in presenting this to the court they receive an authoritative decision. In doing so, the exercise of discretion ought to be guided by a normative framework and a clearer sense of the role of the public prosecutor which recognizes the prosecutor's power to further the public interest through their role and guides this work by more substantially accounting for what it means to prosecute in the public interest.

It may be argued that for prosecutorial discretionary decisions to be legitimate the interpretations and assertions made by the prosecutor must clearly derive from legislation and related policy. That is, the proper scope of the prosecutorial role is narrower than what has been observed in this chapter. Roger's framework, for example, suggests a more constrained role for the public prosecutor than the role in which they seem to increasingly find themselves in the modern era of criminal justice. However, I suggest that we would be amiss to approach the question of the prosecutorial role in the justice system going forward without firm footing in how the prosecutorial role has evolved over time and the space which the CPS and the public prosecutor now find themselves occupying. Our normative thinking ought to progress in line with our analytical understanding of the role, recognizing and responding to the move beyond a role defined in contrast to the police towards a more significant role which ought to be coupled with a robust and principled account of what securing justice entails and requires.

I posit that this normative work as to the prosecutorial role needs to draw on the public interest, in recognition of the growing range of purposes that prosecutorial discretion now serves in the criminal justice system. The prosecutor is shaping criminalization in ways that are more than merely derivative of legislative intent. There is more to cases like *R*, which Rogers raises, and indeed to the prosecutorial day-to-day than prosecutors passively asking. Prosecutors would not have brought *R*, in light of the law at the time, if they did not think they were acting in the public interest. The ability to do more than ask but to assert, with firm footing in the public interest, is why the public prosecutor has come to develop into an important intermediary in an evolving criminal justice system. When discretion is properly exercised, the prosecutor ensures that the law can be both flexible and certain in responding to the community's shifting conceptions of justice. Returning to the example explored herein, we see why the power and responsibility conferred by discretion need to be guided by a sufficiently robust normative framework. When we look at the development of joint enterprise over time as I have set out here, we see that prosecuting sometimes involves more power and responsibility to shape the law than current frameworks (analytical and normative) and guidance would suggest and support. The discussion herein lends weight to a long reaching chain of calls for a more robust normative framework to guide this work: for the public prosecutor as an increasingly powerful actor in the criminal justice system whose role and responsibilities seem to only be expanding in the modern era; and for the CPS as a safeguard on police power *and* as a mediator between the legislature, the courts and the public.

Conclusion – prosecuting in the public interest in the modern era of criminal justice

The CPS and the public prosecutor emerged in 1986 to act as a safeguard on police power and to help achieve consistency and efficiency in the justice system. As the prosecutorial role has grown and evolved, corresponding evolutions in guidance and supporting frameworks have been reactive and piecemeal. Whereas progress has been made in moving from practical aims of efficiency and counterbalancing police power towards an outlining of the underpinning principles this serves and what this requires of the public prosecutor, the need for more substantial and proactive work of this nature to guide the exercise of discretion remains. This chapter has highlighted the importance of that remaining gap by underscoring the power and responsibility increasingly put on the public prosecutor. I have suggested that a revised understanding of the place that the CPS has come to occupy in the criminal justice system as a mediator between the legislature and the courts, and of the role of the public prosecutor in influencing and shaping the scope and terms of criminalization, highlights the extent and import of this gap in our analytical understanding as well as its important normative implications. In closing, I have briefly sketched a route forward. I have suggested that a more robust normative framework is needed to guide prosecutorial work in the modern era of criminal justice, with a clarified sense of what the public interest requires of the public prosecutor.

Notes

* *Acknowledgement: I am grateful for the insightful feedback from colleagues in the Virtual Criminal Law Group, including in particular Dr. JP Fassnidge, Professor Antony Duff and Professor Pamela Ferguson. This chapter has benefitted greatly from conversations with Dr. Jackson Allen.*

1 Andrew Ashworth, 'The Public-Interest Element in Prosecutions' (1987) Sep *Criminal Law Review* 595, 596.

2 House of Commons Justice Committee, 'The Crown Prosecution Service: Gatekeeper of the Criminal Justice System' (The Stationary Office 2009) HC 186 https://publications.parliament.uk/pa/cm200809/cmselect/cmjust/186/186.pdf; Andrew Sanders, 'The CPS: 30 Years On' (2016) 2 *Criminal Law Review* 82.

3 Prosecution of Offences Act 1879; DJ Bentley, *English Criminal Justice in the Nineteenth Century* (Hambledon Press, London; Rio Grande, Ohio 1998) 86; Thomas Hetherington, *Prosecution and the Public Interest* (Waterlow publishers 1989) 14–18, 26.

4 Bentley (n 3) 7–8, 83–4.

5 Hetherington (n 3) 4–10.

6 ibid 6; Joshua Rozenberg, *The Case for the Crown: The Inside Story of the Director of Public Prosecutions* (Equation 1987) 79–83 these being the Royal Commission on Police Powers and Procedure which reported in 1929, the Royal Commission on the Police which reported in 1962, and finally the Royal Commission on Criminal

Procedure led by Sir Cyril Philips which reported in 1981.

7 Sir Cyril Philips, 'The Royal Commission on Criminal Procedure' (House of Commons Library 1981) cm 8092.

8 Sir Henry Fisher, 'Report of an Inquiry by the Hon. Sir Henry Fisher into the Circumstances Leading to the Trial of Three Persons on Charges Arising out of the Death of Maxwell Confait and the Fire at 27 Doggett Road, London SE6' (Her Majesty's Stationary Office 1997) https://assets.publishing.service.gov.uk/media/5a7b9a1ced915d131106050d/0090.pdf.

9 Sir Cyril Philips (n 7) 3–4.

10 Debbie Crisp and David Moxon, 'Case Screening by the Crown Prosecution Service: How and Why Cases Are Terminated' (HMSO 1994) Home Office Research Study 137 para 6.18.

11 Hetherington (n 3) 65; Sir Cyril Philips (n 7).

12 Sanders (n 2); 'An Independent Prosecution Service for England and Wales' (Home Office 1983); Rozenberg (n 6) 82; Crisp and Moxon (n 10) para 6.18.

13 House of Commons Justice Committee (n 2) 3.

14 Ibid 6.

15 Rt. Hon. Sir Iain Glidewell, 'The Review of the Crown Prosecution Service: Summary of the Main Report with the Conclusions and Recommendations' (The Stationary Office) Cm3960 para 27 https://assets.publishing.service.gov.uk/media/5a7c761640f0b62aff6c1d45/3972.pdf.

16 'The Code for Crown Prosecutors' (Crown Prosecution Service 1986) 1st ed para 1.

17 Rozenberg (n 6) 147–8; 'The Code for Crown Prosecutors' (n 16) para 4.

18 'The Code for Crown Prosecutors' (n 16) para 5 (i), (iii)–(x), and (xii).

19 'The Code for Crown Prosecutors' (*CPS*, 26 October 2018) paras 4.6–4.8 https://www.cps.gov.uk/publication/code-crown-prosecutors accessed 28 October 2024.

20 Ibid 4.8.

21 'The Code for Crown Prosecutors' (n 16) para 7.

22 HC Deb 29 January 1951, vol 483, col 681; ibid.

23 Ibid.

24 Ibid 8.

25 Ibid.

26 Ibid 9.

27 Ibid 13; Rozenberg (n 6) 158–9.

28 'The Code for Crown Prosecutors' (n 19) paras 4.9–4.14.

29 Ibid 4.12–4.13.

30 Sanders (n 2) 94; with seriousness gaining further prominence after the Glidewell report Rt. Hon. Sir Iain Glidewell, 'The Review of the Crown Prosecution Service' (The Stationary Office 1998) Cm 3972 para 66.

31 'Annual Report for the Period April 1993–March 1994' (Crown Prosecution Service 1994) app A and B, pp. 43–4.

32 Ibid 5.

33 Ibid 4.

34 'Annual Report for the Period April 1993–March 1994' (n 31) Annex B, Code for Crown Prosecutors (3rd Ed) at para 11.1. It is an important question, which largely lies beyond the scope of this paper, whether efficiency ought to be an express and central aim of the CPS and how this relates to other central values like justice and fairness. The body of CPS documents seems to link these values closely together, where a key measure of efficiency is whether prosecutors are making the right decisions, measured in particular on success rates as indicating proper application of the Code's tests.

35 'Annual Report for the Period April 2000–March 2001' (Crown Prosecution Service 2001) Annex A at paras 2.2–2.5; 'Annual Report for the Period April 2003–March 2004' (Crown Prosecution Service 2004) 8.

36 'The Code for Crown Prosecutors' (Crown Prosecution Service 2004) 5th ed para 2.4.

37 'The Code for Crown Prosecutors' (n 19) para 2.5.

38 Ibid 2.1–2.13.

39 House of Commons Justice Committee (n 2) 9–10.

40 Ibid 41.

41 Ibid 47.

42 'The Crown Prosecution Service: Gatekeeper of the Criminal Justice System: Government Response to the Committee's Ninth Report of Session 2008–09' (The Stationary Office 2012) HC 245 app 2 https://publications.parliament.uk/pa/cm200910/cmselect/cmjust/245/245.pdf.

43 Henrique Carvalho, *The Preventive Turn in Criminal Law* (Oxford University Press 2017).

44 J Horder, *Ashworth's Principles of Criminal Law* (9th edn, Oxford University Press 2019) 4.

45 *R v R* [1992] 1 AC 599.

46 *Jogee* [2016] UKSC 8; [2017] A.C. 387.

47 As referred to in Jogee at [85]; see Chang Wing-Siu [1985] AC 168. See also Findlay Stark, 'The Demise of "Parasitic Accessorial Liability": Substantive Judicial Law Reform, Not Common Law Housekeeping' (2016) 75 *Cambridge Law Journal* 550.

48 *Jogee* at [1–2]; *Chang Wing-Siu* (n 68).

49 Andrew Green and Claire McGourlay, 'The Wolf Packs in Our Midst and Other Products of Criminal Joint Enterprise Prosecutions' (2015) 74 *The Journal of Criminal Law* 280, 281; Stark (n 47) 550–1.

50 See discussion in Green and McGourlay (n 49) 282–3.

51 Ibid.

52 Ibid 280–97.

53 Green and McGourlay (n 49).

54 Here, two clarifications are useful. Firstly, in terms of how a case is brought, there is scope for the defence to also meaningfully impact criminalization – however this lies beyond the scope of this chapter. Secondly, 'the court' here is a simplification that encompasses, for the purposes of this chapter, the role of the jury. The court needs to be satisfied that the conduct in question is such that a jury may reasonably convict the defendant for the offence – that is, the court needs to agree with the prosecutor's interpretation and application of the law in the given case.

55 Jogee at 3; see also Stark (n 47).

56 *Jogee* at [8–11].

57 Jogee at [78]; however see critical discussion which puts pressure on that assessment in Henrique Carvalho, 'Dangerous Patterns: Joint Enterprise and the Culture of Criminal Law' (2023) 32 *Social and Legal Studies* 335; Helen Mills, Matt Ford and Roger Grimshaw, 'The Usual Suspects: Joint Enterprise Prosecutions before and after the Supreme Court Ruling' (Centre for Crime and Justice Studies 2022) https://www.crimeandjustice.org.uk/publications/usual-suspects-second-edition accessed 28 October 2024.

58 Haynes (2019) EWCA crim 1217; Jogee 2016 UKSC 8, (14).

59 Eithne Quinn, Erica Kane and Will Pritchard, 'Compound Injustice: A Review of Cases Involving Rap Music Evidence in England and Wales' (University of Manchester 2024) https://documents.manchester.ac.uk/display.aspx?DocID=72455 accessed 28 October 2024.

60 See discussion in Carvalho (n 57).

61 For an example of this, see Kajsa E Dinesson, 'A Terrorist Mindset: Findings from an Empirical Enquiry into Prosecutions, Evidence, and Mindset Material' [2024] Legal Studies https://www.cambridge.org/core/journals/legal-studies/article/terrorist-mindset-findings-from-an-empirical-enquiry-into-prosecutions-evidence-and-mindset-material/8C72A7563D654CA4E02300741B5BB069 accessed 21 November 2024.

62 Jonathan Rogers, 'Restructuring the Exercise of Prosecutorial Discretion in England' (2006) 26 *Oxford Journal of Legal Studies* 775; Jonathan Rogers, 'The Role of the Public Prosecutor in Applying and Developing the Substantive Criminal Law', in *The Constitution of the Criminal Law* (Oxford University Press 2013).

63 Rogers (n 62).

64 Ibid 775–6, 793–7.

65 Ibid 787–91.

66 The nature of prosecutions as an assertion as opposed to as a question may usefully be seen in contrasting these with examples of legal questioning as, for example, is done through Attorney General's and Lord Advocate's References. Rogers discusses this in terms of the 'fairness test' in Rogers (n 62).

References

'An Independent Prosecution Service for England and Wales' (Home Office 1983).

'Annual Report for the Period April 1993–March 1994' (Crown Prosecution Service 1994).

'Annual Report for the Period April 2000–March 2001' (Crown Prosecution Service 2001).

'Annual Report for the Period April 2003–March 2004' (Crown Prosecution Service 2004).

Ashworth A, 'The Public-Interest Element in Prosecutions' (1987) September *Criminal Law Review* 595.

Bentley DJ, *English Criminal Justice in the Nineteenth Century* (Hambledon Press 1998).

Carvalho H, 'Dangerous Patterns: Joint Enterprise and the Culture of Criminal Law' (2023) 32 *Social and Legal Studies* 335.

Carvalho H, *The Preventive Turn in Criminal Law* (Oxford University Press 2017).

Crisp D and Moxon D, 'Case Screening by the Crown Prosecution Service: How and Why Cases Are Terminated' (HMSO 1994) *Home Office Research Study* 137.

Dinesson KE, 'A Terrorist Mindset: Findings from an Empirical Enquiry into Prosecutions, Evidence, and Mindset Material' [2024] Legal Studies https://www.cambridge.org/core/journals/legal-studies/article/terrorist-mindset-findings-from-an-empirical-enquiry-into-prosecutions-evidence-and-mindset-material/8C72A7563D654CA4E02300741B5BB069 accessed 21 November 2024.

Green A and McGourlay C, 'The Wolf Packs in Our Midst and Other Products of Criminal Joint Enterprise Prosecutions' (2015) 74 *The Journal of Criminal Law* 280.

Hetherington T, *Prosecution and the Public Interest* (Waterlow Publishers 1989).

Horder J, *Ashworth's Principles of Criminal Law* (9th edn, Oxford University Press 2019).

House of Commons Justice Committee, 'The Crown Prosecution Service: Gatekeeper of the Criminal Justice System' (The Stationary Office 2009) HC 186 https://publications.parliament.uk/pa/cm200809/cmselect/cmjust/186/186.pdf.

Mills H, Ford M and Grimshaw R, 'The Usual Suspects: Joint Enterprise Prosecutions before and after the Supreme Court Ruling' (Centre for Crime and Justice Studies 2022) https://www.crimeandjustice.org.uk/publications/usual-suspects-second-edition accessed 28 October 2024.

Montgomery J, Jones C and Biggs H, 'Hidden Law-Making in the Province of Medical Jurisprudence: Hidden Law-Making and Medical Jurisprudence' (2014) 77 *Modern Law Review* 343.
Quinn E, Kane E and Pritchard W, 'Compound Injustice: A Review of Cases Involving Rap Music Evidence in England and Wales' (University of Manchester 2024) https://documents.manchester.ac.uk/display.aspx?DocID=72455 accessed 28 October 2024.
Rogers J, 'Restructuring the Exercise of Prosecutorial Discretion in England' (2006) 26 *Oxford Journal of Legal Studies* 775.
Rogers J, 'The Role of the Public Prosecutor in Applying and Developing the Substantive Criminal Law', in RA Duff, Lindsay Farmer, SE Marshall, Massimo Renzo and Victor Tadros (eds), *The Constitution of the Criminal Law* (Oxford University Press 2013) 53–76.
Rozenberg J, *The Case for the Crown: The Inside Story of the Director of Public Prosecutions* (Equation 1987).
Rt. Hon. Sir Iain Glidewell, 'The Review of the Crown Prosecution Service' (The Stationary Office 1998) Cm 3972.
Rt. Hon. Sir Iain Glidewell, 'The Review of the Crown Prosecution Service: Summary of the Main Report with the Conclusions and Recommendations' (The Stationary Office) Cm 3960 https://assets.publishing.service.gov.uk/media/5a7c761640f0b62aff6c1d45/3972.pdf.
Sanders A, 'The CPS: 30 Years On' (2016) 2 *Criminal Law Review* 82.
Sir Cyril Philips, 'The Royal Commission on Criminal Procedure' (House of Commons Library 1981) Cm 8092.
Sir Henry Fisher, 'Report of an Inquiry by the Hon. Sir Henry Fisher into the Circumstances Leading to the Trial of Three Persons on Charges Arising out of the Death of Maxwell Confait and the Fire at 27 Doggett Road, London SE6' (Her Majesty's Stationary Office 1997) https://assets.publishing.service.gov.uk/media/5a7b9a1ced915d131106050d/0090.pdf.
Stark F, 'The Demise of "Parasitic Accessorial Liability": Substantive Judicial Law Reform, Not Common Law Housekeeping' (2016) 75 *Cambridge Law Journal* 550.
'The Code for Crown Prosecutors' (*CPS*, 26 October 2018) https://www.cps.gov.uk/publication/code-crown-prosecutors accessed 28 October 2024.
'The Code for Crown Prosecutors' (Crown Prosecution Service 1986) 1st ed.
'The Code for Crown Prosecutors' (Crown Prosecution Service 2004) 5th ed.
'The Crown Prosecution Service: Gatekeeper of the Criminal Justice System: Government Response to the Committee's Ninth Report of Session 2008–09' (The Stationary Office 2012) HC 245 https://publications.parliament.uk/pa/cm200910/cmselect/cmjust/245/245.pdf.

2

Prosecution in the public interest

The Scottish dimension

Pamela R. Ferguson

Introduction

Scotland is one of the three legal jurisdictions of the UK, with both Northern Ireland and England &Wales each having its own laws and procedures. Scottish Law has its roots in the civil law/European continental law, stemming from classical Roman Law, but has also been influenced by the common law/English Law. Although this makes Scottish Law a 'hybrid' or 'mixed' system, its criminal trials are conducted largely within the adversarial tradition. Members of the judiciary authorize police warrants to arrest suspects and/or to search suspects' homes or offices, and they decide pre-trial applications for release on bail, but are not otherwise involved in the investigation of crime or the prosecution process. However, as we shall see below, aspects of Scotland's prosecution process have historically been closer to the 'inquisitorial' traditions of continental European countries.

Scottish criminal trials may be taken under 'summary procedure' or 'solemn procedure'. 'Summary procedure' is employed in the Justice of the Peace (JP) courts (the lowest courts), with the charges against the accused being listed on a 'complaint'. The fact-finder is a lay judge who is advised on the law by a legally qualified clerk of court. The maximum penalties that can be imposed in the JP courts are imprisonment for sixty days and/or a fine of £2,500.[1] In the High Court of Justiciary, Scotland's highest domestic criminal court, 'solemn procedure' is used and the fact-finder is a lay-jury of fifteen citizens – provisions which would have reduced this number to twelve, in the Victims, Witnesses, and Justice Reform (Scotland) Bill, were ultimately not enacted by the Scottish Parliament.[2] There is no upper limit to the fines and periods of imprisonment which can be imposed in the High Court. The sheriff courts rank between the JP courts and the High Court. The sheriff courts' process can be either summary or solemn, depending on the seriousness of the charges against the accused. Under summary procedure, the maximum penalty a sheriff court can impose is imprisonment for twelve months and/or a fine of £10,000.[3] In sheriff court cases prosecuted under solemn procedure, the maximum penalty is five years' imprisonment and/or an unlimited fine.[4] In all cases (including solemn ones, where a jury determines the verdict), sentencing is a matter for the judge. It is notable that the relevant legislation on solemn procedure specifies that: 'All prosecutions *for the public interest* before the High Court or before the sheriff sitting with a jury shall proceed on indictment'.[5]

The UK ('Westminster') Parliament can enact laws for Scotland but most law-making powers have been devolved to the Scottish Parliament ('Holyrood') since the latter was re-established in 1999.[6] Scotland has its own, unitary police force ('Police Scotland'[7]). The police may deal with low-level offences,[8] but all other prosecutorial decisions are taken by the Crown Office and Procurator Fiscal Service (COPFS, also referred to as 'the Crown'), headed by the Lord Advocate. Legislation provides that the person with overall responsibility for Police Scotland, the chief constable, must comply with all lawful orders from the Lord Advocate[9] and from the COPFS.[10]

A history of prosecution

Although Scotland has had its own legislature for only twenty-six years, its prosecution service, which is independent from those of the other UK jurisdictions, is of much older vintage.[11] The prosecution of crime in Scotland was, historically, a matter for the victims of crime or their families. This type of 'private prosecution' remains competent in Scotland for serious crimes,[12] but is extremely rare, with the most recent, successful private prosecution having been taken in 1982.[13] There are references dating back to the sixteenth century to a Crown official, the 'King's Advocate',[14] who 'was authorized to act as public prosecutor of crimes'.[15] Legislation enacted by the Scottish Parliament in 1587 empowered the King's Advocate to instigate a prosecution even in cases in which this was not favoured by the victim of the crime.[16] The 1587 statute had as its purpose

> to stop the abuse of private agreements between the parties. It gave the King's Advocate, for the first time, the privilege of pursuing, on his own behalf, in every species of criminal case, instead of being restricted to a limited class. It made him, in fact, public prosecutor.[17]

By the early nineteenth century, prosecutions were generally taken by 'his Majesty's Advocate' who 'prosecutes *for the public interest*, and in the name of his Majesty, as guardian and administrator for all his people, of the laws which secure their tranquillity and welfare'.[18]

The modern prosecution process

It has been rightly said that:

> One of the most important factors in the proper administration of criminal justice is to secure a system of prosecution which will have regard to the public interest uninfluenced by ulterior considerations such as popularity or unpopularity, discrimination or revenge.[19]

In the current era, the Crown Office and Procurator Fiscal Service is a national agency, headed by the Lord Advocate and her deputy, the Solicitor General for Scotland. The day-to-day conducting of prosecutions is carried out in the High Court by advocates depute (senior prosecutors, also referred to as 'Crown Counsel'), and by procurators fiscal and their deputes (legally qualified civil servants) in the sheriff courts and justice of the peace courts.[20]

The 'opportunity principle'

In contrast to many jurisdictions which traditionally operated a 'principle of legality' or mandatory prosecution in cases in which there was sufficient admissible evidence,[21] Scottish prosecutors have always had a great deal of discretion in determining whether or not to prosecute any particular case. Systems which allow prosecutors such discretion are said to operate under the 'opportunity principle' or 'principle of expediency'.[22] The High Court has made clear that 'the decision whether to prosecute or not must in each case rest with [the Lord Advocate] as *master of the instance*'[23] – meaning that generally it is for the Crown to determine whom to prosecute, for which charges, and in which court. The High Court has also affirmed that it is for the COPFS to determine whether or not a prosecution 'is in the public interest'.[24] More than sixty years ago, the Court referred to the Lord Advocate as 'the recognized prosecutor in the public interest':

> It is for him, in the exercise of his responsible office, to decide whether he will prosecute in the public interest and at the public expense, and under our constitutional practice this decision is a matter for him, and for him alone. No one can compel him to give his reasons. ... The basic principle of our system of criminal administration in Scotland is to submit the question of whether there is to be a public prosecution to the impartial and skilled investigation of the Lord Advocate and his department, and the decision whether or not to prosecute is exclusively within his discretion. This system has operated in Scotland for centuries, and … the result has completely proved the justice of these principles, for such has become the public confidence in the decision of the Lord Advocate and his deputes on the grounds of prosecution, that private prosecutions have almost gone into disuse. It is utterly inconsistent with such a system that the Courts should examine … the reasons which have affected the Lord Advocate in deciding how to exercise his discretion, and it would be still more absurd for this Court to proceed to review their soundness.[25]

More recently, the Court noted that: 'The public interest in the investigation and suppression of crime' was 'one of the strongest factors in the historical development of the role of the Lord Advocate as the sole prosecutor in the public interest in our system'.[26]

The meaning of the public interest

The main statute governing criminal procedure in Scotland is the Criminal Procedure (Scotland) Act 1995. This refers to prosecutions as being '*for* the public interest'[27] and defines prosecutors as acting '*in* the public interest'.[28] The 'public interest' is a phrase which encompasses a range of values, including efficiency, finality and procedural integrity. As long ago as 1968, the High Court held that while individual liberty had to be protected against 'undue or unnecessary invasion', this could at times be outweighed by the 'public interest' in identifying those who are suspected of having committed serious crimes, and detecting evidence of their crimes.[29] Dicta from the appeal court have also emphasized that there is a public interest in the alleged victims of crime (referred to as 'complainers', in Scottish Law) and other witnesses being treated with respect at all stages of the criminal process.[30] This is particularly important in trials for sexual offences, to avoid further trauma to complainers who may have already been seriously harmed by the offence itself. Thus in *SJ v HM Advocate*,[31] the appeal court noted that

> it is now well established that the fairness of a trial encompasses more than fairness to an accused, not least the *public interest* in crimes being reported and investigated, and the respectful treatment of those making reports of sexual offences both before and during a trial.[32]

Efficiency

The importance of prosecutions being 'efficient and expeditious' has been stressed by the appeal court.[33] Where an accused person is facing several charges, Scottish practice is that they should generally be prosecuted on the same indictment, that is, at the same trial. This is so even when the charges are not related in terms of type of charge or date of offence. The accused's lawyers may ask the court to permit there to be two (or more) separate trials, where having all charges tried at the same time might be prejudicial to the accused. This could be the case where a jury, having been satisfied that there is sufficient evidence to convict an accused of a minor offence, may, as a result, be more inclined to convict of other, more serious, offences on the same indictment. However, the more common approach is to prosecute all charges in one trial. This is based on a desire to save time and money (efficiency), but also safeguards the accused from having to undergo multiple prosecutions.[34]

Prosecutions must be taken in a timely fashion – the appeal court regards trials being 'brought to a timeous conclusion' as an aspect of the public interest.[35] Legislation provides for quite tight time limits during which trials must begin. Although there is a presumption in favour of bail being granted and accused persons being at liberty while awaiting trial,[36] in solemn cases, in particular, bail might not be granted and the accused person may be remanded in custody prior to trial. The relevant legislation specifies that a person may be remanded in custody pre-trial where 'there is a good reason for refusing bail',[37] and specifies that in making such decisions a court must have 'regard to the public interest'.[38] The maximum period within which a trial must start if an accused person has been denied bail in a solemn case is 140 days,[39] while for those on bail, the trial must generally begin within twelve months from the date when the accused first appeared in court to respond to the indictment.[40] The defence or the prosecution can ask the court to extend these periods if there is a good reason for this,[41] and such motions are often granted. However, the appeal court has referred to the need to balance

> on the one hand the public interest in the prosecution of crime with, on the other hand, the public interest, and the interests of a person against whom proceedings have been brought, in securing that criminal proceedings are pursued efficiently.[42]

This reflects the requirement in Article 5 of the European Convention on Human Rights that prosecutions be conducted within a 'reasonable time'.

Finality

There are limited grounds on which an accused person may appeal against a conviction in Scottish Law, but these include 'any alleged miscarriage of justice', and this may be based on an averment that the verdict was one which 'no reasonable jury, properly directed [on the law by the trial judge], could have returned'.[43] In practice, the appeal court is reluctant to interfere with juries' convictions, since the jurors have seen and heard the witnesses' testimony, unlike the appeal court which generally has to determine the case from written transcripts of the trial.[44] The court has referred to there being a 'legitimate public interest' in not overturning a jury verdict without there being substantial doubt as to its integrity.[45]

Procedural integrity

It would be a mistake to view the public interest as being in tension with the interests of the accused in receiving a fair trial since it is in the public interest for trials to be fair.[46] One aspect of this is that a trial judge must direct a jury that it may convict an accused of a charge which is less serious than the one specified on the indictment. For example, if the charge on the indictment is murder, the jury may instead convict the accused of culpable homicide (where the accused is found to have caused the victim's death, but did not intend to kill, or where the requisite causation and intent have both been proven, but there are other mitigating factors recognized by the law). Alternatively, the jury may find that there is insufficient evidence that the accused did in fact cause the victim's death, and so may return a verdict of guilty of attempted murder, or of assault to severe injury. A key point is that the appeal court has held that the jury is entitled to convict an accused of these less serious crimes, and the judge should direct the jury of its power to do so, even where these alternative verdicts have not been suggested to the jury by the prosecution or the defence lawyers.[47] This approach is taken on the basis that:

> In any criminal prosecution for a serious offence there is an important public interest in the outcome. ... The public interest is that, following a fairly conducted trial, [accused persons] should be convicted of offences which they are proved to have committed and should not be convicted of offences which they are not proved to have committed. ... [This] is the ultimate responsibility of the trial judge.[48]

The decision to prosecute

Police officers complete a 'Standard Prosecution Report' (SPR) for each case they investigate; this ensures that the prosecution has all necessary information about the alleged offence (date, time, place). The SPR will include a list of potential witnesses and other types of evidence, as well as information about the alleged offender, such as any criminal record/previous convictions, 'mental health, alcohol or drug use, risk, vulnerability, disability, attitude to offending, family dynamics and education or employment status'.[49] When completing these Reports, police officers can include their opinion on whether a case could be suitable for diversion from prosecution.[50] It seems, however, that officers suggest this in less than half of all suitable cases.[51] His Majesty's Inspectorate of Prosecution in Scotland (HMIPS) has recently recommended that:

> Police Scotland should ensure that reporting officers have an appropriate level of awareness of the overarching principles of diversion from prosecution, including the role of partner agencies, and a good working knowledge of the national guidelines on diversion.[52]

The COPFS website begins its description of its role in Scotland's criminal justice system by stating that once a crime has been reported to it: 'A procurator fiscal ... will assess the evidence. If there is enough evidence the procurator fiscal will decide what action to take, if any, in the public interest'.[53] This process is known as 'marking', and cases are marked by staff in the COPFS's National Initial Case Processing unit – this centralization is designed 'to promote consistency and efficiency in the marking of cases, and to facilitate a national approach to prosecution'.[54] A prosecution can be taken only if there is sufficient, admissible evidence to prove: (i) that the crime was committed, and (ii) that the accused was the person responsible for having committed it. This can be a difficult hurdle for the prosecution to overcome, since Scotland operates a general corroboration requirement: there must be at least two independent sources of evidence to establish each of these factors.[55]

Where no corroboration has been found which can support a complainer's evidence, a case may be 'marked' as 'no proceedings' or 'no proceedings meantime'. However, even in cases where there is sufficient, admissible evidence, the COPFS's *Prosecution Code* includes an additional test, namely that the 'public interest' must be taken into account in deciding whether or not to prosecute a case.[56] The *Code* specifies thirteen 'public interest considerations' to which prosecutors must have regard. These are:

i. The nature and gravity of the offence
ii. The impact of the offence on the victim and other witnesses
iii. The age, background and personal circumstances of the accused (this can include any previous convictions which an accused person may have)
iv. The age and personal circumstances of the victim and other witnesses
v. The attitude of the [alleged] victim
vi. The motive for the crime
vii. The age of the offence (there is no statute of limitations in Scottish criminal cases; however, if there has been a long lapse of time since the offence was allegedly committed, this may mean that prosecution is no longer in the public interest)
viii. Mitigating circumstances (this could include that the accused acted under 'extreme provocation' or that the accused has offered to provide financial compensation to the victim)
ix. The effect of prosecution on the accused
x. The risk of further offending [by the accused person]
xi. The availability of a more appropriate civil remedy (it may be that the case would be better dealt with in the non-criminal courts as a breach of contract, or by means of a delictual action)
xii. Powers of the court (for instance, to award compensation payable by the accused to the victim; to disqualify the accused from driving, etc.)
xiii. Public concern (this includes local community interests).[57]

Although the expense of taking a prosecution is specified as a factor to be taken into consideration in the prosecution policies in some jurisdictions,[58] this is not explicitly included in the Scottish *Code*. However, in practice, Scottish prosecutors operate under the principle of *de minimis non curat lex:* the law does not concern itself with trivial matters. This criterion allows prosecutors to use their discretion not to prosecute minor offences.

The decision *not* to prosecute

A key part of prosecutorial discretion in Scotland is the power of the Crown to decline to prosecute a case. As Lord Carloway, formerly the Lord Justice General (Scotland's most senior judge), has explained:

> An option not to prosecute a person for a particular crime has always been available in Scotland; it being a matter for [the Lord Advocate] to decide whether to do so in the public interest.[59]

A highly experienced advocate depute has pointed out that the Crown must

> prosecute fairly in the public interest. If the evidence does not match up to the requirements of evidence, whether that be through its quality, reliability or quantity, there might be no substantial prospect of a conviction at all. The prosecutor is not there to represent the victim to get the case limping into court under any circumstances.[60]

When a decision is taken not to prosecute a case, this may be recorded as having been due to a range of factors. Of the thirteen considerations listed above, numbers (vii), (viii), (ix) and (xi) are more likely to weigh in favour of a decision *not* to prosecute.

The right to a review

In compliance with the UK's obligations under the EU Directive *on establishing minimum standards on the rights, support and protection of victims of crime,*[61] the Lord Advocate was required by legislation to 'make and publish' rules to allow complainers to seek a review of a decision by the COPFS not to prosecute an accused person.[62] Each Member State can determine its own review procedure, and some require the alleged victim to pay for this. Scotland does not charge for this service. The 'right to a review' is described in the *Lord Advocate's Rules:*

Review of a Decision Not to Prosecute.[63] The task of the reviewer is to determine whether the original decision was reasonable, taking into account all the circumstances, the COPFS prosecution policies and the Prosecution Code.[64] As one commentator notes, 'The focus of this test is therefore whether the original decision can be *justified* rather than whether it was the *correct* decision in the circumstances'.[65] This is in contrast to the scheme which applies in England and Wales, where a reviewer is asked to consider whether the original decision 'was *unreasonable* or whether it was *wrong*'.[66] The Scottish right to a review applies only where the decision has been to take no action against an accused person: it does not apply to a decision to apply some diversionary measure.[67] This complies with the requirements of the EU Directive.[68]

Alternatives to prosecution

A Scottish prosecutor may decide that it is not in the public interest to take a case to court, but may nonetheless determine that the case should be dealt with by one of a number of alternatives to prosecution. These include the accused being given a formal verbal or written 'warning' from the prosecutor or, if the accused has alcohol, drug or mental health issues, their case being 'diverted' to a social service agency for treatment or support.[69] According to the *National Guidelines on Diversion from Prosecution in Scotland* (2020), diversionary measures offer 'an appropriate person-centred response' which consider both the offence and the (alleged) offender, in the hope that quick input from social services can 'prevent further offending'.[70] Dorothy Bain, KC, the current Lord Advocate, has explained that

> diversion should be considered for all individuals reported to [the COPFS] where there is an identifiable need which has contributed to the offending which can best be met through a diversion scheme. Prosecutors will consider all the circumstances and determine the appropriate outcome in the public interest. … Any decision to prosecute the person is normally deferred until completion of a diversion program of support.[71]

In its *National Strategy for Community Justice* (2022) the Scottish Government emphasized its desire to: 'Optimise the use of diversion and intervention at the earliest opportunity':

> Where appropriate and relevant, effectively diverting people away from prosecution – or away from the justice system entirely – can allow individuals to

> address a range of issues, behaviours or needs which have contributed to their alleged offending at the earliest opportunity. This improves outcomes for both individuals and communities, and can lead to less offending and reoffending and, ultimately, fewer victims and harm to society. We also recognise that those who come into contact with the justice system often present with higher levels of vulnerability than the general population and often have complex needs. We therefore want to ensure that, wherever appropriate, people are diverted away from the justice system at the earliest opportunity following arrest, and that suitable, appropriately informed and tailored opportunities, which reflect the nature and severity of the alleged offence, are provided to address underlying needs and causes of offending behaviour.[72]

Accused persons must agree to their cases being disposed of in this way. From 2022–3 to 2023–4 there were 3,400 cases diverted from prosecution to social services agencies. This represents a 28 per cent increase, and is the highest percentage in the most recent ten-year period.[73] It seems that 90 per cent of those who are offered case diversion are successful in completing this.[74]

Another alternative, which applies to minor road traffic offences, is for fiscals to offer an accused person a fiscal fixed penalty of between £50 and £300.[75] For other offences, a fiscal may offer an accused person one of a range of 'conditional disposals' or 'direct measures', in lieu of prosecution. These measures are available for offences which would otherwise be tried under summary procedure (i.e. less serious types of offences). They are: payment of a fine directly to the prosecution (a 'fiscal fine' of between £50 and £300[76]); a fiscal work order: undertaking unpaid labour of between ten and fifty hours[77] (e.g. for a charity); or payment of financial compensation (up to £5,000) to the complainer.[78] In 2023–4, there were 102 fiscal work orders, 25 per cent fewer than in the previous year.[79] The latest data (from 2022 to 2023) show that of the 145,000 reports received by procurators fiscal during that period, 68,000 people received a conviction in court for one or more crimes or offences.[80] No action was taken in 13,000 cases. Of those dealt with by 'direct measures', for 10,500 cases, this was by way of a fiscal fine; a further 10,900 received the offer of a fiscal fixed penalty; and 3,200 were given a warning from the fiscal.[81] These alternatives to prosecution operate in an 'opt-out' fashion: the offer is made by the fiscal and is taken to have been accepted by the accused unless the latter notifies the clerk of court that they do not accept the offer. A prosecution for the original offence will then generally be taken.

The Scottish prosecutor's discretion to act in the 'public interest' does not end at the point at which a decision is made to prosecute an alleged offender, but persists as the case proceeds towards trial. In a recent report, HMIPS noted that:

> Throughout the life of a case, the decision to prosecute should be kept under continuous review. The marking depute's initial decision may no longer be appropriate if new evidence emerges or circumstances change. As court deputes manage and prepare the case, they should also be reassessing whether there is a sufficiency of evidence and whether it is in the public interest to prosecute.[82]

This means that the prosecution can decide to terminate proceedings at any time prior to a guilty verdict being returned at trial.

The trial

In her study of several European prosecution systems,[83] Julia Fionda found that:

> Scottish [procurators fiscal] see their role in the courtroom very much in terms of presenting all relevant evidence, whether favourable or unfavourable to the prosecution case. It is for the court to decide the outcome; prosecutors simply aim for a reasonable sentence in any case and act in the public interest. The traditional two-sided adversarial fight seen in English trials is less evident in a Scottish trial, and elements of the inquisitorial systems of Northern Europe are stronger.[84]

This means that a prosecutor may decide during a trial to accept an offer from an accused person to plead guilty to a less serious charge to the one being tried. For example, in a murder prosecution in 2018, the accused's daughter was called as a witness for the Crown. Following the daughter's testimony, the advocate depute who was prosecuting the case decided to accept the accused's plea of guilty to the crime of 'culpable homicide'. Unlike the crime of murder which has a penalty of 'life imprisonment' fixed by law, a trial judge who is sentencing someone for culpable homicide has a wide discretion in determining the appropriate sentence. In accepting a plea of guilty to this less serious crime, the advocate depute explicitly referenced the fact that he was acting 'as a prosecutor in the public interest'.[85] This meant that no further evidence was heard, and the jury was dismissed. One might have thought that the prosecutor was usurping the role of the lay jurors in taking away from them the determination of whether the accused was guilty of murder or of culpable homicide. However, the trial court stressed that the decision was made as part of the advocate depute's 'prerogative as a prosecutor acting in the public interest'.[86] Indeed, the court stressed that the Crown had discharged its duty to act in the public interest in a 'scrupulous' manner.[87]

Judges are conscious of the need to keep the public interest in mind when determining whether or not to allow certain types of evidence to be led at trial. This applies particularly when the evidence is of questionable provenance, such as where the police have not followed proper procedures in obtaining it. The appeal court has emphasized that it is required to balance the rights of the individual not to be subject to sharp police practices against the importance of ensuring that the police are able to investigate crimes. Thus, a court should avoid

> hamstringing the police in their investigation of crime with a series of academic vetoes which ignore the realities and practicalities of the situation and discount completely the public interest.[88]

At the same time, while noting the public interest 'in placing highly relevant evidence before the jury', the Court has emphasized that this interest 'can never be of such overriding importance that it will persuade the Court to permit the leading of evidence that would breach the fundamental requirement of fairness'.[89]

The fair treatment of complainers

It is important to stress that a Scottish prosecutor's duty to consider the wider public interest means that they are not the 'complainer's lawyer'. As Fiona Raitt explains:

> There is no lawyer-client relationship between a prosecutor and a complainer – and thus none of the characteristics of that relationship based upon trust, confidentiality and legitimate partisanship. The Crown's role as a public prosecutor and officer of the court inevitably restricts the scope for supporting the complainer [whose] interests are subordinated to wider concerns, possibly without even the opportunity of being canvassed before a judge.[90]

This can lead to tension in prosecutors' relationships with complainers. As HMIPS has noted:

> In all their contact with victims, one challenge faced by prosecutors is the need to convey their role as acting in the public interest rather than being a representative for the victim. While the interests of victims and the public interest may sometimes align, this is not always so.[91]

A study in 2019, which involved interviews with seventeen complainers in sexual offences cases, found that they were far from satisfied with their experiences of the prosecution process.[92] Complainers had assumed that the prosecutor's job was to 'win their case' and be 'on their side'.[93] The report concluded that

> The requirement for the COPFS [to] prosecute in the public interest, rather than [in the interests] … of the victim, contributed to victim-survivors feeling very let down by prosecutors and unprepared for the evidence that they were about to give.[94]

It was noted above that the Scottish prosecutor is regarded as the 'Master of the Instance'. This means that once complainers have reported their case to the police, they thereafter have little say in determining whether a prosecution will, or will not, go ahead. The High Court has held that it is not appropriate for the COPFS to consult complainers or their families as part of its decision to accept an accused person's pre-trial plea to a less serious offence. As the Court explained,

> in exercising the judgment whether it is appropriate to prosecute, the Lord Advocate, as an independent prosecutor, may take into account the sentiments of a complainer; but a decision not to proceed is the decision of the Lord Advocate, who, as such independent prosecutor, is not in any sense a representative or agent of a complainer. If, having taken a decision in light of those sentiments, those sentiments or wishes change, that can hardly be a reason, consistent with the concept of an independent prosecutor, for sanctioning the reversal of a decision not to prosecute and undermining the finality intended by the legislature.[95]

As discussed earlier in this chapter, complainers/victims have a right to a review of a decision not to prosecute, but once the prosecutor has decided that a case should proceed to trial, complainers have no right to have the case dropped. In *Opuz v Turkey*,[96] the European Court of Human Rights recognized that there was a lack of consensus among Member States as to whether prosecutions were required to be continued even if the alleged victim decided to withdraw the complaint. The Court listed a number of factors which prosecutors could consider, including the seriousness of the offence; whether the alleged victim has physical or psychological injuries; any impact the alleged offence has had on any children in the alleged victim's household; the accused's previous convictions (particularly if these are for crimes of violence) and how likely the accused is to re-offend; whether the accused is alleged to have used a weapon, planned the attack or threatened the alleged victim since the attack, the history of the relationship between the accused and the alleged victim, any continuing relationship between and parties, and the impact on that relationship if the prosecution is continued against the alleged victim's wishes. Nevertheless, the ECtHR held that 'the more serious the offence or the greater the risk of further offences, the more likely that the prosecution should continue in the public interest, even if victims withdraw their complaints'.[97] A Scottish Government website advises complainers:

> You cannot ask to drop the charges at a later date. Once the details of the crime have been passed to the procurator fiscal, it's up to them to decide whether it is in the public interest to proceed with the case or not.[98]

Conclusion

As this chapter has demonstrated, concern for the 'public interest' permeates the Scottish prosecution process, beginning with the initial decision on whether to take no action, to dispose of a case by one of a range of alternative measures, or to prosecute the case in court. Where the decision is to prosecute, public interest considerations continue to apply for the duration of the trial process. However, as David Garland argues, we should recognize that complainers' interests cannot necessarily be 'subsumed within the "public interest" that guides the prosecution and penal decisions of the state'.[99]

Legislations

Bail and Release from Custody (Scotland) Act 2023
Coronavirus (Recovery and Reform) (Scotland) Act 2022
Criminal Procedure (Scotland) Act 1995
Police and Fire Reform (Scotland) Act 2012
Road Traffic Offenders Act 1988
Scotland Act 1998
Victims and Witnesses (Scotland) Act 2014
Victims, Witnesses, and Justice Reform (Scotland) Bill
Scottish Statutory Instrument
Coronavirus (Recovery and Reform) (Scotland) Act 2022 (Extension of Temporary Justice Measures) Regulations 2024 (SSI 2024/322)
EU Law

Council Framework Decision 2001/220/JHA
Directive 2012/29/EU *establishing minimum standards on the rights, support and protection of victims of crime*

Cases

Ashif and Ashraf v HM Advocate [2015] HCJAC 100
Beggs v HM Advocate [2025] HCJAC 69
Collins v HM Advocate [2013] HCJAC 167
Ferguson v HM Advocate [2008] HCJAC 71
Gordon v HM Advocate [2018] HCJAC 21
Hay v HM Advocate 1968 JC 40
HM Advocate v ARK and AR [2013] HCJAC 107
HM Advocate v Cairns 1967 JC 37
HM Advocate v Cooney [2022] HCJAC 10
HM Advocate v PG and JM [2024] HCJAC 43
Jackson v HM Advocate [2017] HCJAC 72
King's Advocate v Lord Dunglas (1836) 15 S 314
LB v HM Advocate 2003 JC 94
Lord Advocate's Reference (No. 1 of 2023) [2023] HCJAC 40
MacDonald v HM Advocate [2020] HCJAC 21
McBain v Crichton 1961 JC 25
Miln v Cullen 1967 JC 21
Opuz v Turkey (2010) 50 EHRR 28.
R v Coutts [2006] 1 WLR 2154
SJ v HM Advocate [2020] HCJAC 18
Toal v HM Advocate [2012] HCJAC 123
Van Phan v HM Advocate [2018] HCJAC 7
X v Sweeney 1982 JC 70

Notes

1 Criminal Procedure (Scotland) Act 1995, s 7(6)(a) and (b).

2 Victims, Witnesses, and Justice Reform (Scotland) Bill, s 34(2). This would have amended the Criminal Procedure (Scotland) Act 1995, s 88(2). (Note that unlike Bills in the Westminster Parliament, those of the Scottish Parliament have 'sections', rather than 'clauses').

3 Criminal Procedure (Scotland) Act 1995, s 5(2)(a) and (d).

4 Ibid s 3(3).

5 Ibid s 64(1) (emphasis added).

6 See the Scotland Act 1998, s 1(1): 'There shall be a Scottish Parliament'.

7 Police Scotland was formed in 2013 by the Police and Fire Reform (Scotland) Act 2012, s 6. Prior to then, there were eight regional forces. For further discussion of police powers and limitations on these powers, see Pamela R Ferguson, *The Law of Criminal Procedure in Scotland* (SULI/W Green 2023) Chapter 7.

8 The Police may issue a recorded police warning (RPW) or an Anti-Social Behaviour Fixed Penalty Notice (ASBFPNs) for minor offences. They issued 21,127 RPWs in 2022–3 and 4,722 SBFPNs: Scottish Government, *Criminal Proceedings in Scotland: 2022–23* (2024), 49.

9 Police and Fire Reform (Scotland) Act 2012, s 17(3)(b). See also the Criminal Procedure (Scotland) Act 1995, s 12 which provides that the Lord Advocate may issue occasional instructions to the police chief constable regarding the reporting of offences. This allows the Lord Advocate to issue policy guidelines for particular types of offences and offenders.

10 Police and Fire Reform (Scotland) Act 2012, s 17(3)(a).

11 See Ferguson (n 7) paras 8-002 and 8-003.

12 That is, crimes prosecuted before a judge and a lay jury ('solemn procedure').

13 *X v Sweeney* 1982 JC 70. For the background to the case, see R Harper and A McWhinnie, *The Glasgow Rape Case* (Hutchinson 1983).

14 George WT Omond, *The Lord Advocates of Scotland: From the Close of the Fifteenth Century to the Passing of the Reform Bill* (D. Douglas 1883) 1.

15 *King's Advocate v Lord Dunglas* (1836) 15 S 314, 327.

16 Ibid. See also David Hume, *Commentaries on the Law of Scotland Respecting Crimes*, Vol II (4th edn, Bell & Bradfute 1844) 130.

17 Omond (n 14) 50.

18 Hume (n 16) 118 (emphasis added). See also Archibald Alison, *Practice of the Criminal Law of Scotland* (Blackwood 1833) xi, referring to the prosecution of crimes as 'a matter of public interest'.

19 TB Smith, 'Public Interest and Safeguards for the Suspect' (1965) 11 *McGill Law Journal* 43, 44.

20 For a history of this office, see R Shiels, 'Procurators Fiscal from 1885 to 1918: The Move from Men of Business to Professional Public Prosecutors: Part 1' (2010) *Scottish Criminal Law* 1027, and by the same author 'Procurators Fiscal from 1885 to 1918: The Move from Men of Business to Professional Public Prosecutors: Part 2' (2010) *Scottish Criminal Law* 1137.

21 Mirjan Damaška, 'Structures of Authority and Comparative Criminal Procedure' (1975) 84 *Yale Law Journal* 480, 503–4.

22 Ibid.

23 *HM Advocate v Cairns* 1967 JC 37, 41 (emphasis added).

24 *HM Advocate v ARK and AR* [2013] HCJAC 107, [19].

25 *McBain v Crichton* 1961 JC 25, 29.

26 *HM Advocate v Cooney* [2022] HCJAC 10, [33].

27 Criminal Procedure (Scotland) Act 1995, s 64(1) (emphasis added).

28 Ibid s 307(1) (emphasis added).

29 *Hay v HM Advocate* 1968 JC 40, 46.

30 *Beggs v HM Advocate* [2025] HCJAC 69, [39] and [40]; *MacDonald v HM Advocate* [2020] HCJAC 21, [33].

31 [2020] HCJAC 18.

32 Ibid [27] (emphasis added). See also John D Jackson and Sarah J Summers, 'Seeking Core Fair Trial Standards across National Boundaries: Judicial Impartiality, the Prosecutorial Role and the Right to Counsel' in John D Jackson and Sarah J Summers (eds), *Obstacles to Fairness in Criminal Proceedings: Individual Rights and Institutional Forms* (Hart Publishing 2018) 104: there is 'an important public interest attached to the right to a fair trial': this 'operates not just for the benefit of defendants but for the benefit of society as well'.

33 *Ashif and Ashraf v HM Advocate* [2015] HCJAC 100, [57].

34 See Hume, *Commentaries* (n 16) 172.

35 *Jackson v HM Advocate* [2017] HCJAC 72, [17].

36 Criminal Procedure (Scotland) Act 1995, s 23B. This will be amended by the Bail and Release from Custody (Scotland) Act 2023 when the relevant provisions of that Act are brought into force.

37 Criminal Procedure (Scotland) Act 1995, s 23B(1)(a).

38 Ibid.

39 Ibid s 65(4)(aa)(ii) (High Court) and 65(4)(b)(ii) (sheriff courts).

40 Ibid s 65(1)(b). Longer periods had been introduced during the COVID-19 pandemic, under the Coronavirus (Recovery and Reform) (Scotland) Act 2022, s 50 and schedule, Part 5, Chapter 1, para 22 (accused remanded in custody, pre-trial) and para 20 (accused at liberty, pre-trial). These provisions were due to expire on 30 November 2024 but this has been further extended until 30 November 2025 by the Coronavirus (Recovery and Reform) (Scotland) Act 2022 (Extension of Temporary Justice Measures) Regulations 2024 (SSI 2024/322).

41 Criminal Procedure (Scotland) Act 1995, s 65(3).

42 *Collins v HM Advocate* [2013] HCJAC 167, [14] per Lord Eassie. See also [21].

43 Criminal Procedure (Scotland) Act 1995, s 106(3)(b).

44 Although the appeal court has power to hear evidence from witnesses (ibid s 104(1)(b) and (2)), an appeal in Scotland is not a re-hearing of all the evidence which was led at the original trial.

45 *Toal v HM Advocate* [2012] HCJAC 123, [108].

46 See TB Smith, 'Public Interest and the Interests of the Accused in the Criminal Process – Reflections of a Scottish Lawyer' (1958) 32 *Tulane Law Review* 349. See also *SJ v HM Advocate* [2020] HCJAC 18, [27].

47 *Ferguson v HM Advocate* [2008] HCJAC 71.

48 Lord Bingham in *R v Coutts* [2006] 1 WLR 2154, [12], cited ibid at [31].

49 HM Inspectorate of Prosecution in Scotland, *Joint Review of Diversion from Prosecution* (2023) para 9.

50 Ibid. Diversion is considered further, below.

51 Ibid 6.

52 HM Inspectorate of Prosecution in Scotland, *The Prosecution of Domestic Abuse Cases at Sheriff Summary Level* (2024) 9, Recommendation 8.

53 COPFS website: 'Scotland's criminal justice system' (last updated 22 July 2024), available at: https://www.copfs.gov.uk/the-justice-process/scotland-s-criminal-justice-system/ .

54 *Joint Review of Diversion from Prosecution* (n 49) para 64.

55 In recent years, the corroboration requirement has been interpreted by the Scottish appeal court in a more liberal fashion: see *Lord Advocate's Reference (No. 1 of 2023)* [2023] HCJAC 40, and *HM Advocate v PG and JM* [2024] HCJAC 43.

56 Crown Office and Procurator Fiscal Service, *Prosecution Code* (most recently updated on 14 July 2023) 2. This is available at: https://www.copfs.gov.uk/publications/prosecution-code/html/.

57 Ibid 3–5.

58 Australia: Commonwealth Director of Public Prosecutions, *Prosecution Policy of the Commonwealth: Guidelines for the Making of Decisions in the Prosecution Process* (2021), para 2.10 (q); Public Prosecution Service for Northern Ireland, *Code for Prosecutors* (2023), para 4.14 (xiii); Sweden: *Swedish Code of Judicial Procedure* (1998), Chapter 23, Section 4a, para 1.

59 *Van Phan v HM Advocate* [2018] HCJAC 7, [38].

60 Evidence from Derek Ogg, QC, to: Justice Committee of the Scottish Parliament, *Role and Purpose of the Crown Office and Procurator Fiscal Service* (2017) para 213.

61 Directive 2012/29/EU *establishing minimum standards on the rights, support and protection of victims of crime*, art 11. This Directive replaces the Council Framework Decision 2001/220/JHA.

62 Victims and Witnesses (Scotland) Act 2014, s 4(1).

63 COPFS, *Lord Advocate's Rules: Review of a Decision Not to Prosecute – Section 4 of the Victims and Witnesses (Scotland) Act 2014*. These rules came into force on 1 July 2015.

64 COPFS, *Victims' Right to Review* (last updated 15 November 2024), available at: https://www.copfs.gov.uk/services/victim-services/victims-right-to-review/.
65 S Colman, 'A Comparison of the Implementation of the Victims' Right to Review in England and Wales, Scotland and Northern Ireland' [2018] 5 Criminal Law Review 365, 375 (emphases added).
66 Ibid (emphases in original).
67 (n 63) 2. These measures are discussed further below.
68 (n 61) art 11(5).
69 This process began following the recommendations of the Stewart Committee, *Keeping Offenders Out of Court: Further Alternatives to Prosecution*, Cmnd 8958 (HMSO, 2nd report, 1983).
70 Community Justice Scotland, *National Guidelines on Diversion from Prosecution in Scotland* (2020) 3.
71 COPFS, 'Lord Advocate statement on Diversion from Prosecution' (2021), available at: https://www.copfs.gov.uk/about-copfs/news/lord-advocate-statement-on-diversion-from-prosecution/.
72 Scottish Government, *National Strategy for Community Justice* (2022) 7.
73 Scottish Government, *Justice Social Work Statistics in Scotland: 2023–24 – Part 1* (2024) 3.
74 *Joint Review of Diversion from Prosecution* (n 49) 8.
75 Road Traffic Offenders Act 1988, s 75(2).
76 Criminal Procedure (Scotland) Act 1995, s 302(7A). Payment may be made by instalments. The maximum has been temporarily increased to £500 until 30 November 2025, by the Coronavirus (Recovery and Reform) (Scotland) Act 2022, s 52 and sch, para 1, as amended by the Coronavirus (Recovery and Reform) (Scotland) Act 2022 (Extension of Temporary Justice Measures) Regulations 2024 (SSI 2024/322), reg 2(2).
77 Criminal Procedure (Scotland) Act 1995, s 303ZA(2).
78 Ibid s 302A. This may be paid by instalments.
79 *Justice Social Work Statistics in Scotland: 2023–24* (n 73) 3.
80 *Criminal Proceedings in Scotland: 2022–23* (n 8), 14, Chart 1.
81 Ibid. All figures are rounded in the Report to the nearest 100 (ibid, Note 1).
82 (n 52) para 219.
83 Namely: the Netherlands, England & Wales, Germany and Scotland.
84 J Fionda, *Public Prosecutors and Discretion: A Comparative Study* (Clarendon Press 1995) 66.
85 *Gordon v HM Advocate* [2018] HCJAC 21, [28].
86 Ibid [40].
87 Ibid.

88 *Miln v Cullen* 1967 JC 21, 29–30.

89 *LB v HM Advocate* 2003 JC 94, [14].

90 FE Raitt, *Independent Legal Representation for Complainers in Sexual Offence Trials* (Rape Crisis Scotland 2010), paras 7.10 to 7.11. This document is included as an appendix in J Chalmers, F Leverick, and A Shaw (eds), *Post-Corroboration Safeguards Review: Report of the Academic Expert Group* (2014).

91 *The Prosecution of Domestic Abuse Cases at Sheriff Summary Level* (n 52) para 360.

92 O Brooks-Hay, M Burman and L Bradley, *Justice Journeys: Informing Policy and Practice Through Lived Experience of Victim-Survivors of Rape and Serious Sexual Assault* (Scottish Centre for Crime and Justice Research 2019) 19.

93 Ibid.

94 Ibid.

95 *Collins* (n 42) [18].

96 (2010) 50 EHRR 28.

97 Ibid [139].

98 See https://www.mygov.scot/police-investigation/the-decision-to-take-a-case-to-court#:~:text=Asking%20to%20drop%20the%20charges,if%20you%20have%20any%20concerns.

99 D Garland, *The Culture of Control: Crime and Social Order in Contemporary Society* (Oxford University Press 2001) 11.

References

Alison A, *Practice of the Criminal Law of Scotland* (Blackwood 1833).

Brooks-Hay O, Burman M and Bradley L, *Justice Journeys: Informing Policy and Practice through Lived Experience of Victim-Survivors of Rape and Serious Sexual Assault* (Scottish Centre for Crime and Justice Research 2019).

Chalmers J, Leverick F and Shaw A (eds), *Post-Corroboration Safeguards Review: Report of the Academic Expert Group* (2014).

Colman S, 'A Comparison of the Implementation of the Victims' Right to Review in England and Wales, Scotland and Northern Ireland' (2018) 5 *Criminal Law Review* 365.

Commonwealth Director of Public Prosecutions, *Prosecution Policy of the Commonwealth: Guidelines for the Making of Decisions in the Prosecution Process* (2021).

Community Justice Scotland, *National Guidelines on Diversion from Prosecution in Scotland* (2020).

Crown Office and Procurator Fiscal Service, *Lord Advocate's Rules: Review of a Decision Not to Prosecute – Section 4 of the Victims and Witnesses (Scotland) Act 2014* (2015).

Crown Office and Procurator Fiscal Service, *Lord Advocate Statement on Diversion from Prosecution* (2021).

Crown Office and Procurator Fiscal Service, *Prosecution Code* (2023).

Crown Office and Procurator Fiscal Service, *Victims' Right to Review* (2024).

Damaška M, 'Structures of Authority and Comparative Criminal Procedure' (1975) 84 *Yale Law Journal* 480.

Ferguson PR, *The Law of Criminal Procedure in Scotland* (SULI/W Green 2023).

Fionda J, *Public Prosecutors and Discretion: A Comparative Study* (Clarendon Press 1995).

Garland D, *The Culture of Control: Crime and Social Order in Contemporary Society* (Oxford University Press 2001).

Harper R and McWhinnie A, *The Glasgow Rape Case* (Hutchinson 1983).

HM Inspectorate of Prosecution in Scotland, *Joint Review of Diversion from Prosecution* (2023).

HM Inspectorate of Prosecution in Scotland, *The Prosecution of Domestic Abuse Cases at Sheriff Summary Level* (2024).

Hume D, *Commentaries on the Law of Scotland Respecting Crimes*, Vols II (4th edn, Bell & Bradfute 1844).

Jackson JD and Summers SJ (eds), *Obstacles to Fairness in Criminal Proceedings: Individual Rights and Institutional Forms* (Hart Publishing 2018).

Justice Committee of the Scottish Parliament, *Role and Purpose of the Crown Office and Procurator Fiscal Service* (2017).

Omond GWT, *The Lord Advocates of Scotland: From the Close of the Fifteenth Century to the Passing of the Reform Bill* (D Douglas 1883).

Public Prosecution Service for Northern Ireland, *Code for Prosecutors* (2023).

Raitt FE, *Independent Legal Representation for Complainers in Sexual Offence Trials* (Rape Crisis Scotland 2010).

Scottish Government, *Criminal Proceedings in Scotland, 2022–23* (2024).

Scottish Government, *Justice Social Work Statistics in Scotland: 2023–24 – Part 1* (2024).

Scottish Government, *National Strategy for Community Justice* (2022).

Shiels R, 'Procurators Fiscal from 1885 to 1918: The Move from Men of Business to Professional Public Prosecutors: Part 1' (2010) *Scottish Criminal Law* (November) 1027.

Shiels R, 'Procurators Fiscal from 1885 to 1918: The Move from Men of Business to Professional Public Prosecutors: Part 2' (2010) *Scottish Criminal Law* (December) 1137.

Smith TB, 'Public Interest and the Interests of the Accused in the Criminal Process – Reflections of a Scottish Lawyer' (1958) 32 *Tulane Law Review* 349.

Smith TB, 'Public Interest and Safeguards for the Suspect' (1965) 11 *McGill Law Journal* 43.

Stewart Committee, *Keeping Offenders Out of Court: Further Alternatives to Prosecution*, Cmnd 8958 (2nd report, HMSO 1983).

Swedish Code of Judicial Procedure (1998).

3

Rule of law and public interest in Polish criminal proceeding from an axiological perspective

Bartłomiej Oręziak and Marcin Wielec

Introduction

According to Poland's supreme legal act, the Constitution of the Republic of Poland of 2 April 1997 (hereinafter: CRP)[1] – Poland is a democratic state governed by the rule of law, implementing the principles of social justice (Article 2 of the CRP). This means that Poland is a country where law takes precedence over the state, and governance is based on the rule of law rather than the rule of individuals or the majority.[2] Article 2 of the CRP, as interpreted by the Polish Constitutional Tribunal, represents a composite expression of numerous rules and principles that, while not explicitly stated in the CRP's text, inherently derive from the axiology and essence of a democratic state governed by the rule of law.[3] One such principle is the principle of the rule of law, which also encompasses the principle of legality.[4] Parallel to these legal principles operates the concept of public interest, which represents *the raison d'état.* Although the CRP does not explicitly define public interest, it manifests across multiple provisions and functionally connects with the principles of the rule of law and legality. The significance of these legal concepts in Poland is also evident in their reflection not only in the CRP, but also in sectoral laws such as the Act of 6 June 1997, Code of Criminal Procedure (hereinafter: CCP).[5] The CCP defines the course of criminal proceedings under the jurisdiction of Polish courts. This legal act serves as the primary source of norms for formal criminal law in Poland. According to Article 87 of the CRP, the sources of universally binding law in the Republic of Poland include the CRP, statutes, ratified international agreements and regulations. Additionally, on the territory of the authorities that issued them, acts of local law also constitute sources of universally binding law.

This catalogue is exhaustive, and nothing else in Poland can serve as a source of law in the positivist sense.[6] However, it should be noted that no legal system is established without reasons underlying the decision to normative concretization of legal norms. From this naturalistic perspective on legal systems,[7] law reflects the values that a society seeks to realize through the application of legal instruments. Consequently, from a scientific and theoretical standpoint, it is justified to discuss the significance of values in law in the context of legal systems.[8] It can be concluded that the formal aspect of sources of law determines how law should be enacted and in what form. The closed catalogue specifying that law comprises the CRP, statutes, ratified international agreements and regulations does not determine the substantive content of legal norms. It seems that this content is determined by the values respected by society. It is no coincidence that Article 4 of the CRP states that the supreme power in the Republic of Poland belongs to the Nation, which exercises its authority either through its representatives or directly.

This means that Poland is a country governed by the rule of law, where laws are enacted in a strictly defined form, and their content should be determined by the values that society – represented by the Nation as the sovereign authority – seeks to realize through the law. Here, the concept of public interest reemerges, indeed. It becomes apparent that there are certain values in the law that serve society as a whole, such as those related to security, public order or public health. At the same time, there are values in the law that, although they also pertain to society as a whole, are perceived on an individual level. These include values expressed through personal safety, bodily integrity or respect for human rights and freedoms. Only a combination of these collective and individual values should ultimately determine the substantive content of the law and define the extent to which the law can go to realize values aligned with the public interest, understood as the raison d'état – namely, the interests of society considered on a global scale.

The chapter is divided into five parts. The first discusses the definition and theoretical basis of the rule of law. Then its main addressees and unilateral influence on public authority are indicated. The next part is devoted to an analysis of the legal and institutional mechanisms that guarantee compliance with this principle in Poland. The fourth part deals with the relationship between the rule of law and criminal proceedings and the role of the prosecutor's office. The last part of the chapter presents the role of the prosecutor's office in protecting the rule of law and the public interest. The methodology adopted combines normative analysis with axiological interpretation, showing the impact of values on the organization and practice of criminal procedure in Poland. Axiological analysis examines the values underlying the law and their influence on the creation, interpretation and application of norms. It includes an assessment of how social and individual values, such as security, order, dignity or human rights, shape the law. It also considers how the rule of law and the public interest reflect deeper social and cultural ideals.

The rule of law: Seeking a definition

In democratic states, the idea of the rule of law, embodying the principle of the rule of law, is a fundamental concept. However, the model of a state based on this idea is not something new. It, indeed, is generally accepted that this concept – 'the idea of basing the existence (and prosperity) of the state on the absolute adherence to legal norms (primarily statutory law)' –originated in antiquity, appearing in the works of Plato, Roman jurists and in Byzantium.[9] These observations highlight the strong bonds between the rule of law, legal systems and the state. These elements are undoubtedly interdependent and mutually reinforcing. In scholarly discourse, these connections have been distinctly recognized.

One notable scholar who explored the relationship between law and the state, L.L. Fuller described law as 'an activity aimed at subjecting human behavior to defined rules of conduct'.[10] In his concept of the so-called internal morality of law, the rule of law is realized when, first, the law is sufficiently general to ensure impartiality; second, the law is properly promulgated, meaning it is public and transparent; third, the law does not have retroactive effect; fourth, the law is clear and easy to interpret; fifth, the law avoids contradictions between norms; sixth, the law is relatively stable over time; seventh, the law does not require the impossible from its subjects; and eighth, official actions are consistent with the law.[11] Furthermore, most dictionary definitions describe the rule of law as a system 'organized in accordance with the law, governed by the law'[12] and this is connected with rightly statement that 'the highest instance of authority remains the law [...]'.[13]

Regarding the types of the rule of law, legal theory recognizes a distinction between the formal rule of law and the substantive rule of law. The former, i.e. the formal rule of law, is understood as a directive rooted in the foundations of the state's constitutional framework. In this sense, the rule of law obliges state authorities to strictly adhere to the law and operate in accordance with universally binding legal norms.[14] The second type, namely the substantive rule of law, goes beyond fulfilling the requirements of the formal rule of law by additionally incorporating the principle of law being equal for all and respecting fundamental freedoms and the rights of individuals and citizens. The substantive rule of law is grounded in the principle of universal equality before the law, which derives, among other sources, from the previously mentioned Article 2 of the Constitution of the Republic of Poland (CRP). It is also emphasized that the substantive rule of law is closely linked to the concept of substantive justice. Although the substantive rule of law directly references the principle of equality before the law, scholars stress that 'this is not a principle of absolute equality. Under this principle, differential treatment of various categories of subjects may be justified. The distinction between justified and unjustified inequalities can only be determined based on a system of moral values [...]'.[15] In summary of the presented distinction, the first concept – the formal rule of law – defines a lawful state as one in which the law is adhered to by public authorities, regardless of the content of that law. In contrast, the second concept – the substantive rule of law – focuses on the nature of the law itself, emphasizing what the law should be and the substantive content of the legal norms that must be observed.[16]

To summarize the aforementioned definitions of the rule of law, it can be specified that the rule of law 'in the narrow sense, is the obligation to adhere to the legal order, while in the broader sense, it encompasses the totality of norms constituting the legal order, defining the framework for the application of law, the procedures leading to it, institutions that combine substantive and procedural elements in their actions, and all of this in relation to the subjects of the law'.[17]

The rule of law: The addressee of the value

The constitutional dimension of the rule of law is more visible and appreciated in legal scholarship, as the activities of key state organs in the legislative and executive spheres are more prominently highlighted there. Scientifically – in legal studies – the issue of the rule of law primarily belongs to the domains of legal theory and philosophy, as well as to some extent constitutional law, since, as a pillar of statehood, it inherently aligns with the constitutional relationships of the state. Moreover, it is correct to view the rule of law as being primarily associated with the public dimension of the state, rather than with private interests. Public authorities, in fulfilling their mandates, must act properly – meaning in accordance with the rule of law – as they are the first and most critical actors for the organization and functioning of the state. This requirement, however, is not equally imposed on individuals. While individuals are also subject to the legal regime and must comply with it, the law applies to them more as a synchronizer and regulator of social relations, influencing them preventively and restoratively. If an individual violates the law, they will face appropriate consequences, which are enforced by the relevant state authority, depending on the type, impact and scope of the violation. A private individual does not have any independent decision-making authority to legally influence the position of another individual in the public sphere. By contrast, a public authority has significant powers to affect an individual's position – such as their rights and obligations – within the limits recognized by law. At the same time, the individual has a legitimate expectation that this authority will respect their legally granted rights. In cases of unlawful actions by the authority, the individual also has appropriate recourse mechanisms to respond.

In light of the above, it can be inferred that the value of the rule of law is not based on a feedback mechanism, as can be observed, to some extent, in the value of dignity. The rule of law is rather unidirectional, as this value primarily affects public authorities, which are its main addressees. Even in definitional descriptions, it is emphasized that the rule of law obliges state authorities to comply with the law, act solely on the basis of legal provisions, and strictly in accordance with the law. Its purpose, however, is to ensure that citizens' rights granted by law are respected and to protect them from the arbitrariness of state authorities.[18] The addressees of the value of the rule of law are therefore always public authorities, which are simply obligated to comply with the law. This naturally results in the respect of all rights granted to individuals.[19] At the same time, it is the law that determines what rights an individual has and what obligations are imposed upon them. However, when public authorities intervene in these granted rights, as long as such actions remain within the legal boundaries assigned to those authorities, they are considered lawful actions under the rule of law, which the individual is expected to accept.

The rule of law: Legal and institutional guarantees

For an effective fulfilment of the principles of the rule of law, an appropriate institutional framework is required. This framework involves the functioning of entities endowed with powers aimed at realizing the value of the rule of law. These entities safeguard and uphold the rule of law by ensuring that other entities, directly or indirectly linked to public authority, do not exceed the boundaries set by law, while themselves remaining bound by the rule of law. In this sense, democratic systems often establish institutional structures specifically responsible for ensuring compliance with the rule of law. The CRP, in addition to defining the foundations of the rule of law (Article 2 CRP), provides for a range of institutions tasked with its protection. These include, among others, the Supreme Audit Office, the Ombudsman, the State Tribunal and the Constitutional Tribunal.[20] The objectives of these institutions differ individually, but they are united by the overarching purpose of overseeing other state organs. In case of any violations of the value of the rule of law – essentially actions contrary to the law – they aim to address these violations, eliminate them and, where possible, mitigate their consequences. The existence of an institutional structure dedicated to the protection of the rule of law is essential. Without such institutions, the rule of law would remain merely an abstract, meaningless and unenforceable concept. It is therefore accepted that the realization of the rule of law is directly tied to the legal actions of state authorities, in the areas of both lawmaking and law enforcement.[21]

The principle of legality is closely tied to the rule of law. It requires that state authorities not only comply with and respect the law but also act solely and strictly within its boundaries. In Poland, the legal basis for the principle of legality is provided in Article 7 of the CRP, which states: 'Public authorities shall operate on the basis of, and within the limits of, the law'. This principle is also reflected in other legal acts, including the CCP.

The rule of law: Its relationship to criminal proceedings and the office of the prosecutor

The question arises regarding the relationship between the rule of law and criminal proceedings in Poland. It appears that criminal proceedings, with their distinctive nature, represent an area where the value of the rule of law holds exceptional significance. Considering the unique character of criminal proceedings, which involve significant interference with the individual, it becomes evident how crucial and autonomous the role of the rule of law is in this domain.[22]

Undoubtedly, this type of legal procedure, in the form of criminal proceedings, requires the continuous involvement of public authorities, whose decision-making processes encompass essential actions that, to varying degrees, impact individuals. Criminal proceedings are conducted primarily in the public interest, with limited connections to private interests. Given that criminal proceedings are associated with one of the state's branches of power (the judiciary) and significantly affect an individual's position in society in the context of their rights, only the lawful actions of the criminal justice authorities – being public bodies – ensure that the process is conducted correctly. Thus, there is no doubt that the significance of the rule of law becomes particularly prominent in criminal proceedings, where the interests of public authorities frequently intersect with those of individuals, although decision-making typically remains within the purview of public authorities. Consequently, criminal procedure represents a critical domain where ensuring the effective implementation of the rule of law is essential. This assertion, however, also extends successfully to proceedings before public administration bodies, administrative courts and other areas of public decision-making.[23]

Considering the range of participants in criminal proceedings, their roles, assigned powers, and the outlined significance of the rule of law, it is evident that the burden of implementing the rule of law is not equally distributed among them. Neither the accused nor the victim is an entity predisposed to protect or uphold the rule of law, as neither possesses the appropriate status for this purpose, and their procedural roles are entirely different. Most importantly, they are not public entities. Thus, it is beyond question that the rule of law in this context pertains exclusively to the actions of public authorities. It does not apply to individuals, who can only demand that public authorities uphold and implement the rule of law.

In criminal proceedings in Poland, the participants include several public entities, notably the prosecution service, which serves as a cardinal organ of criminal proceedings. However, the constitutional position of the prosecution extends far beyond the scope of criminal proceedings, as its statutory mandate encompasses the broad safeguarding of the rule of law (sensu largo). Although in this role the prosecution primarily formulates and supports the accusation in virtually every case of a legal order violation, its mandate to protect the rule of law also includes participation in administrative and judicial-administrative proceedings, and even in civil proceedings. This diversity of contexts in which prosecutors operate has been recognized since the inception of this office.[24] Therefore, it is a mistake to reduce the role of the prosecution solely to criminal proceedings, where it indeed plays a crucial role. However, granting it the ability to operate in other procedural contexts, such as administrative or civil proceedings, positions it as a powerful institution designed to safeguard the rule of law in its entirety (in extenso) within the state. The rule of law has a universal dimension, encompassing the overarching obligation of all public authorities to comply with the law, regardless of the area in which they operate.

In the case of the prosecution service, the pivotal importance lies in the content of Article 2 of the Act on the Prosecution Service,[25] which explicitly highlights that the primary task of the prosecution is to safeguard the rule of law, followed by the duty to oversee the prosecution of crimes. Additionally, it is worth noting that the legislator deliberately uses the term 'safeguarding' rather than terms such as 'controlling', 'monitoring' or 'securing'. The term 'safeguarding' is significantly more precise and effective in its meaning, as it implies the existence of active measures to respond to any observed violations of the rule of law. 'Safeguarding' also encompasses supervision,[26] meaning the continuous analysis and monitoring of the activities of public administration bodies to ensure their compliance with applicable laws. In essence, it involves verifying whether these bodies act in accordance with the principles of the rule of law.[27] The prosecution service is, therefore, a guardian of the rule of law, endowed with significant prerogatives to enforce it, essentially in relation to all public authorities and, naturally, individuals as well.

Considering the above-mentioned, there is no doubt that the office of the prosecutor is inherently linked to the realization of the rule of law. It is universally accepted that the prosecution acts as an institution ensuring the rule of law, as its fundamental mandate is to safeguard the rule of law and oversee the prosecution of crimes.[28] The prosecutor is portrayed as a 'guardian' of the rule of law, a body responsible for ensuring the lawful and proper functioning of state authorities.[29] It is also emphasized that a prosecutor operating in contexts such as administrative and judicial-administrative proceedings serves as a 'custodian of the public interest'.[30]

The above perspective has a direct connection to the study of criminal procedure, where the prosecutor is positioned within three procedural roles:

first, as the authority conducting pre-trial proceedings; second, as the public prosecutor; and third, as the advocate of the public interest (or advocate of the rule of law).[31] From the standpoint of the rule of law, the last model is particularly significant, as it assigns the prosecution the role of an advocate for the public interest, or simply, an advocate of the rule of law.

In the context of the current discussion, attention is drawn to the term 'advocate', which, according to dictionary definitions, also means proponent, supporter, promoter, representative, spokesperson or someone who defends someone or something and supports a particular cause.[32] In criminal procedure, the concept of 'advocates' does not formally appear in the Code of Criminal Procedure (CCP). Neither the previous nor the current CCP in Poland uses this term. Instead, it is a theoretical construct based on numerous provisions of the CCP that define the procedural roles of entities fitting within the scope of the term 'advocate'.[33]

The prosecutor's office and the public interest

Another element directly linked to safeguarding the rule of law that warrants attention is the concept of the social interest or public interest. It is worth noting that both terms appear within the framework of Polish criminal proceedings. Although their meanings differ slightly, for the purposes of this analysis, they can be treated as synonyms. The social or public interest serves as one of the guiding principles for the prosecutor's actions as an advocate of the rule of law. Additionally, it functions as a general clause, meaning a vague term whose precise meaning is determined by context, including even non-systemic dimensions.[34] A general clause is a term that is inherently ambiguous, which is why various attempts have been made to define it.[35] Among other things, it is emphasized that general clauses are

> a clear legislative construct (an element of a legal provision) formulated in legal language, granting authorization to the authority applying the law to determine the behavior of the decision's addressee or to establish the basis for qualifying the behavior of the norm's addressee. This is done based on criteria (norms, evaluations) expressed (named) in the legal text but not incorporated (for various reasons) into the system of legal provisions.[36]

The social interest serves as a motivator for prosecutorial actions in the role of the aforementioned advocate of the rule of law. Social interest demands that every authority acts lawfully. Thus, it is not without reason to assert that the concept of an advocate of social interest, and therefore simultaneously an advocate of the rule of law,[37] encompasses the prosecutor's two other roles: as the authority in preparatory proceedings and as the public prosecutor.

In Poland, the prosecutor's role as both the authority in preparatory proceedings and the public prosecutor depends on the specific stage of the criminal proceedings.[38] A prosecutor acting as the authority in preparatory proceedings undertakes actions specifically reserved for this distinct stage of criminal proceedings. At this stage, the prosecutor generally acts independently, serving as the so-called master of the proceedings (dominus litis).[39] On the other hand, the prosecutor as the public prosecutor operates during the judicial stage of criminal proceedings, performing a different set of tasks. According to Article 10 § 1 of the CCP, the authority responsible for prosecuting crimes is obligated to initiate and conduct preparatory proceedings, while the public prosecutor is also required to file and support an indictment for offences prosecuted ex officio. Thus, it is rightly emphasized that the prosecutor's role as an advocate of the rule of law in criminal proceedings is

> crucial and fundamental; it serves as a unique common denominator for all actions undertaken by the prosecutor throughout the course of criminal proceedings. This role should be upheld consistently by the prosecutor during all stages of criminal proceedings, alongside the two other procedural roles previously mentioned. Its interaction with these roles is determined in each instance by the specific action the prosecutor may undertake at various stages of the criminal process.[40]

The position of the prosecutor as an advocate of the public interest is derived, among other things, from Article 6 of the Act of 28 January 2016, on the Prosecution Service,[41] which states that the prosecutor is obligated to undertake actions specified in the law, guided by the principles of impartiality and equal treatment of all citizens.[42] Moreover, within the provisions of the CCP, in addition to the tasks typically associated with the prosecution service, such as overseeing preparatory proceedings and ultimately drafting, filing and supporting indictments, there are also actions that directly relate to the prosecutor's role as an advocate of the rule of law.

One provision that legitimizes the prosecutor's active involvement in criminal proceedings by justifying it with the existence of a public interest is Article 60 § 1 of the CCP. According to this provision, in cases involving crimes prosecuted by private indictment, the prosecutor may initiate proceedings or join proceedings already initiated if the public interest so requires. In such instances, the proceedings are conducted ex officio, and the victim who initially filed the private complaint retains the rights of a subsidiary prosecutor. Article 60 CCP thus allows for the prosecutor's intervention in cases of crimes prosecuted by private indictment, based on the justification of public interest. However, the provision does not provide a detailed definition of what constitutes the public interest in this context.[43] It appears that the scope of the term public interest should encompass all situations in which a private prosecution offence infringes upon the interests of the general public. The assessment of whether a public interest exists lies solely with the prosecutor and is not subject to judicial review. Furthermore, Article 60 CCP does not require the prosecutor to explicitly justify the reasons that led them to determine that the public interest necessitates their intervention.[44] The study of criminal procedure emphasizes that 'the public interest in prosecuting private indictment offenses arises when the criminal act directly infringes not only the legally protected interests of the victim but also general societal goods'.[45]

Regarding the prosecutor's obligation to respond when assessing whether a public interest exists, it seems reasonable to assert that, upon a positive determination of the existence of a public interest, the prosecutor cannot refrain from intervening, as such inaction would represent an impermissible expression of opportunism. The previously mentioned principle of legality also extends to the obligation to prosecute private indictment offences if the public interest so requires. There is no room for 'discretionary judgment' in this matter. It is further emphasized that 'submitting a notification to the prosecutor regarding a private indictment offense obliges the prosecutor to examine whether there is a public interest in prosecuting the offense, and they cannot automatically issue a decision refusing to initiate preparatory proceedings'.[46] The scope of the term 'public interest' should encompass all situations where a private indictment offence infringes upon the interests of the general public. It is important to remember that a victim's request for the prosecutor to assume prosecution arises from the victim's helplessness, vulnerability or some other impediment they face. The assessment of public interest and the associated need for intervention rests solely with the prosecutor, and the lack of a definition for the term 'public interest' highlights the subjective nature of such judgements. When interpreting this term and identifying its specific elements, it is reasonable to include factors such as the victim's helplessness, difficulties in gathering evidence or the particularly complex nature of the case. Consequently, factors such as the anonymity of the perpetrators or the victim's inability to directly identify them should be considered part of this group of elements.[47] A similar situation arises with the prosecutor's involvement in criminal proceedings initiated through the submission of a subsidiary indictment, which allows for an independent prosecution in cases that fall under the public prosecution procedure.[48] This type of prosecutorial activity should also be analysed in the context of the prosecutor's status as an advocate of the rule of law.

Additionally, the prosecutor, as an advocate of the rule of law, may act on behalf of a party weakened by unforeseen circumstances during the proceedings, pursuing their position in the name of the general interest. The legal basis for this is provided in Article 52 § 1 of the CCP, which states that in the event of the victim's death, the rights that would have belonged to the victim may be exercised by close relatives or dependents. In the absence or non-disclosure of such persons, the prosecutor may act ex officio. As a side note, it is worth pointing out that this example, derived from the provision of Article 52 CCP, represents a multifaceted realization of values. As previously discussed, the exercise of rights by the entities specified in Article 52 CCP also serves to uphold the value of human dignity. This demonstrates that values in criminal proceedings frequently intersect and complement each other, which is a natural occurrence stemming from the integrity of values.

Another example of the prosecutor's role as an advocate of the rule of law (or advocate of the public interest) is the authority provided under Article 425 §3 and §4 of the CCP. According to these provisions, the prosecutor, as a public prosecutor, is not bound by the gravamen principle when filing appeals. Generally, the appealing party may only challenge decisions or findings that infringe upon their rights or harm their interests. However, this limitation does not apply to the public prosecutor, who is also entitled to file an appeal in favour of the accused. It is rightly stated that

> at this stage of the proceedings, the prosecutor, while still a party to the process in the classical sense, also assumes a special role, being not only an advocate of the prosecution but also a guardian of the public interest. […] The fact that the prosecutor can file a cassation appeal in favor of the accused, in addition to representing the public interest, implies that the prosecutor may act not only in the exercise of their own procedural rights but also – acting in the interest of the accused – exercise the rights of the latter as another party to the proceedings.[49]

Based on the analysis of the above-mentioned institutions within criminal proceedings, it is quite clear that the prosecutor – acting as an advocate of the rule of law – functions as an authority dedicated to implementing the principles of the rule of law. Through the prerogatives granted to it, the prosecution service upholds the rule of law in the interest of the public as a whole. Furthermore, the category of 'advocates' occupies a position somewhere between the parties to the criminal proceedings and the representatives of those parties, endowed with the authority to act directly based on statutory provisions.[50]

It is worth considering whether the institutional status of the prosecution service in Poland is currently somewhat weak, especially when compared to the highly respected role of the prosecutor as an advocate of the rule of law. One might reasonably adopt the view that, to highlight the prosecutor's significant role in criminal proceedings as an advocate of the rule of law, it is necessary to consider the frequently discussed concept in legal scholarship of constitutionalizing the prosecution service. This would involve elevating the prosecution service to a constitutional organ by embedding the foundations of its operation and organization into the highest-ranking legal act – the CRP.

This perspective is justified by the fact that the lack of constitutional roots for the prosecution service, to some extent, undermines its purpose and significantly weakens its institutional standing. Since other entities equipped with strictly supervisory powers are enshrined in the CRP, it is reasonable to propose a de lege ferenda recommendation to reintroduce the prosecution service into constitutional provisions. The aim would be to elevate the status of the prosecution service, which, in comparison to other supervisory bodies with constitutional roots – such as the Supreme Audit Office, the Ombudsman or the National Broadcasting Council – is significantly constitutionally marginalized and often compared institutionally to professional legal associations.

As is evident, numerous institutions tasked with ensuring compliance with the law have their foundations in the CRP. Constitutional provisions include entities such as the Ombudsman, the Children's Ombudsman and even purely administrative bodies like the National Broadcasting Council. The suggestion of constitutionalizing the prosecution service is, of course, a de lege ferenda proposal. It is justified, among other reasons, by the fact that the prosecution service's primary mission is to implement the constitutional value of the rule of law, as confirmed by Article 2 of the Act on the Prosecution Service (2016).

For the prosecution service to effectively fulfil its role as a guardian of the rule of law, its model – in statu esse – must be versatile and comprehensive.

Assuming that the prosecution service is a guardian of the rule of law, restricting its role to that defined by its criminal procedural specificity – narrowing it to a law enforcement body – would significantly marginalize the institution. Limiting the prosecutor's role to that of an accuser in criminal proceedings would confine the concept of the guardian of the rule of law to matters of exclusively criminal provenance. Currently, the prosecution service successfully acts on behalf of the public as an advocate of the rule of law in administrative, judicial-administrative and civil proceedings (e.g. cases involving incapacitation). Therefore, it is fitting that, given its broad treatment as a guardian and advocate of the rule of law, the scope of the prosecution service's activities in the Polish legal system should not be restricted solely to the criminal realm. Prosecutors operate in civil and administrative proceedings – areas entirely distinct from the criminal procedural sphere – fulfilling their role as advocates of the rule of law.

Broadly understood, the rule of law encompasses the protection of fundamental rights guaranteed to individuals by the state. The word 'prosecution service' itself originates from the Latin term, *procurare*, meaning 'to take care of interests' or 'to manage'.[51] The prosecution service embodies the representation of both public interests and the possibility of representing individual interests, all within the framework of upholding the rule of law. It seems evident, however, that a strong prosecution service is necessary – one that should not only hold the status of a constitutional organ but also possess the competencies to serve as the primary and impartial authority in the state.

This authority would ensure the proper, equitable and uniform realization of the value of the rule of law. There is considerable merit in the assertion that, during the preparatory stage of proceedings, the rule of law requires the prosecutor to exhibit strong objectivity rather than being guided by opportunism or conformity. Placing an individual under suspicion or later indictment demands integrity and diligence from the prosecutorial authority. Acting as an advocate of the rule of law, the prosecutor ensures adherence to the law, which should be created in the spirit of efficiency and benefit for the nation, as the source of the mandate to undertake appropriate actions on behalf of state authorities. Therefore, in cases of violations of the rule of law, it is imperative for the prosecutor to take appropriate measures to rectify the breach and restore a lawful state of affairs.

In summary, regarding the realization of the rule of law by the prosecutor, it must ultimately be emphasized that ensuring the rule of law through prosecutorial actions is motivated by the common good (the social or public interest). This is particularly significant in situations where there is a disparity in competencies between public authorities and individuals. In such cases, the prosecutor's role as an advocate of the rule of law becomes especially vital. The prosecution service, as an institution tasked with safeguarding the rule of law, seeks to mitigate the procedural or competency deficiencies of individuals. Acting as an advocate of the rule of law, the prosecutor strives to achieve public objectives while simultaneously addressing the individual goals of the affected person.

Conclusion

The above analysis demonstrated that, based on the legal provisions in force in Poland within the context of criminal proceedings, it is possible to reflect on the concept of the rule of law as a value present in the legal order. This presence, however, is not characterized by stasis or passivity but rather by dynamism and activity. Although the rule of law lacks a formal legal definition, it holds meaning grounded in axiological principles. In this respect, the value of the rule of law also incorporates the important element of the principle of legality, which serves as a directive for action based on and within the limits of the law. Within the same framework lies the concept of the public interest, whose perception and implementation are influenced by the value of the rule of law itself. The exemplification of this value in the Polish normative order, as described and outlined in this analysis, has its designated addressees as well as a foundation of legal and institutional guarantees.

In the realm of Polish criminal proceedings, conducted in accordance with the provisions of formal criminal law – primarily contained in the CCP but also reflecting principles enshrined in the CRP – there exists a procedural body that is pivotal for the realization of the value of the rule of law while also serving as an executor of the public interest. The axiological and legal analysis conducted here has revealed that in Poland, this body is the prosecutor, who combines the dual roles of guardian of the rule of law and advocate of the public interest. However, the prosecutor is not entirely free in performing these duties.

First and foremost, under the principle of the rule of law, the prosecutor is bound by the provisions of universally binding law, as, like any state authority, they can act only within the boundaries of and on the basis of the law. Yet, as this analysis has shown, this is not as straightforward as it may appear. The prosecutor's work is governed by something that, while legally difficult to define, nevertheless holds binding force. This element ensures that the prosecutor's actions transcend the formalities of being a state organ; their conduct is not solely directed by procedural law but also incorporates something far more substantive. This refers to the metaphysical dimension of law, akin to the discourse on legal sources, which imbues the provisions of general clauses with substantive content. In other words, this is what determines, for example, how to interpret actions taken in the 'public interest'. Consequently, the prosecutor, as the guardian of the rule of law and advocate of the public interest in Polish criminal proceedings, is also compelled to refer to values widely recognized by Polish society and rooted in European culture. These values necessitate that the prosecutor's actions align with the rule of law and the public interest, as understood through this cultural and societal lens.

In concluding this analysis, it should be emphasized that the rule of law requires the prosecutor, as its guardian, not only to comply with the law – acting on its basis and within its limits – but also to actively work towards ensuring the best possible realization of the value of the rule of law within the state. Secondly, the prosecutor is responsible for fulfilling the public interest as its advocate in Polish criminal proceedings. This means that the realization of the public interest must respect the rule of law, and thus it must be based on legal grounds. One might conclude that, to serve the public interest, the prosecutor merely needs to rely on the appropriate legal basis. However, this is not entirely true, as the concept of the public interest is shaped by the axiology of law, which defines its boundaries through the axiological perspective of the value of the rule of law.

Legislations

Constitution of the Republic of Poland 1997

Act of 26 July 2024 amending certain acts to improve the operations of the Armed Forces of the Republic of Poland, the Police, and the Border Guard in the event of a threat to state security

Act of 28 January 2016 - Law on the Public Prosecutor's Office

Announcement of the Marshal of the Sejm of the Republic of Poland of 20 February 2024 on the publication of the consolidated text of the Act - Law on the Public Prosecutor's Office

Cases

Judgment of the Constitutional Tribunal (Poland) 16 June 1999, P 4/98
Judgment of the Court of Appeal in Szczecin 10 April 2014, case no II AKa 48/14, LEX no 1459031
Judgment of the Supreme Court 6 September 2001, case no V KKN 216/01, OSP No 3 (2002) item 44

Notes

1 Constitution of the Republic of Poland 1997.

2 Wiesław Skrzydło, *Polskie prawo konstytucyjne* (LexisNexis 2003) 109; Dorota Fleczer and Krzysztof Małysa, 'Wokół problematyki praworządności' (2022) 22 (2) *Roczniki Administracji i Prawa* 31, 32.

3 Judgment of the Constitutional Tribunal (Poland) 16 June 1999, P 4/98.

4 Hanna Suchocka, 'Geneza i ewolucja bezpośredniego stosowania Konstytucji RP' (2022) 226 (2) *Studia Prawnicze* 9; Michał Bitner and Michał Kulesza, 'Zasada legalizmu a zdolność kontraktowa jednostek samorządu terytorialnego' (2009) 6 *Samorząd Terytorialny* 5; Anna Rakowska-Trela, 'Prezydent Rzeczypospolitej Polskiej jako strażnik konstytucji' (2023) 104 *Acta Universitatis Lodziensis. Folia Iuridica* 141.

5 Act of 26 July 2024 amending certain acts to improve the operations of the Armed Forces of the Republic of Poland, the Police, and the Border Guard in the event of a threat to state security.

6 Ryszard Mojak, 'System źródeł prawa w Konstytucji Rzeczypospolitej Polskiej z 2 kwietnia 1997 r' (2009) 12 *Studia Iuridica Lublinensia* 27–50; Izabela Malinowska, 'Źródła prawa w Konstytucji RP z 1997 roku' (2017) 6 *Przegląd Sejmowy* 282; Andrzej Jackiewicz, 'Uwagi na temat "niedomknięcia" źródeł prawa powszechnie obowiązującego w Konstytucji Rzeczypospolitej Polskiej z 2 kwietnia 1997 r', in Stanisław Bożyk (ed), *Prawo, parlament i egzekutywa we współczesnych systemach rządów. Księga poświęcona pamięci Profesora Jerzego Stembrowicza* (Temida 2 2009) 61; Paweł Bucoń, 'U źródeł prawa pozytywnego' (2012) 29 *Modern Information Technologies and Innovation Methodologies of Education in Professional Training Methodology Theory Experience Problems* 131–7.

7 Marzena Kordela, 'Aksjologia źródeł prawa' (2016) 78 (2) *Ruch Prawniczy, Ekonomiczny i Socjologiczny* 15; Karol Wojtyła, 'Osoba ludzka a prawo naturalne' (1970) 18 (2) *Roczniki Filozoficzne/Annales de Philosophie/Annals of Philosophy*

53; Jerzy Laskowski, 'Prawo naturalne' (1991) 34 (1–2) *Prawo Kanoniczne* 151; Wojciech Łączkowski, 'Prawo naturalne a prawo stanowione. Uwagi prawnika' (1999) 12 *Ethos* 173; Adriana Kurasz, 'Czy istnieje prawo naturalne?' (2007) 9 (1) *Studia Ełckie* 35; Jacek Salij, 'Prawo naturalne i prawa stanowione w ujęciu św. Tomasza z Akwinu' (2017) 26 (2) *Łódzkie Studia Teologiczne* 103; Oliver Wendell Holmes, 'Natural law', in Andrew Delbanco (ed), *Writing New England: An Anthology from the Puritans to the Present* (Harvard University Press 2001) 328; Brian Bix, 'Natural law theory', in *A Companion to Philosophy of Law and Legal Theory* (2nd edn, Wiley-Blackwell 2010) 209; Brian Tierney, 'Natural Law and Natural Rights: Old Problems and Recent Approaches' (2002) 64 (3) *The Review of Politics* 389.

8 Marcin Wielec, *Wartości – analiza z perspektywy osobliwości postępowania karnego* (Wydawnictwo Academicon 2017); Remigiusz Sobański, 'Prawo jako wartość' (1999) 42 (3–4) *Prawo Kanoniczne* 11–26; Wojciech Łączkowski, 'Prawo i moralność' (2000) 9 *Poznańskie Studia Teologiczne* 205; Sławomir Tkacz, 'Prawo a wartości w teorii prawa Józefa Nowackiego' (2017) 6 (2) *Filozofia Publiczna i Edukacja Demokratyczna* 255; Roman Kwiecień, 'Wartości i prawo a kreatywność porządku prawnego' (2010) 1 (1) *Forum Prawnicze* 30; Jerzy Leszczyński, 'Wartości w teorii prawa Jerzego Wróblewskiego' (2013) 2 (2) *Filozofia Publiczna i Edukacja Demokratyczna* 258; Tomasz Barankiewicz, 'Aksjologiczna problematyka prawa' (2019) 14 (1) *Roczniki Nauk Prawnych* 45; Łukasz Pikuła, 'Bezpieczeństwo prawne jako podstawowa wartość prawa w systemie prawa' (2017) 39 *Przegląd Prawno-Ekonomiczny* 130.

9 Krzysztof Wroczyński, 'Demokratyczne państwo prawne' (1994) 3 *Człowiek w Kulturze* 197.

10 Lon L Fuller, *Moralność prawa* (Wydawnictwo PWN 2004) 106.

11 Roman Tokarczyk, 'Relacje moralności i prawa w doktrynie Lona L. Fullera' (1977) 15 *Etyka* 77.

12 Stanisław Skorupka, Halina Auderska and Zofia Łempicka, *Mały słownik języka polskiego* (Wydawnictwo Naukowe PWN 1969) 627.

13 Gustav Radbruch, *Filozofia prawa* (Wydawnictwo PWN 2009) 88.

14 Józef Nowacki, *Praworządność. Wybrane problemy teoretyczne* (Państwowe Wydawnictwo Naukowe 1977) 65.

15 Jerzy Skorupka, *O sprawiedliwości procesu karnego* (Wolters Kluwer Polska 2013) 212.

16 Stefan Korycki, Jerzy Kuciński and Jerzy Zaborowski, *Zarys prawa* (LexisNexis 2004) 28.

17 Roman Tokarczyk, *Filozofia prawa* (LexisNexis 2009) 249.

18 Ludwik Czopek, *Popularna Encyklopedia Powszechna* (Fogra 2004) 239.

19 Irena Lipowicz, *O mądre prawo i wrażliwe państwo* (Biuro Rzecznika Praw Obywatelskich 2013) 199.

20 Dariusz Dudek, Zbigniew Husak and Grzegorz Kowalski, *Konstytucyjny system organów państwa* (C H Beck 2013) 261.

21 Przemysław Krzykowski, 'Znaczenie zasady praworządności przy wydawaniu decyzji administracyjnych przez organy administracji publicznej' (2009) 9 *Studia Prawnoustrojowe* 215.

22 John Griffiths, 'Ideology in Criminal Procedure or a Third Model of the Criminal Process' (1969) 79 *Yale Law Journal* 359, 378.

23 Sergii Smokov, Valentyna Horoshko, Maksym Korniienko and Serhii Medvedenko, 'Rule of Law as a Principle of Criminal Procedure (on materials of the European Court of Human Rights)' (2022) 14 (3) *Pakistan Journal of Criminology* 37.

24 Ryszard Stefański, 'Prokurator jako organ postępowania karnego', in Piotr Hofmański (ed), *System prawa karnego procesowego*, vol V (Wolters Kluwer, Warsaw 2015) 732.

25 Act of 28 January 2016 – Law on the Public Prosecutor's Office.

26 Stanisław Skorupka, Halina Auderska and Zofia Łempicka, *Mały słownik języka polskiego* (Wydawnictwo Naukowe PWN 1989) 784.

27 Wiesław Czerwiński, *Mit leninowskiej koncepcji prokuratury* (Prokuratura Okręgowa w Zielonej Górze 1990) 10 https://zielona-gora.po.gov.pl/magazyn/upload/lektury_elektroniczne/mit-leninowskiej-koncepcji-prokuratury.doc accessed 14 April 2025.

28 Yvon Dandurand, 'The Role of Prosecutors in Promoting and Strengthening the Rule of Law' (2007) 47 *Crime, Law and Social Change* 247, 258.

29 Bennett L Gershman, 'The Most Dangerous Power of the Prosecutor' (2008) 29 *Pace Law Review* 1, 19.

30 Marek Szubiakowski, Marek Wierzbowski and Aleksandra Wiktorowska, 'Postępowanie administracyjne – ogólne, podatkowe i egzekucyjne', in Marek Wierzbowski (ed), *Postępowanie administracyjne – ogólne, podatkowe i egzekucyjne* (C.H. Beck, Warsaw 1998) 251.

31 Edward Samborski, *Zarys metodyki pracy prokuratora* (LexisNexis 2010) 19.

32 Stanisław Dubisz, *Uniwersalny słownik języka polskiego* (Wydawnictwo Naukowe PWN 2003) 1112.

33 Radosław Olszewski and Dariusz Świecki (eds), *Polskie postępowanie karne* (Wolters Kluwer Polska 2022) 335.

34 Leszek Leszczyński and Grzegorz Maroń, 'Pojęcie i treść zasad prawa oraz generalnych klauzul odsyłających. Uwagi porównawcze' (2013) 60 (1) *Annales Universitatis Mariae Curie-Skłodowska* 81, 82.

35 Artur Żurawik, 'Klauzula generalna "dobrych obyczajów" – ujęcie teoretyczne' (2009) 71 (1) R*uch Prawniczy, Ekonomiczny i Socjologiczny* 35.

36 Leszek Leszczyński, *Tworzenie generalnych klauzul odsyłających* (Wydawnictwo Uniwersytetu Marii Curie-Skłodowskiej 2000) 17.

37 Marian Cieślak, *Polska procedura karna. Podstawowe założenia teoretyczne* (Państwowe Wydawnictwo Naukowe 1984) 42; Wiesław Daszkiewicz, *Proces karny. Część ogólna* (Uniwersytet Mikołaja Kopernika 1995) 213; Olszewski and Świecki (n 33) 389; Stanisław Waltoś, *Proces karny. Zarys systemu* (10th edn, Wolters Kluwer Polska 2009) 203.

38 Ryszard Stefański, 'Przegląd uchwał Izby Karnej Sądu Najwyższego w zakresie postępowania karnego za 2013 r' (2014) 3 *Ius Novum* 90, 104.

39 Robert Olszewski, 'Role prokuratora w postępowaniu karnym' (2014) 1 *Prokuratura i Prawo* 43, 45.

40 Olszewski (n 39) 51.

41 Announcement of the Marshal of the Sejm of the Republic of Poland of 20 February 2024 on the publication of the consolidated text of the Act – Law on the Public Prosecutor's Office.

42 Katarzyna Boratyńska, Łukasz Chojniak and Wojciech Jasiński, *Postępowanie karne* (2nd revised edn, C H Beck 2016) 146.

43 Damian Gil, *Postępowanie w sprawach z oskarżenia prywatnego* (Wolters Kluwer Polska 2011) 126.

44 Judgment of the Court of Appeal in Szczecin 10 April 2014, case no II AKa 48/14, LEX no 1459031.

45 Marek Czekaj, 'Ingerencja prokuratora w sprawach o przestępstwa prywatnoskargowe' (1999) 7–8 *Prokuratura i Prawo* 46.

46 Katarzyna Dudka, 'Wybrane problemy dochodzenia w sprawach o przestępstwa prywatnoskargowe' (2005) 6 *Prokuratura i Prawo* 32; Anna Matusiak, 'Pojęcie interesu publicznego jako przesłanki udziału prokuratora w postępowaniu' (2013) 13 (3) *Zeszyty Prawnicze* 147.

47 Marcin Janik, 'Glosa do wyroku NSA z dnia 21 lutego 2014 r., I OSK 2324/12' (2014) 6 *Zeszyty Naukowe Sądownictwa Administracyjnego* 144.

48 Dariusz Świecki (ed), *Kodeks postępowania karnego*, vol I (Wolters Kluwer Polska 2015) 309.

49 Judgment of the Supreme Court 6 September 2001, case no V KKN 216/01, OSP No 3 (2002) item 44; Wincenty Grzeszczyk, 'Glosa do wyroku SN z dnia 6 września 2001 r., V KKN 216/01' (2002) 3 *Orzecznictwo Sądów Polskich* 44.

50 Marian Cieślak, *Polska procedura karna* (Państwowe Wydawnictwo Naukowe 1984) 42.

51 Irena Kamińska-Szmaj (ed), *Słownik wyrazów obcych* (Wydawnictwo EUROPA 2001) 640.

References

Barankiewicz T, 'Aksjologiczna problematyka prawa' (2019) 14 (1) *Roczniki Nauk Prawnych* 45.

Bitner M and Kulesza M, 'Zasada legalizmu a zdolność kontraktowa jednostek samorządu terytorialnego' (2009) 6 *Samorząd Terytorialny* 5.

Boratyńska K, Chojniak Ł and Jasiński W, *Postępowanie karne* (2nd revised edn, C H Beck 2016).

Bucoń P, 'U źródeł prawa pozytywnego' (2012) 29 *Modern Information Technologies and Innovation Methodologies of Education in Professional Training Methodology Theory Experience Problems* 131.

Cieślak M, *Polska procedura karna* (Państwowe Wydawnictwo Naukowe 1984).

Czekaj M, 'Ingerencja prokuratora w sprawach o przestępstwa prywatnoskargowe' (1999) 7–8 *Prokuratura i Prawo* 46.

Czopek L, *Popularna Encyklopedia Powszechna* (Fogra 2004).

Dandurand Y, 'The Role of Prosecutors in Promoting and Strengthening the Rule of Law' (2007) 47 *Crime, Law and Social Change* 247.

Daszkiewicz W, *Proces karny. Część ogólna* (Uniwersytet Mikołaja Kopernika 1995).

Dubisz S, *Uniwersalny słownik języka polskiego* (Wydawnictwo Naukowe PWN 2003).

Dudek D, Husak Z and Kowalski G, *Konstytucyjny system organów państwa* (C H Beck 2013).

Dudka K, 'Wybrane problemy dochodzenia w sprawach o przestępstwa prywatnoskargowe' (2005) 6 *Prokuratura i Prawo* 32.

Fleczer D and Małysa K, 'Wokół problematyki praworządności' (2022) 22 (2) *Roczniki Administracji i Prawa* 31.

Fuller LL, *Moralność prawa* (Wydawnictwo PWN 2004).

Gershman BL, 'The Most Dangerous Power of the Prosecutor' (2008) 29 *Pace Law Review* 1, 19.

Griffiths J, 'Ideology in Criminal Procedure or a Third Model of the Criminal Process' (1969) 79 *Yale Law Journal* 359.

Grzeszczyk W, 'Glosa do wyroku SN z dnia 6 września 2001 r., V KKN 216/01' (2002) 3 *Orzecznictwo Sądów Polskich* 44.

Holmes OW, 'Natural Law', in Andrew Delbanco (ed), *Writing New England: An Anthology from the Puritans to the Present* (Harvard University Press 2001) 328–32.

Jackiewicz A, 'Uwagi na temat "niedomknięcia" źródeł prawa powszechnie obowiązującego w Konstytucji Rzeczypospolitej Polskiej z 2 kwietnia 1997 r', in Stanisław Bożyk (ed), *Prawo, parlament i egzekutywa we współczesnych systemach rządów. Księga poświęcona pamięci Profesora Jerzego Stembrowicza* (Temida 2 2009) 203–15.

Janik M, 'Glosa do wyroku NSA z dnia 21 lutego 2014 r., I OSK 2324/12' (2014) 6 *Zeszyty Naukowe Sądownictwa Administracyjnego* 144.
Kamińska-Szmaj I (ed), *Słownik wyrazów obcych* (Wydawnictwo EUROPA 2001).
Kordela M, 'Aksjologia źródeł prawa' (2016) 78 (2) *Ruch Prawniczy, Ekonomiczny i Socjologiczny* 15.
Korycki S, Kuciński J and Zaborowski J, *Zarys prawa* (LexisNexis 2004).
Krzykowski P, 'Znaczenie zasady praworządności przy wydawaniu decyzji administracyjnych przez organy administracji publicznej' (2009) 9 *Studia Prawnoustrojowe* 215.
Kurasz A, 'Czy istnieje prawo naturalne?' (2007) 9 (1) *Studia Ełckie* 35.
Kwiecień R, 'Wartości i prawo a kreatywność porządku prawnego' (2010) (1) *Forum Prawnicze* 30–43.
Łączkowski W, 'Prawo i moralność' (2000) 9 *Poznańskie Studia Teologiczne* 205.
Łączkowski W, 'Prawo naturalne a prawo stanowione. Uwagi prawnika' (1999) 12 *Ethos* 173.
Laskowski J, 'Prawo naturalne' (1991) 34 (1–2) *Prawo Kanoniczne* 151.
Leszczyński J, 'Wartości w teorii prawa Jerzego Wróblewskiego' (2013) 2 (2) *Filozofia Publiczna i Edukacja Demokratyczna* 258.
Leszczyński L and Maroń G, 'Pojęcie i treść zasad prawa oraz generalnych klauzul odsyłających. Uwagi porównawcze' (2013) 60 (1) *Annales Universitatis Mariae Curie-Skłodowska* 81.
Lipowicz I, *O mądre prawo i wrażliwe państwo* (Biuro Rzecznika Praw Obywatelskich 2013) 199.
Malinowska I, 'Źródła prawa w Konstytucji RP z 1997 roku' (2017) 6 *Przegląd Sejmowy* 282.
Matusiak A, 'Pojęcie interesu publicznego jako przesłanki udziału prokuratora w postępowaniu' (2013) 13 (3) *Zeszyty Prawnicze* 147.
Nowacki J, *Praworządność. Wybrane problemy teoretyczne* (Państwowe Wydawnictwo Naukowe 1977).
Olszewski R, 'Role prokuratora w postępowaniu karnym' (2014) 1 *Prokuratura i Prawo* 43.
Olszewski R and Świecki D (eds), *Polskie postępowanie karne* (Wolters Kluwer Polska 2022).
Pikuła Ł, 'Bezpieczeństwo prawne jako podstawowa wartość prawa w systemie prawa' (2017) 39 *Przegląd Prawno-Ekonomiczny* 130.
Radbruch G, *Filozofia prawa* (Wydawnictwo PWN 2009).
Rakowska-Trela A, 'Prezydent Rzeczypospolitej Polskiej jako strażnik konstytucji' (2023) 104 *Acta Universitatis Lodziensis. Folia Iuridica* 141.
Salij J, 'Prawo naturalne i prawa stanowione w ujęciu św. Tomasza z Akwinu' (2017) 26 (2) *Łódzkie Studia Teologiczne* 103.
Samborski E, *Zarys metodyki pracy prokuratora* (LexisNexis 2010).

Skorupka J, *O sprawiedliwości procesu karnego* (Wolters Kluwer Polska 2013).

Skorupka S, Auderska H and Łempicka Z, *Mały słownik języka polskiego* (Wydawnictwo Naukowe PWN 1969).

Skrzydło W, *Polskie prawo konstytucyjne* (LexisNexis 2003).

Smokov S, Horoshko V, Korniienko M and Medvedenko S, 'Rule of Law as a Principle of Criminal Procedure (on materials of the European Court of Human Rights)' (2022) 14 (3) *Pakistan Journal of Criminology* 37.

Sobański R, 'Prawo jako wartość' (1999) 42 (3–4) *Prawo Kanoniczne* 11–26.

Stefański R, 'Prokurator jako organ postępowania karnego', in Piotr Hofmański (ed), *System prawa karnego procesowego, vol V* (Wolters Kluwer, Warsaw 2015) 726–77.

Stefański R, 'Przegląd uchwał Izby Karnej Sądu Najwyższego w zakresie postępowania karnego za 2013 r' (2014) 3 *Ius Novum* 90.

Suchocka H, 'Geneza i ewolucja bezpośredniego stosowania Konstytucji RP' (2022) 226 (2) *Studia Prawnicze* 9.

Świecki D (ed), *Kodeks postępowania karnego, vol I* (Wolters Kluwer Polska 2015).

Szubiakowski M, Wierzbowski M and Wiktorowska A, 'Postępowanie administracyjne – ogólne, podatkowe i egzekucyjne', in Marek Wierzbowski (ed), *Postępowanie administracyjne – ogólne, podatkowe i egzekucyjne* (C.H. Beck, Warsaw 1998) 1–45.

Tierney B, 'Natural Law and Natural Rights: Old Problems and Recent Approaches' (2002) 64 (3) *The Review of Politics* 389.

Tkacz S, 'Prawo a wartości w teorii prawa Józefa Nowackiego' (2017) 6 (2) *Filozofia Publiczna i Edukacja Demokratyczna* 255.

Tokarczyk R, *Filozofia prawa* (LexisNexis 2009).

Tokarczyk R, 'Relacje moralności i prawa w doktrynie Lona L. Fullera' (1977) 15 *Etyka* 77.

Waltoś S, *Proces karny. Zarys systemu* (10th edn, Wolters Kluwer Polska 2009).

Wielec M, *Wartości – analiza z perspektywy osobliwości postępowania karnego* (Wydawnictwo Academicon 2017).

Wojtyła K, 'Osoba ludzka a prawo naturalne' (1970) 18 (2) *Roczniki Filozoficzne/Annales de Philosophie/Annals of Philosophy* 53.

Wroczyński K, 'Demokratyczne państwo prawne' (1994) 3 *Człowiek w Kulturze* 197.

Żurawik A, 'Klauzula generalna "dobrych obyczajów" – ujęcie teoretyczne' (2009) 71 (1) *Ruch Prawniczy, Ekonomiczny i Socjologiczny* 35.

4

Public interest and the principle of opportunity in the prosecution of crimes committed by minors in cases of sexual violence in Spain

Adán Carrizo González-Castell

Introduction

Article 19 of Organic Law 5/2000, of 12 January, Regulating the Criminal Responsibility of Minors, from now on LORPM, expressly states that the Public Prosecutor's Office may withdraw the continuation of the case, taking into account the seriousness and circumstances of the facts and the minor. In that way, the Spanish legislator introduced the principle of opportunity in our juvenile criminal proceedings, as opposed to the principles of officiality and legality which, in general, govern the Spanish criminal procedural model, and which prevent the waiver of the exercise of the criminal action, except in a few exceptions. For instance, the case of minor offences, contained in Article 963 of Spanish Criminal Procedure Act, which allows the dismissal of proceedings at the request of the Public Prosecutor's Office when the offence '*is of very little seriousness in view of the nature of the act, its circumstances, and the personal circumstances of the perpetrator*' or '*there is no relevant public interest in prosecuting the act*'.

It is precisely this concept of relevant public interest that we intend to analyse in this chapter, assessing the extent to which criminal prosecution of certain facts could be waived, in view of the best interests of the minor that the Public Prosecutor's Office may appreciate in this type of proceedings, examining the conditions for it to be able to desist from the initiation of the case. This is in

This chapter has been made in the framework of the Research Project entitled *Agenda 2030 y acceso igualitario a la justicia de personas vulnerables desde una perspectiva de género* (PIC-2022-06) funded by the Universidad de Salamanca. Principal Investigator: Adán Carrizo González-Castell.

contrast to the principle of free opportunity, in order to avoid the possible adverse effects of a future conviction on young offenders and where the Public Prosecutor's Office, after analysing the information on the case, has the option of requesting a dismissal without being subject to closed conditions, or at least with these conditions being much more lax and susceptible to assessment, with the flexibility of these conditions being what differentiates the two models.

All of this, in a way that is compatible with the rights of the victims, especially those who are also minors, in the regulatory framework established by the Organic Law 10/2022, of 6 September, on the Comprehensive Guarantee of Sexual Freedom,[1] popularly known as the 'only yes is yes' law. It includes the generalized prohibition of the use of mediation and conciliation for victims of sexual aggression, which is added to that already existing in the area of gendered violence, contained in Article 44.5 of Organic Law 1/2004, of 28 December, on Comprehensive Protection Measures against Gendered Violence.[2]

In this sense, the Twelfth Final Provision, which includes the amendments made to Law 4/2015, of 27 April, on the Statute of the Victim of Crime,[3] from now on EVD, redrafts Article 3.1 of this text and thus, after establishing the victim's right to protection, information, support, assistance, care and reparation, it establishes that, in any case, mediation and conciliation will be forbidden in cases of sexual violence and gendered violence. It is surprising, to say the least, that a law such as the EVD, which in its Preamble states, among its main objectives, its intention to return to the victims the protagonism of the criminal conflict,[4] incorporates a prohibition that precisely denies it in the commission of certain crimes, preventing a positive intervention by the State aimed at restoring the situation in which the victims found themselves before suffering the crime or, at least, at mitigating the effects of what has been called secondary victimization.

This is so, because if we really seek to offer the victim a reparation that goes beyond a simple economic compensation, and even beyond the criminal process itself, minimizing the traumatic effects of the crime, regardless of their procedural situation and outside the criminal process itself, it must be started from the recognition of their dignity as victims and their ability to freely decide whether or not they want to access the restorative justice services that the principle of opportunity allows, with no other limitation from our point of view than their consent and that this can be developed in conditions of equality.[5]

However, the possibility that there may be crimes for which access to these restorative justice services may be prohibited is not an innovation introduced by Organic Law 10/2022, since Article 15 of the EVD itself, which contains the guarantees of access to restorative justice services for victims, already requires that it is not prohibited for the crime committed. This would be added to those that the offender has acknowledged the essential facts from which their responsibility derives; that the victim has given their consent, after having received full and impartial information about its content, its possible outcomes and the procedures in place to enforce it; that the offender has given their consent; and that the mediation procedure does not pose a risk to the victim's safety, nor is there a danger that its conduct could cause further material or moral harm to the victim.

Nevertheless, what is new is that, in a clear and precise manner, and after the multiple doctrinal debates that the issue had given rise to, Article 19.2 of the aforementioned Organic Law 5/2000, of 12 January, Regulating the Criminal Responsibility of Minors, has been modified in the sense of establishing that, when the measure of withdrawal requested by the Public Prosecutor's Office is a consequence of the commission of any of the offences referred to in the Organic Law 10/2022, or are related to gendered violence, it will not have the effect of conciliation. This will be in this form unless the victim expressly requests it and the minor has also completed the accessory measure of sex education and education for equality, all in line with the new wording given to Articles 7.5 and 10.2.c) LORPM, where the judge is also obliged to impose the obligation to undergo training programmes on sex education and education for equality in certain cases.

However, it is not the compulsory nature of this accessory measure that is of particular concern to us, but the fact that in these cases the victim must expressly request it, leaving the final decision in their hands, which leads us to wonder about the role of the best interests of the minor, which is supposed to guide all the actions of this law, as opposed to the public interest and the rights of the victims, a concern that we will try to resolve in the following section of our study.

The best interests of the minor as a basis for the inclusion of the principle of opportunity in Organic Law 5/2000 – Regulating the criminal responsibility of minors

The best interests of the minor as the basis for the use of the principle of opportunity in the LORPM are materialized, in our opinion, in the formally criminal but materially educationally punitive nature of the juvenile process and of the measures applicable to minor offenders.

There is no doubt that the process is of a criminal nature and that what is being purged through it is a true legal responsibility in relation to acts classified as offences in the Criminal Code. But what cannot be ignored is that, as it is of an educational nature, other essential aims of adult criminal law must be rejected, such as proportionality between the act and the sanction or intimidation of the addressees of the rule, avoiding any possible counterproductive effect for the minor.

This allows the Juvenile Judge, or the Juvenile Section of the Courts of First Instance, following the recent approval of Organic Law 1/2025, of 2 January, on Measures for the Efficiency of the Public Justice Service,[6] to annul the measure imposed, to reduce its duration or to substitute it with another, provided that the modification is in the best interests of the minor and that the reproach deserved their conduct is sufficiently expressed to the minor.[7] This is fully consistent with international regulations on the matter, especially with the *Convention on the Rights of the Child*, approved by the United Nations General Assembly on 20 November 1989.[8]

This formally criminal but materially educational sanctioning nature, to which we referred earlier, is manifested in the introduction of the principle of opportunity in juvenile criminal proceedings, through the regulation of Article 19 LORPM, which contains the dismissal of the case by conciliation or reparation between the minor and the victim. This is an article subject to reform by Organic Law 10/2022, and which, however, fits perfectly with the principles that the LORPM itself expresses in its Explanatory Memorandum, and which are nothing more than a reflection of the guidelines established in the *Opinion of the European Economic and Social Committee on the prevention of juvenile delinquency, the ways of dealing with it and the role of juvenile justice in the European Union.*[9]

In this regard, Article 19 LORPM expressly states that the Public Prosecutor's Office may withdraw the continuation of the case. To this end, it takes into account the seriousness and circumstances of the facts and of the minor, particularly the lack of serious violence or intimidation in the commission of the acts, and the circumstance that the minor has also reconciled with the victim or has undertaken to repair the damage caused to the victim or the injured party by the offence, or has undertaken to comply with the educational activity proposed by the technical team in its report, although limiting this only to cases in which the act imputed to the minor constitutes a less serious or minor offence.[10]

In that way, our legislator introduced the principle of opportunity in our juvenile criminal proceedings, as opposed to the principles of officiality and legality which currently govern the Spanish criminal procedural model, and which prevent the waiver of criminal prosecution, except for a few exceptions. This is the case of minor offences, contained in Article 963 of our Criminal Procedure Act, which allows the dismissal of proceedings at the request of the Public Prosecutor's Office when the crime *'is of very little seriousness in view of the nature of the act, its circumstances and the personal circumstances of the perpetrator'* or *when 'there is no relevant public interest in prosecuting the act'*.[11]

What it can be clearly stated, however, is that in the two cases in which the Prosecutor is given the power to request the early termination of proceedings for reasons of strict opportunity, whether in juvenile or minor offences, we are dealing with the introduction of the principle of regulated opportunity, as a series of conditions which are set out for the Prosecutor's Office to be able to desist from the initiation of proceedings. This is in contrast to the principle of free opportunity, in order to avoid the possible adverse effects of a future conviction on young offenders and where the prosecution, after analysing the information on the case, has the option of requesting a dismissal without being subject to closed conditions, or at least with these conditions being much more lax and susceptible to assessment, and it is the flexibility of these conditions that differentiates the two models.[12]

Thus, and returning to the regulation of mediation in juvenile criminal proceedings, it should be pointed out that, for the purposes of the withdrawal contained in Article 19.1 LORPM, *conciliation* will be understood to have taken place when the minor acknowledges the harm caused and apologizes to the victim, and the victim accepts their apology. On the other hand, *reparation* will be understood to be the commitment assumed by the minor with the victim or injured party to carry out certain actions for the benefit of the victim or the community, followed by their effective implementation, without prejudice to the agreement reached by the parties in relation to civil liability.[13]

In that way, it can be seen how the key element of voluntariness plays a fundamental role when it comes to understanding that reparation has taken place, as it is not only enough for the minor to recognize the harm caused and apologize to the victim, but it will also be necessary for the victim to accept the apology. This is something that could cause certain problems, especially in cases where the victim is also a minor. In these cases, in accordance with the provisions of Article 19.6 LORPM, both the apology and the commitment must be accepted, not only by the victim, but also by their legal representatives with the approval of the Juvenile Judge, which, although it is true that this is an important guarantee, in a certain way it could distort the spirit of the mediation itself.[14]

Limits to the principle of opportunity in the prosecution and trial of crimes committed by minors in cases of sexual or gendered violence

The Seventh Final Provision of Organic Law 10/2022 introduces the need for the victim to expressly request conciliation in cases of sexual and gendered violence in order for conciliation to be understood to have been carried out, and for the minor to have completed the accessory measure of sex education and education for equality.

Regarding the prohibition of gendered violence, and without prejudice to whether it is possible to talk about the existence of this type of violence between minors, what the current wording of Article 19.2 LORPM does clarify is that mediation in matters of sexual and gendered violence is not prohibited in juvenile proceedings, but only that, in order for conciliation to be understood to have taken place, the two aforementioned requirements must be fulfilled.

This new wording, therefore, seems to agree with those of us who did not consider that the prohibition contained in the fifth paragraph of Article 87 *ter* of the Organic Law of the Judiciary was applicable to juvenile proceedings,[15] since this prohibition falls within the competences of the Court for Violence against Women. Therefore, it should only affect this body, without making any mention of the Juvenile Courts, competent for the application of the LORPM, which design a stage in which, from our point of view, mediation is perfectly possible without limitation of any kind, even more so when, according to different studies, the advantages of its application in these cases are being observed.[16]

This position was already reinforced by the supplementary nature of the Criminal Procedure Act over the LORPM in matters not expressly provided for by the latter or that are not contrary to its inspiring principles, or by *Directive 2012/29/EU of the European Parliament and of the Council, of 25 October 2012, establishing minimum standards on the rights, support and protection of victims of crime*, which does not restrict anything regarding the possibility of using this mechanism. Nevertheless, it states in its Explanatory Memorandum that, when referring a case to restorative justice services or carrying out a restorative justice process, consideration should be given to factors such as the nature and seriousness of the crime, the degree of harm caused, the repeated violation of a victim's physical, sexual or psychological integrity, power imbalances and the age, maturity or intellectual capacity of the victim, which may limit or reduce the victim's ability to make an informed choice or may cause harm to the victim.[17]

In view of the seriousness of the crime, in matters of sexual or gendered violence, it is expressly stated that, in order for the conciliation to be understood as having been carried out, the victim must expressly request it. This limitation, which does not raise any doubts in matters of sexual violence, does make us wonder, however, whether it can be talked about gendered violence between minors.

In order to answer this question, the first thing it must be analysed is what the Spanish legislator understands by gendered violence, referring to Organic Law 1/2004, of 28 December, on Comprehensive Protection Measures against Gendered Violence, which, despite being the result of an enormous consensus when it was passed, seems clearly outdated, insofar as it would only receive the denomination of gendered violence that which, as a manifestation of discrimination, the situation of inequality and the power relations of men over women, is exercised against women by those who are or have been their spouses or by those who are or have been linked to them by similar relationships of affection even without cohabitation.[18]

We understand this concept as outdated because, in line with the Sustainable Development Goals of the *2030 Agenda*, States should promote the necessary measures to eliminate discrimination against women in access to the justice system for the protection of their rights and legitimate interests, achieving effective equality of conditions and paying special attention to cases of violence against women. These are understood, in accordance with Article 1 of the *UN Declaration on the Elimination of Violence against Women*, number 48/104 of 20 December 1993, as any act of gender-based violence that results in, or is likely to result in, physical, sexual or psychological harm or suffering to women, including threats of such acts, coercion or arbitrary deprivation of liberty, whether occurring in public or in private life.

Along the same lines, the Istanbul Convention,[19] extends the concept of gendered violence to all types of violence against women contained therein, making express reference not only to violence perpetrated by a male who is or has been a spouse or who is or has been linked to the victim by similar relations of affection, even without cohabitation, but also to many others, such as physical, psychological and sexual violence, including rape, female genital mutilation, forced marriage, sexual harassment and gender-based harassment, forced abortion and forced sterilization. Even in those cases in which there is no relationship with the aggressor as required for the application of Organic Law 1/2004, of 28 December, on Comprehensive Protection Measures against Gendered Violence, to which we have referred.[20]

However, until this necessary claim is made, in order to assess the possibility that gendered violence may or may not exist among minors, it must be abided by Spanish law, which requires the existence of a relationship of affection, analogous to that of marriage, which would require a degree of maturity that many authors refuse to recognize in a minor.

Perhaps the solution to this question would have been easier if our LORPM had opted for the so-called system of discernment, instead of a mixed system combined with a purely biological one, when determining the criminal age, where the age from which criminal responsibility is demanded for the criminal conduct carried out, is not determined by a fixed and generally valid limit, in accordance with a chronological age of the subject, but has to be resolved with respect to each offender, making the criminal response depend on a prior judgement about the offender. This is known as the judgement of discernment, which may allow us to assess whether the affective relationship was analogous to the marital relationship or not.[21]

Insofar as this is not the case, it must be taken into account what is stated in Circular 6/2011, of 2 November, on criteria for the unity of specialized action of the Public Prosecutor's Office in relation to violence against women, which states that, although Articles 315 of the Civil Code and 12 of the Constitutional text set the age of majority at eighteen years of age, and this is the reason for the question being raised before the Courts of Justice as to whether or not underage women can be passive subjects of gendered violence in terms of whether or not they have the necessary capacity to decide to enter into a sentimental relationship, the truth is that there are also many other rules which grant minors the capacity to carry out legally effective acts on their own. For instance, making wills, contracting marriages with dispensation, exercising parental authority over their children, albeit with certain limitations, which would lead us to conclude that, although full capacity is granted at the age of majority, women who have not reached the age of majority have the capacity to decide to enter into a sentimental relationship which places them, without any doubt, under the sphere of criminal guardianship granted to women victims of gendered violence, without lacking a common project with their partner; cohabiting with the parents or being financially dependent on them; or there having been a temporary break in the relationship, can justify not granting said guardianship.

In this sense, Article 17 of Organic Law 1/2004, of 28 December, on Comprehensive Protection Measures against Gendered Violence states that '*all women victims of gendered violence, regardless of their origin, religion or any other personal or social condition or circumstance, are guaranteed the rights recognised in the Law*' without the law requiring, conditioning or defining the circumstances that must be present in order for a sentimental relationship to be accredited, although this must be the object of proof.

All this allows us to conclude that, although it can be admitted the existence of gendered violence in the field of relationships between minors, we do not share the opinion expressed in Opinion 7/2012 on criteria for action in cases of gendered violence, of the Prosecutor of the Coordinating Chamber for Minors, which considers that the application of the extrajudicial solutions of Article 19 LORPM should be exceptional in cases of violence against women, arguing that '*to carry out a conciliation without further ado, for this type of facts, would mean transmitting to possible juvenile aggressors the message, not only misleading but dangerous, that with an eventual pardon these conducts can be settled*'. We are aware, and we share the demand that the use of these solutions should always take into account the interests of the victim, which should not lead us to forget the best interests of the minor, which should inspire all actions carried out within the framework of juvenile justice.

For this reason, we are in favour of carrying out a prior and rigorous analysis of the circumstances of the specific case, so that it can be assessed whether or not it is appropriate to use it. And not only, as we have said, to respect the best interests of the minor, but also because we consider that mediation can be, as with adult female victims, an ideal mechanism to empower them, making them the protagonist of their own decisions, along the lines of what we have always been in favour of eliminating the general prohibition of mediation contained in Article 44.5 of Organic Law 1/2004, considering that it implies a total lack of confidence in the woman's capacity to make decisions since, although it is true that mediation requires a situation of equality in order to be carried out, it is also true that it could, as we propose, be entrusted to the judge to carry out the control that would allow mediation to be carried out in cases of gendered violence, when it is considered that it could be carried out under conditions of equality.[22]

Thus, we share the opinion of those who think that mediation can be very positive in preventing the repetition of the trial, thus avoiding possible secondary victimization, with all that this entails, provided that the accused undertakes, in addition to a possible commitment not to communicate with the victim in the future, the carrying out of extrajudicial educational or training activities or work related to the offence, aimed at preventing the repetition of such behaviour in the future. This is something which seems to be the aim of the new accessory measure consisting of undergoing training programmes on sex education and education in equality.[23]

Conclusion

Although references to the principle of opportunity and the use of mediation have been a constant in international victim legislation,[24] in our opinion, it was not this restorative vocation that motivated the inclusion of mediation in Article 19 LORPM, but rather the primacy of the best interests of the minor, configuring this mediatory action, within the minor's own criminal proceedings, not in itself as an alternative mechanism to the judicial process, but as an alternative solution to the sentence eventually handed down by the judge, acquiring, from our point of view, the legal nature of a non-mandatory phase of the juvenile criminal process. This is an option for which we are inclined over those who advocate a fully alternative model of mediation to the process, that is, isolated from it.[25]

In any case, and starting from this premise, we would only oppose the application of mediation, and therefore the principle of opportunity, in those crimes in which the court appreciates that violence or intimidation of a serious nature or finds the existence of inequality between the parties, and should use the opinion of the technical teams to make these assessments, taking into account the circumstances of the specific case, without any limitation other than those expressed and the will of the victim who, in many cases, can choose not to participate in mediation. In this sense, we are aware that it will be much easier to resort to mediation when dealing with punishable acts in which the possible violence or intimidation has been of a minor nature, as it is clear that, in cases of more serious violence or intimidation, the victim's predisposition to participate in mediation could be lower.[26]

In relation to future reflections, and without forgetting that prevention will always be better than repression, applying a guarantee model and measures with an eminently educational content, our proposal would be not only to reduce the use of the traditional justice system as much as possible, implementing new justice systems with specially trained personnel and professionals that allow diversifying the criminal reaction with flexible measures that can be adjusted and adapted to the circumstances of the minor, according to the specific circumstances of each case, but also to give a greater role to the community and other groups in social life in the solution of the conflict and in the search for viable alternatives, such as the family, the school, the community or social organizations, without ruling out the replication of this model in the criminal process for adults.[27]

It is precisely this invitation to give a greater role to the community that connects us directly with the different models of restorative justice. For example, conferences or circles, whether healing or sentencing, where the aim is to involve as many people as possible who have been affected by a crime in the decision-making process regarding the best way to respond to said criminal act, and which perhaps have not been sufficiently developed in our country, opting decisively for mediation and not taking advantage of the participation of other agents who could contribute a broader point of view and a greater understanding of the conflict through their professional perspective.[28]

As the LORPM points out in its explanatory memorandum, in juvenile criminal law, the best interests of the minor must prevail as a determining factor in the procedure and the measures adopted. This interest must be assessed with technical and not formalistic criteria by teams of specialized professionals, who are not only responsible for mediating between victim and offender, but also for informing the Public Prosecutor's Office both of the commitments made and their degree of compliance; because if the minor does not comply with the reparation or the educational activity agreed in terms of sex education and education in equality, as required by Organic Law 10/2022, of 6 September, on the Comprehensive Guarantee of Sexual Freedom, the Public Prosecutor's Office should, according to Article 16.5 LORPM continue with the processing of the case file.[29]

For this reason, and due to the importance that this technical team develops in juvenile proceedings, we would like to conclude our work by demanding that the necessary personal and material resources be provided to make effective the guarantee of professional specialization, through initial and continuous training, foreseen in Article 23 of Organic Law 10/2022, of 6 September, on the Comprehensive Guarantee of Sexual Freedom, where special reference is made to that which should be received by those professionals who have direct and habitual contact with minors, such as educational, social and health intervention and social services staff, members of the Security Forces and Corps and of the Judicial and Prosecutorial Careers, staff in the service of the Administration of Justice, workers in penitentiary establishments or internment and custody centres, lawyers and solicitors, among others. Only in this way can we speak of an application of the law that meets the necessary conditions for justice to fulfil its dual task of punishing the guilty party and contributing to repairing the harm caused to the victims, exploring all the formulas that the principle of opportunity offers and that could serve to jointly respond to both interests.

Notes

1 Organic Law 10/2022, of 6 September, on the Comprehensive Guarantee of Sexual Freedom. BOE of 7 September 2022.

2 Organic Law 1/2004, of 28 December, on Comprehensive Protection Measures against Gendered Violence. BOE of 29 December 2004.

3 Law 4/2015, of 27 April, on the Statute of the Victims of Crime. BOE of 28 April 2015.

4 In this sense, Silvia Barona Vilar, 'Mirada restaurativa de la justicia penal en España, una bocanada de aire en la sociedad global líquida del miedo y de la securitización', in Helena Soleto Muñoz, Ana Carrascosa Miguel (dirs), *Justicia restaurativa: una justicia para las víctimas* (Tirant lo Blanch 2019).

5 On victim reparation in restorative justice see Helena Soleto Muñoz, 'Justicia restaurativa para la mejor reparación a la víctima', in Helena Soleto Muñoz, Ana Carrascosa Miguel (dirs), *Justicia restaurativa: una justicia para las víctimas* (Tirant lo Blanch 2019).

6 Organic Law 1/2025, of 2 January, on Measures for the Efficiency of the Public Justice Service. BOE of 3 January 2025.

7 In accordance with Article 13 LORPM, the Judge for Minors competent for the execution may adopt this decision, *ex officio* or at the request of the Public Prosecutor's Office or the minor's lawyer, but always after hearing them and following a report from the technical team and, where appropriate, from the public entity for the protection or reform of minors. However, and since the entry into force of Organic Law 10/2022, of 6 September, on the Comprehensive Guarantee

of Sexual Freedom, when the offence committed is within the scope of application of this law, the measure may only be lifted if it is accredited that the person subject to the measure has fulfilled the obligation to undergo training programmes on sex education and education in equality, provided for in Section 5 of Article 7 of the LORPM.

8 Other international conventions and treaties related to juvenile justice can also be consulted at Inmaculada Sánchez Barrios, 'Menores infractores y principio de oportunidad. Regulación internacional', in Lorenzo Mateo Bujosa Vadell, Fernando Martín Diz (dirs), *Menores y justicia juvenil* (Thomson Reuters Aranzadi 2021).

9 *Opinion of the European Economic and Social Committee on the prevention of juvenile delinquency, the treatment of juvenile delinquency and the role of juvenile justice in the European Union* (2006/C 110/13). *Official Journal of the European Union* C 110/75 of 9 May 2006, in which the model of criminal responsibility for minors is promoted over other more traditional models that have proved clearly ineffective in the face of new delinquency, not only because of their slowness but also because they have failed to reduce the rate of recidivism.

10 In this sense, Esther Pillado González, 'La mediación como manifestación del principio de oportunidad en la Ley de Responsabilidad Penal de Menores', in Esther Pillado González (coord), *Mediación con menores infractores en España y los países de su entorno* (Tirant lo Blanch 2012).

11 On the application of the principle of opportunity in juvenile criminal proceedings, see Selena Tierno Barrios, 'Mediación penal y justicia de menores: una manifestación del principio de oportunidad', in Lorenzo Mateo Bujosa Vadell, Fernando Martín Diz (dirs), *Menores y justicia juvenil* (Thomson Reuters – Aranzadi 2021).

12 Rubén López Picó, 'Sobreseimiento del expediente de reforma por conciliación o reparación entre el menor infractor y la víctima del delito; una manifestación del principio de oportunidad en el proceso penal de menores', in Lorenzo Mateo Bujosa Vadell, Fernando Martín Diz (dirs), *Menores y justicia juvenil* (Thomson Reuters – Aranzadi 2021). On the principle of opportunity in our domestic law, see Isabel Hernández Gómez, 'Justicia restaurativa, mediación penal y principio de oportunidad', in José María Roca Martínez (dir), *El acceso a la Justicia* (Tirant lo Blanch 2018).

13 On criminal mediation in juvenile proceedings, see Ignacio Colomer Hernández, 'La mediación penal con menores infractores en la LORPM', in Esther Pillado González (coord), *Mediación con menores infractores en España y los países de su entorno* (Tirant lo Blanch 2012).

14 On the importance of the victim's acceptance of such apologies, as an essential element of this mechanism, see Isabel González Cano, 'Valoración de las reformas

procesales operadas por la LO 6/2004, de 4 de diciembre, por la que se modifica la Ley Orgánica de Responsabilidad Penal de los menores' (2007) 3 *Diario La Ley* 1.

15 This is the opinion of María Jesús Molina Caballero, 'Algunas fronteras de la Ley Integral contra la violencia de género: jurisdicción de menores y mediación' (2015) 17–24 *Revista Electrónica de Derecho Penal y Criminología* 1.

16 Adrián Gómez Conesa, 'Mediación y violencia de género. Análisis y propuestas a partir de la evidencia empírica' (2021) 9825 *Diario La Ley* 1, Sección Tribuna, points out that empirical research does not support such a categorical and radical prohibition of the application of criminal mediation in cases of gendered violence and that, on the contrary, the mechanisms of restorative justice are beneficial to the needs of victims of gendered violence.

17 Directive 2012/29/EU of the European Parliament and of the Council of 25 October 2012 establishing minimum standards on the rights, support and protection of victims of crime and replacing Council Framework Decision 2001/220/JHA of 15 March 2001 on the standing of victims in criminal proceedings. *Official Journal of the European Union* L 315/57 of 14.11.2012.

18 When the Law was passed, some authors criticized the limitations of Article 1.1 of Law 1/2004, of 28 December, on Comprehensive Protection Measures against Gendered Violence, which, in the opinion of Eva María Martínez Gallego, *Ley de Medidas de Protección Integral contra la Violencia de Género* (Iustel 2005),detracts from the Legislator's merits by limiting the scope of application of the Law to domestic violence, without taking into account other cases of violence against women in other spheres.

19 Council of Europe Convention on preventing and combating violence against women and domestic violence, done at Istanbul on 11 May 2011, whose instrument of ratification was published in BOE no. 137 of 6 June 2014. On this topic see María Gemma Gallego Sánchez, 'El Convenio de Estambul: por qué un convenio sobre la violencia contra la mujer?' (2016) 1 *Cuadernos Digitales de Formación, Consejo General del Poder Judicial* 1.

20 For an approach to the practical problems posed by this divergence see María Tardón Olmos, 'Definiciones del Convenio de Estambul y ámbito de aplicación, en relación con la Ley 1/2004' (2016) 1 *Cuadernos Digitales de Formación, Consejo General del Poder Judicial* 1.

21 In some connection with this judgement of discernment, the original wording of the LORPM, provided in its Article 1.2 the possibility of extending the scope of application of the criminal responsibility of minors to persons aged between eighteen and twenty-one, when the crime committed was less serious, the subject was not a repeat offender and there had been no violence or intimidation or danger to the life or health of persons, a possibility whose effective application was successively suspended until its complete disappearance through the approval of Organic Law 8/2006, of 4 December, which modifies Organic Law 5/2000,

of 12 January, Regulating the Criminal Responsibility of Minors, yet another criminal policy option. On the demanded reform of the minimum age of criminal responsibility, see Tomás Montero Hernanz, 'Sobre las propuestas de reforma de la Ley Orgánica 1/2000', in Lorenzo Mateo Bujosa Vadell, Fernando Martín Diz (dirs), *Menores y justicia juvenil* (Thomson Reuters – Aranzadi).

22 We share the opinion of, among others, Cristina Castillo Roldán, 'Violencia de género. ¿Crisis de la justicia? Avanzar hacia la justicia restaurativa' (2020) 9681 *Diario La Ley* 1, or Isabel Huertas Martín, 'Reflexiones sobre la prohibición de la mediación en la violencia de género', in Ana María Rodríguez Tirado (coord), *Cuestiones actuales de Derecho Procesal. Reformas procesales. Mediación y arbitraje* (Tirant lo Blanch 2017), when stating that the particular circumstances of each case must be assessed individually, so that, if there is a situation, even if it is minimal, of equality between the parties that allows each one to defend their interests and freely express their opinions, accept or reject proposals, mediation will be possible. On the contrary, Fernando Martín Diz, *La mediación: sistema complementario de Administración de Justicia* (Consejo General del Poder Judicial 2010), does not agree as he considers that the inequality between victim and aggressor in these cases is evident and, in his opinion, insurmountable.

23 In this sense we share the opinion of Manuel José García Rodríguez, 'La mediación entre el menor infractor y la víctima ¿un mecanismo válido para resolver los conflictos de violencia de género en el sistema de justicia penal juvenil?' (2021) 9908 *Diario La Ley* 1, Sección Doctrina.

24 Not only at the level of the European Union, but also in the framework of the Council of Europe, whose Recommendation [85] 2 of 28 June 1985 of the Committee of the Council of Europe on the position of the victim in criminal law and criminal procedure gives a wide margin to reparation and the advantages that mediation and conciliation systems can offer, or Recommendation [87] 21, on assistance to victims and the prevention of victimization which already expressly refers to mediation, and even more strongly, Recommendation [99] 19 of the Committee of the Council of Ministers of the Council of Europe, which defines criminal mediation as 'any process which enables the victim and the offender to participate actively, if they freely consent, in the resolution of the difficulties caused by the offence with the help of an independent third party (the mediator)'. On this subject, see Begoña Castro Jover, 'La mediación penal como práctica restaurativa en la fase de ejecución penal' (2020) 9710 *Diario La Ley* 1.

25 On the *intrajudicial* nature of mediation in Spain, see María Avilés Navarro, 'La mediación intrajudicial en España' (2020) 9576 *Diario La Ley* 1, or Daniel Montesdeoca Rodríguez, 'Luces y sombras de la mediación penal' (2020) 9704 *Diario La Ley* 1.

26 We say that this will be the case, in general, since, for example, criminal mediation in the United States has developed a process that is the reverse of this, that is: it

began by being applied only to minor crimes and, at present, at the request of the victims, it has been extended to serious crimes, including murders and sexual assaults, in which the meeting of victims and perpetrators is absolutely necessary to restore the safety of the former. César Estirado de Cabo, 'Cuestiones relevantes de Derecho sustantivo y procesal respecto de la incorporación de la mediación a la jurisdicción penal de adultos en las fases de instrucción y enjuiciamiento' (2008) *Estudios de Derecho Judicial. La mediación civil y penal. Un año de experiencia, Consejo General del Poder Judicial* 136–207, or Coral Arangüena Fanego, 'La mediación penal en el ámbito de la violencia de género ¿ha llegado el momento para replantearse su prohibición?' in Xavier Abel Lluch (coord), *Las medidas preventivas de conflictos jurídicos en contextos económicos inestables* (J. M. Bosch Editor 2014).

27 This is the opinion of María Auxiliadora García Fernández, 'Una mediación especializada: intervención con menores' (2015) 8627 *Diario La Ley* 1, when she states that the triumph of the resocializing thesis in certain countries, such as Argentina, Chile, England, France or the United States has turned the institution of mediation into an appropriate tool, not only to solve conflicts, but also as an effective means to prevent the commission of future crimes. Similarly, Silvia Barona Vilar, 'Mediación penal. Integration of mediation in criminal justice. Supuestos especiales', in Virginia Pardo Iranzo (coord), *La mediación: algunas cuestiones de actualidad* (Tirant lo Blanch 2015), highlights the importance of experience in juvenile matters for the development of adult criminal mediation.

28 For an approach to this form of restorative justice, see Rodrigo Miguel Barrio, 'La Justicia Restaurativa y el interés por el delito: los círculos restaurativos como posible método de resocialización del victimario' (2018) 9297 *Diario La Ley* 1, and on the application of these models can be found Mar Jimeno Bulnes, 'Sobre la mediación, justicia restaurativa y otras justicias', in Helena Soleto Muñoz, Ana Carrascosa Miguel (dirs), *Justicia restaurativa: una justicia para las víctimas* (Tirant lo Blanch 2019).

29 Except in those cases in which it has not been possible to carry out the proceedings for reasons beyond the minor's control, in which case the investigation should be concluded and the judge should be asked to dismiss and close the proceedings.

References

Arangüena Fanego C, 'La mediación penal en el ámbito de la violencia de género ¿ha llegado el momento para replantearse su prohibición?' in Xavier Abel Lluch (coord), *Las medidas preventivas de conflictos jurídicos en contextos económicos inestables* (J. M. Bosch Editor 2014).

Avilés Navarro M, 'La mediación intrajudicial en España' (2020) 9576 *Diario La Ley* 1.

Barona Vilar S, 'Mediación penal. Integración de la mediación en la justicia penal. Supuestos especiales', in Virginia Pardo Iranzo (coord), *La mediación: algunas cuestiones de actualidad* (Tirant lo Blanch 2015).

Barona Vilar S, 'Mirada restaurativa de la justicia penal en España, una bocanada de aire en la sociedad global líquida del miedo y de la securitización', in Helena Soleto Muñoz, Ana Carrascosa Miguel (dirs), *Justicia restaurativa: una justicia para las víctimas* (Tirant lo Blanch 2019).

Castillo Roldán C, 'Violencia de género. ¿Crisis de la justicia? Avanzar hacia la justicia restaurativa' (2020) 9681 *Diario La Ley* 1.

Castro Jover B, 'La mediación penal como práctica restaurativa en la fase de ejecución penal' (2020) 9710 *Diario La Ley* 1.

Colomer Hernández I, 'La mediación penal con menores infractores en la LORPM', in Esther Pillado González (coord), *Mediación con menores infractores en España y los países de su entorno* (Tirant lo Blanch 2012).

de Cabo C, Estirado, 'Cuestiones relevantes de Derecho sustantivo y procesal respecto de la incorporación de la mediación a la jurisdicción penal de adultos en las fases de instrucción y enjuiciamiento' (2008) *Estudios de Derecho Judicial. La mediación civil y penal. Un año de experiencia, Consejo General del Poder Judicial* 136–207.

Gallego Sánchez MG, 'El Convenio de Estambul: ¿por qué un convenio sobre la violencia contra la mujer?' (2016) 1 *Cuadernos Digitales de Formación, Consejo General del Poder Judicial* 1.

García Fernández MA, 'Una mediación especializada: intervención con menores' (2015) 8627 *Diario La Ley* 1.

García Rodríguez MJ, 'La mediación entre el menor infractor y la víctima ¿un mecanismo válido para resolver los conflictos de violencia de género en el sistema de justicia penal juvenil?' (2021) 9908 *Diario La Ley* 1, Sección Doctrina.

Gómez Conesa A, 'Mediación y violencia de género. Análisis y propuestas a partir de la evidencia empírica' (2021) 9825 *Diario La Ley* 1, Sección Tribuna.

González Cano I, 'Valoración de las reformas procesales operadas por la LO 6/2004, de 4 de diciembre, por la que se modifica la Ley Orgánica de Responsabilidad Penal de los menores' (2007) 3 *Diario La Ley* 1.

Hernández Gómez I, 'Justicia restaurativa, mediación penal y principio de oportunidad', in José María Roca Martínez (dir), *El acceso a la Justicia* (Tirant lo Blanch 2018).

Huertas Martín I, 'Reflexiones sobre la prohibición de la mediación en la violencia de género', in Ana María Rodríguez Tirado (coord), *Cuestiones actuales de Derecho Procesal. Reformas procesales. Mediación y arbitraje* (Tirant lo Blanch 2017).

Jimeno Bulnes M, 'Sobre la mediación, justicia restaurativa y otras justicias', in Helena Soleto Muñoz, Ana Carrascosa Miguel (dirs), *Justicia restaurativa: una justicia para las víctimas* (Tirant lo Blanch 2019).

López Picó R, 'Sobreseimiento del expediente de reforma por conciliación o reparación entre el menor infractor y la víctima del delito; una manifestación del principio de oportunidad en el proceso penal de menores', in Lorenzo Mateo Bujosa Vadell, Fernando Martín Diz (dirs), *Menores y justicia juvenil* (Thomson Reuters- Aranzadi 2021).

Martín Diz F, *La mediación: sistema complementario de Administración de Justicia* (Consejo General del Poder Judicial 2010).

Martínez Gallego EM, *Ley de Medidas de Protección Integral contra la Violencia de Género* (Iustel 2005).

Miguel Barrio R, 'La Justicia Restaurativa y el interés por el delito: los círculos restaurativos como posible método de resocialización del victimario' (2018) 9297 *Diario La Ley* 1.

Molina Caballero MJ, 'Algunas fronteras de la Ley Integral contra la violencia de género: jurisdicción de menores y mediación' (2015) 17–24 *Revista Electrónica de Derecho Penal y Criminología* 1.

Montero Hernanz T, 'Sobre las propuestas de reforma de la Ley Orgánica 1/2000', in Lorenzo Mateo Bujosa Vadell, Fernando Martín Diz (dirs), *Menores y justicia juvenil* (Thomson Reuters - Aranzadi 2021).

Montesdeoca Rodríguez D, 'Luces y sombras de la mediación penal' (2020) 9704 *Diario La Ley* 1.

Pillado González E, 'La mediación como manifestación del principio de oportunidad en la Ley de Responsabilidad Penal de Menores', in Esther Pillado González (coord), *Mediación con menores infractores en España y los países de su entorno* (Tirant lo Blanch 2012).

Rodríguez Tirado AM, 'Los sistemas de justicia restaurativa y la mediación penal. Efectos en el sistema procesal penal español', in Ana María Rodríguez Tirado (coord), *Cuestiones actuales de Derecho Procesal. Reformas procesales. Mediación y arbitraje* (Tirant lo Blanch 2017).

Sánchez Barrios I, 'Menores infractores y principio de oportunidad. Regulación internacional', in Lorenzo Mateo Bujosa Vadell, Fernando Martín Diz (dirs), *Menores y justicia juvenil* (Thomson Reuters Aranzadi 2021).

Soleto Muñoz H, 'Justicia restaurativa para la mejor reparación a la víctima', in Helena Soleto Muñoz, Ana Carrascosa Miguel (dirs), *Justicia restaurativa: una justicia para las víctimas* (Tirant lo Blanch 2019).

Tardón Olmos M, 'Definiciones del Convenio de Estambul y ámbito de aplicación, en relación con la Ley 1/2004' (2016) 1 *Cuadernos Digitales de Formación, Consejo General del Poder Judicial* 1.

Tierno Barrios S, 'Mediación penal y justicia de menores: una manifestación del principio de oportunidad', in Lorenzo Mateo Bujosa Vadell, Fernando Martín Diz (dirs), *Menores y justicia juvenil* (Thomson Reuters - Aranzadi 2021).

5

Opportunity principle and legal persons

Compliance and criminal mediation as manifestations of the modern criminal justice system in Spain

Selena Tierno Barrios

Introduction

One of the most important legal debates that can be highlighted within the criminal justice system concerns the necessary balance that criminal proceedings must strike between safeguarding public order and safety on the one hand, and the protection of fundamental rights and freedoms on the other.[1,2]

A dilemma ('guarantees *versus* efficiency'), which represents nothing more than an old dilemma in the field of criminal procedure between a more efficient system, but one that limits the fundamental rights of the accused, in favour of the powers entrusted to the bodies responsible for criminal prosecution, as well as in favour of the agility of the process, *versus* a more guaranteeing system that promotes the defence of citizens in the face of abuses of power.[3]

This is the context in which the opportunity principle is framed in response to another issue of utmost importance in this area, namely the particular crisis suffered by the Spanish criminal justice system, which is generally accused of being slow, expensive, inefficient and unfair.[4]

In response to which reform proposals are being put forward in the search for instruments that contribute to its modernization, speed and capacity to offer adequate protection to the interests of citizens, but all in a perfect balance with respect for and guarantee of fundamental rights. In this sense, it is not surprising that there is a demand for a greater commitment to the application of the principle of minimum intervention in criminal law, or the decriminalization of certain low-injury conduct or minor offences, promoting the use of the opportunity principle or allowing recourse to self-compositive formulas for conflict resolution such as mediation.[5]

This raises the concept of public interest in the criminal justice system, which is closely connected with the opportunity principle and with the rethinking of the role that the Public Prosecutor's Office could play in the future in Spain, given that at present the direction of the pre-trial phase of criminal proceedings is attributed to the investigating judge.[6]

In that way, among the factors that are usually highlighted as causes of this particular crisis that criminal justice suffers, it is found the sometimes disproportionate response offered both from the substantive and procedural sphere in the criminal systems of post-industrial societies in relation to the magnitude of the injury produced or the danger generated that is the object of prevention or repression, leading to a rethinking of the purposes of punishment and questioning its true effectiveness as an element of general prevention, hence the search for a certain flexibility with regard to the compulsory exercise of criminal action, that is, criteria of convenience or opportunity, as well as the search for alternative formulas to the judicial process and the application of custodial sentences.[7]

To all this it must also be added the traditional neglect and neutralization of the victim in the criminal justice system and, in contrast, the recent and progressive interest in the role that the victim should occupy in it and the necessary protection of their rights and needs, promoting the reparative effects of the conflict generated by the commission of the criminal act. In all these cases, therefore, the opportunity principle seems to fit in as an instrument of criminal policy through which to alleviate the crisis of criminal justice.[8]

In this sense, in the constant search to find the panacea that will put an end to all the ills that plague the Administration of Justice, in the criminal order it is worth looking at the objectives set by recent criminal policies aimed at increasing the levels of efficiency so desired and which have resulted in this area in *(i)* the regulation of the criminal liability of legal persons and, in connection with this, the regulation of compliance programmes[9]; and *(ii)* the use of alternative – complementary – means of conflict resolution in the criminal order, framed within the current of restorative justice, with particular emphasis on criminal mediation.[10]

Therefore, the purpose of this research work will be to analyse how this principle, as well as the concept of public interest, fits into each of the aforementioned areas in the framework of criminal proceedings against legal persons. All of this with the aim of defining the delineations that are presupposed for a modern criminal system and to highlight the procedural challenges that need to be addressed.

The opportunity principle and the public interest in the Spanish criminal justice system

The opportunity principle has been incorporated into Spanish criminal procedure to a greater or lesser extent through the latest reforms of criminal procedural legislation – especially since the one adopted in 2015 – being defended by some sectors of the doctrine in favour of what is known as the principle of 'regulated opportunity', insofar as the prosecution of certain criminal offences is subject to the will of the prosecution when certain requirements expressly determined by law are met, hence the term 'regulated'.[11]

In that way, by virtue of it, the holder of the criminal action is attributed the power to dispose of its exercise in response to motives of social interest or public utility, as long as the conditions set out in the rule are met, which translates as a consequence into the power, either to initiate criminal proceedings or to obtain the dismissal of the case.[12]

In short, we are dealing with a power of disposal granted to the parties making it possible, for reasons of public interest, to exclude the penalty provided for in a certain rule as a legal consequence to be applied to a case of the commission of a criminal act.[13]

In this sense, apart from being seen as a magic remedy for, if not ending, at least alleviating to some extent, the crisis that criminal justice has been suffering for several decades now, there are also important reasons that are often put forward as arguments in defence of the incorporation of the opportunity principle in our criminal procedure system, such as taking into consideration the public or social interest. This is in order to improve the state's *ius puniendi*, but also insofar as it makes it possible to better compensate the victim by contributing to their adequate protection, and finally, because it favours the social reintegration of the offender by avoiding the criminogenic effects of short custodial sentences and, therefore, the phenomenon of the stigmatization of the convicted person.[14]

However, the compatibility of the opportunity principle with due process must also be considered in depth, because criteria based on expediency may not necessarily fit in adequately with the right to the presumption of innocence or to a public trial with all the guarantees. Nor with the principle of equality or legal certainty, given that if opportunity is based on reasons of convenience, opportunity represents then a wide range in which a great diversity of proposals, tendencies and objectives can be accommodated, which means that the discretionary powers granted in this respect do not have to be compatible with those guarantees in any case.[15]

Therefore, as far as adult criminal proceedings are concerned, since there are important differences in comparison with juvenile proceedings, one of the most outstanding manifestations of the opportunity principle is the possibility granted to the Public Prosecutor's Office under Article 963.1.1ª of the Criminal Procedure Act (from now on, LECrim) to request the dismissal of the proceedings in the framework of the procedure for the trial of minor offences when the minor offence that has been denounced is of little seriousness in view of the nature of the act, its circumstances and the personal circumstances of the perpetrator, and, furthermore, there is no relevant public interest in the prosecution of the act.[16]

In the latter case, it is understood that in minor property offences there is no such relevant public interest when no complaint has been filed by the injured party and the damage caused has been repaired. Therefore, in view of the above circumstances, the court shall adopt a decision ordering the dismissal of the proceedings, as well as the closure of the proceedings and shall immediately notify all those who have been summoned of the suspension of the trial, namely the complainant and defendant, injured parties and witnesses who could provide evidence of the events that took place. Likewise, the dismissal of the proceedings shall be notified to the injured parties of the offence committed.[17]

However, the legislator does not specify in a concrete manner the cases that allow the Public Prosecutor's Office to proceed with the request for dismissal, but resorts to the use of indeterminate legal concepts that provide little or no guidance as to the opportunity criteria established, namely, the low seriousness of the crime and the absence of public interest in the prosecution of the act, hence the approval by the State Attorney General's Office of Circular 1/2015, of 19 June.[18]

In accordance with the guidelines of the Circular, the criteria of opportunity that should guide the actions of the Public Prosecutor's Office with regard to the exercise of the criminal action – particularly, to waive it – are configured as elements of cumulative concurrence based in the first place on the low seriousness of the crime, which is subordinated in this case to a series of factors to be evaluated, such as the nature of the act, its circumstances and the personal circumstances of the perpetrator.

Regarding this first element, it is considered that the model of opportunity adopted by the legislator in the reform is limited to what are known as petty crimes in which the public interest is assessed according to the cost of the material and personal resources involved in prosecuting them. In that way, if the criminal act does not represent a minimum material relevance that compensates for the cost of initiating criminal proceedings, it is decided not to prosecute, which is precisely the criterion adopted by the legislator, but leaving the decision in the hands of the Public Prosecutor's Office through the corresponding weighing of interests, in short, the material unlawfulness of the conduct in terms of both the action and the result, which will be assessed according to the circumstances of the perpetrator and the act. However, if minor offences are already by their very nature the least relevant group of offences of all the offences typified in the Criminal Code (from now on, CP), to demand that in order to request the dismissal of the case it must be a very minor offence, it reduces the application of the opportunity principle to the minimum expression. Thus, it should be noted that the maximum precautions are imposed by the Spanish legal system on the waiver of *ius puniendi*.[19]

Secondly, with regard to the element of the absence of public interest in the prosecution of the act, it should be emphasized that the concept of public interest in the exercise of criminal action is largely identified with that relating to the material unlawfulness of the conduct, leading to an overlap between the two elements required. However, there are certain factors external to the criminal act committed which should not go unnoticed when analysing and assessing the need for punishment. We are referring, in this case, to the consolidation of the legal system that has been violated, there being a greater interest in prosecution in those cases in which there are frequent acts that threaten the community as a whole, or in those in which greater protection of the victim is required. In relation to this element, the legislator establishes what should be understood by the absence of relevant public interest in cases of minor property crimes, identifying it with the reparation of the damage caused and the absence of a complaint by the injured party, that is, the victim's legitimate expectations of civil and criminal reparation.[20]

Restorative justice and criminal mediation

In close connection with the opportunity principle and representing one of the areas that is becoming particularly popular within the justice system, it must be highlighted the use of mediation in the criminal order as a mechanism for resolving conflicts of this nature, given that it is also understood that for its adequate implementation it necessarily requires, as a basic presupposition, a wide margin of discretion with respect to the criminal action; that is, it is also an institution that finds its support in the opportunity principle.[21]

The appearance of restorative justice must be placed in a context of evolution and transformation of the criminal system which, together with the consolidation during the twentieth century of the postulates about the preventive function of criminal law in the face of the lack of response of the retributive criminal model to the social demands, certain restorative practices are being incorporated. In this regard, the deficiencies of this retributive model, namely the ineffective preventive nature of penalties, the neglect of the victim, and a formalist and slow criminal process, showed the impossibility of responding to all types of criminality, which meant conceiving criminal law as an instrument of general prevention, reparation and rehabilitation or re-socialization, and not only of punishment. Nevertheless, it is not always possible to achieve the fulfilment of these three functions through the criminal process, hence the need to resort to other means of restorative practices which have gradually been incorporated into legal systems.[22]

In that way, restorative justice is mainly articulated around three pillars: the active protagonism of the parties in the resolution of the conflict, the integral reparation of the damage caused by the criminal act beyond a simple economic reparation, and the promotion of dialogue to achieve an agreement between the parties in order to reach an adequate solution, which will be examined below.[23]

Regarding the active protagonism of the parties, it must be said that one of the main characteristics that define restorative justice and that have led to its appearance is the recognition of the protagonist role of the victim of the crime in the solution of the criminal conflict.[24]

This is because for centuries they have been the great forgotten party of the criminal procedural system insofar as the State assumed the competence to react to the commission of a criminal act and exercised the main role in criminal protection as the crime was considered to have been committed against the State and society, so that the victims could not intervene in the reaction to it, thus eliminating any possibility of revenge. In this sense, there is an expropriation of the conflict from the victim, who is neutralized and exposed to what has been called 'secondary victimization' because the criminal procedural system does not offer an adequate response to the protection of their interests and needs. Therefore, restorative justice is based on the rediscovery of the victim, favouring their participation in the criminal process and giving them back the leading role that they really have in the solution of the conflict.[25]

In this regard, at the international level, there are various normative instruments that aim to recognize the rights of victims, and in particular, their participation in criminal proceedings.[26]

For instance, it can be mentioned that different initiatives emanating from international organizations such as the United Nations, including the 'Declaration of Basic Principles of Justice for Victims of Crime and Abuse of Power', approved by the General Assembly in Resolution 40/34 of 29 November 1985, which refers to mediation as one of the instruments for victim participation in criminal proceedings. Furthermore, it must also be taken into account the regulations enacted by the institutions of the European Union, such as Council Framework Decision 2001/220/JHA of 15 March 2001 on the standing of victims in criminal proceedings, and subsequently, Directive 2012/29/EU of the European Parliament and of the Council of 25 October 2012 establishing minimum standards on the rights, support and protection of victims of crime and replacing the previous Framework Decision.[27]

However, these international normative instruments that addressed the protagonism and revaluation of the victim in the criminal process took time to be reflected in the Spanish legal system, as it was not until 2015 when, through Law 4/2015, of 27 April, on the statute of the victim of crime, the possibility of using restorative justice practices was provided for, although it should be noted that mechanisms aimed at assisting victims were previously put in place, such as the creation of assistance offices and the enactment of specific laws aimed at providing reparation for certain particularly vulnerable groups of victims, namely victims of terrorism, violent crimes and crimes against sexual freedom, and gendered violence. Nevertheless, none of these cases contain any regulation of mediation, being limited only to reparation, assistance and protection, and even prohibited in cases of gendered violence and, more recently, in the area of sexual violence with the approval of Organic Law 10/2022, of 6 September, on the comprehensive guarantee of sexual freedom, better known as the 'only yes is yes' law.[28]

In that way, the only area in which this restorative practice is allowed is the juvenile justice system, regulated by Organic Law 5/2000 of 12 January, regulating the criminal responsibility of minors.[29]

Restorative justice, however, also recognizes the essential role that the offender plays in the reparation process of the victim in the sense that they are capable of reaching agreements and collaborating in the reparation process, and all of this because this new model of criminal justice focuses not only on the punishment of the offender, but on the voluntary acknowledgement of the perpetrator of the criminal act committed – always respecting the procedural guarantees provided – on their responsibility and commitment to the victim to repair the harm caused, while at the same time favouring their social reintegration.[30]

Secondly, with regard to the reparation of the damage, it should be pointed out that another of the fundamental pillars on which restorative justice is based is to achieve a reparation of the damage caused by the criminal act, which is commonly described as 'integral'; that is, it does not seek a simple reparation of an economic or material nature, but rather a moral or, if preferred, an emotional reparation, which really implies a compensation or restitution for the victim for the damages derived from the crime.[31]

Finally, the last characteristic common to any restorative practice is the creation of a space for dialogue that makes it possible to reach an agreement between victim and offender with the aim of solving the criminal conflict in an adequate and satisfactory way, and all this based on the participation of the parties in the resolution of the controversy, in such a way that the technique of dialogue allows the offender to assume and take responsibility for the damage caused by the commission of the crime, but also favours the externalization of emotions and feelings by the victim, thus contributing to their recovery.[32]

In this order of things, one of the main formulas through which restorative justice is manifested is the one related to criminal mediation, being the maximum exponent and the most recognized and most deeply rooted instrument in the framework of this model of justice, at least in Spain as well as in European countries of our environment, since apart from this formula, there are also other well-known restorative practices in Common Law countries, such as conferences and sentencing circles.[33]

In this regard, focusing our attention on criminal mediation, this practice is defined as a procedure whereby victim and offender actively participate voluntarily in the resolution of a conflict of a criminal nature with the intervention of an impartial third party whose role is to assist and guide the parties involved with the aim of reaching an agreement on their own to put an end to the dispute and to be able to resolve the conflict.[34]

Criminal liability of legal persons and compliance programmes

Returning to the idea of the crisis plaguing criminal justice and the various attempts at solutions that have occupied the legislator's work for decades through multiple reforms,[35] this brings to mind not only the promotion of the opportunity principle and the rise of *Alternative Dispute Resolution* (ADR), but also the criminal liability of legal persons as a reaction to the clear increase in criminal conflicts and the emergence of new and increasingly complex forms of crime resulting from globalization.[36]

It is, therefore, in this area relating to the criminal liability of legal persons and, especially, in the latest reforms that have taken place in terms of the possibility of exemption or mitigation of this liability through regulatory compliance programmes, better known as compliance programmes, where we will focus our analysis of criminal mediation.

Organic Law 5/2010 of 22 June 2010 included in the Spanish legal system the possibility of attributing criminal liability to legal persons. However, this first regulation did not contemplate the possibility that they could be exempted from liability if they could prove that they had done everything possible to avoid committing the corresponding offence but only established certain mitigating factors. Within this framework, the most important change came with the reform of the Criminal Code in 2015 through Organic Law 1/2015, of 30 March, introducing certain exempting and mitigating circumstances of this liability based on the company or organization having an 'organizational and management model'. To this end, the compliance programme must meet a series of requirements such as the preparation of a 'criminal risk map', the implementation of financial resource management models to avoid the existence of 'b boxes', the creation of internal whistleblowing systems or channels or the adoption of a disciplinary system, for example, as established in Article 31 *bis* 5 of the CP.[37]

In that way, if *(i)* the management body of the entity has adopted and effectively implemented this organization and management model at a time prior to the commission of the offence, including supervision and control measures that are deemed appropriate in order to prevent offences of the same nature or to significantly reduce the risk of commission of the offence; *(ii)* the supervision of the operation and compliance of the model has been entrusted to a body of the legal person with autonomous powers of initiative and control, or to a body entrusted with the function of supervising the effectiveness of the entity's internal controls; *(iii)* the natural persons responsible for the offence have committed it by fraudulently circumventing the organizational and management model; and *(iv)* the supervision, monitoring and control functions have not been omitted or have not been exercised in an insufficient manner, the legal person will in this case be exempt from criminal liability, as per Article 31 *bis* 2 CP, if the offence has been committed 'in the name or on behalf of the legal person, and for its direct or indirect benefit, by its legal representatives or by those who, acting individually or as members of an organ of the legal person, are authorized to take decisions on behalf of the legal person or have powers of organization and control within the legal person', a case referred to in Article 31 *bis* 1 a) CP.[38]

In another case, if the offence has been committed

> in the exercise of corporate activities and on behalf of and for the direct or indirect benefit of the same, by those who, being subject to the authority of the natural persons mentioned in the previous paragraph, have been able to carry out the acts because of a serious breach by them of the duties of supervision, monitoring and control of their activity in view of the specific circumstances of the case [art. 31 *bis* 1 b) CP],

the legal person will be exempt from liability, requiring only in this case that it has adopted and effectively implemented, at a time prior to the commission of the criminal act, an appropriate organizational and management model in order to prevent crimes of the same nature as the one committed, or to significantly reduce the risk of their commission, in accordance with the provisions of Article 31 *bis* 4 CP.[39] Likewise, the adoption of effective measures aimed at the prevention and investigation of future offences that could be committed within the legal person is foreseen as an attenuating circumstance of criminal liability in Article 31 *quater* 1 d) CP.

Therefore, compliance programmes not only have the potential to exonerate from criminal liability those entities that have effectively implemented them, but also fulfil a preventive function in the sense of constituting instruments through which to prevent or avoid, as far as possible, the commission of unlawful acts within those entities.[40] Thus, through the implementation of these programmes, the aim is to create an 'organizational culture' within the entity, that is, a culture based on compliance with the law.[41]

Restorative justice approach in the 'compliance culture'

In this order of things, it can be seen how the promotion of the opportunity principle can be observed in a clearer way in the very singular stage that the introduction of compliance programmes implies, translated into business self-regulation and the powers conferred, therefore, to the entities to prevent and manage criminal risks, but also to detect, investigate and sanction disciplinary offences committed in their midst.[42]

Hence, one might ask how restorative justice, first of all, and criminal mediation, in a more specific way, can fit into this stage, which is also enveloped by a spirit that aspires not only to a culture of legality but also, in a more ambitious way, to business ethics, connecting also with corporate social responsibility.[43]

That is to say, what role can restorative justice play in the field of criminal liability of legal persons, contributing, in a kind of creation of synergy, to achieve, on the one hand, the ultimate objectives that inspire compliance programmes in the prevention and investigation of the criminal act[44] and making possible, in turn, on the other hand, the purposes pursued by the very current of restorative justice, such as the adequate response to the needs of the victim and the comprehensive reparation of the damage caused.[45]

In this sense, taking up again what was pointed out in the introduction to this chapter, we will consider examining the possible contributions that the restorative justice current, through the instrument of criminal mediation, can provide to compliance programmes. And this is because, in the same context of crisis that criminal justice has been suffering for decades in which the introduction of compliance programmes has been taking place, the restorative justice movement constitutes a change of paradigm of the current model strongly marked by a retributive accent and based mainly on the principle of legality and the exclusive exercise by the State of *ius puniendi*, whose purpose is to promote the 'humanization' of criminal law with special reference to the victims of crime, contributing to their reparation.[46]

We can therefore highlight below some elements that we believe can be transferred to the field in question, thus allowing a re-reading of the philosophy that inspires their implementation in the framework of compliance programmes within companies.

Firstly, let us consider that the whistleblowing channels that make up compliance programmes constitute a surveillance and supervision mechanism through which it is possible to detect infractions and irregular or corrupt practices within organizations with the aim of investigating them – known as 'internal corporate investigations'[47] – and sanctioning them through the organization's disciplinary system, or by reporting the information to the public authorities. In this sense, both the internal investigations and the criminal process itself follow the dynamics of a procedure of an adversarial nature to which the restorative justice current is opposed in view of its previously mentioned foundations. Thus, in the context of conflicts between an entity or organization and the reporting person, or between the latter and other members of the company, this adversarial nature could be replaced by a cooperative dynamic in which the protagonism of the parties involved would be promoted through their participation in a dialogue with a view to reaching an agreement that would lead to the mutual satisfaction of interests and the resolution of the conflict generated, for example, in cases of harassment or discrimination. The introduction of the elements of apology, forgiveness and commitment in the implementation of future improvement measures could represent a sign of greater effectiveness and usefulness than a sanction such as dismissal.[48]

Secondly, the comprehensive reparation of the damage caused by the commission of the criminal act defended by restorative justice seems to be an appropriate formula in order to compensate the informant for the damages that they may suffer from the entity as a result of the information that they have provided to the whistleblowing channel.[49] An integral reparation[50] that fits into the spectrum of mechanisms with which to promote the restoration of immaterial damages and broken relationships between the informant and the entity, and which can satisfy the needs of that person insofar as they do not necessarily have to correspond to the desire for punishment or compensation through financial compensation.[51]

Finally, restorative justice can also lead to a rethinking of the disciplinary system linked to the internal whistleblowing channel as integral elements of compliance programmes in the sense of bringing about a change in its functioning insofar as it follows a similar dynamic to the action exercised by the State through *ius puniendi*. The introduction of a restorative perspective would mean eliminating the requirement to necessarily impose a sanction in any case, which may even lead to the dismissal of one of the workers and in respect of which the company may not really be interested in the outcome.[52]

Conclusion

In a context in which, as a consequence of the crisis that has been affecting the administration of justice in a particularly serious way for decades and, specifically, in the field of criminal justice, the examination of those proposals aimed at increasing levels of efficiency in a stage marked by the progressive extension of the opportunity principle and the importance that the concept of public interest is gaining in this sense, becomes a particularly important task which we have redirected in this chapter to the study of compliance programmes and *Alternative Dispute Resolution* in order to promote or optimize their maximum deployment within the criminal justice system while respecting the constitutionally established guarantees in this sense.

In that way, focusing this research, on the one hand, on compliance programmes within the framework of the criminal liability of legal persons, and criminal mediation, on the other hand, as one of the main practices that make up the current of restorative justice, we have carried out an analysis of both material blocks in order to find a synergy that allows us to achieve the aforementioned purpose of increasing the levels of effectiveness of criminal justice without forgetting the recognized guarantees, which has allowed us to examine the fit of the opportunity principle and the concept of public interest in the Spanish criminal process, thus highlighting the challenges presented by the criminal justice system of our time.

Notes

1 This chapter has been made in the framework of a contract obtained through the FPU (training for university teachers) programme from Ministerio de Universidades of Gobierno de España as Postdoctoral Researcher (POP) within the Procedural Law Area of Universidad de Salamanca. This chapter has also been carried out within the framework of the Research Projects 'Cumplimiento normativo y protección penal de la Administración Pública' (PID2022-138775NB-I00) financed by MCIN/AEI/10.13039/501100011033/ and 'FEDER Una

manera de hacer Europa', whose Principal Investigator is Dr. Nicolás Rodríguez-García, and 'Externalización de la investigación en el ámbito empresarial y efectos en el proceso penal' (PIC2-2023-03) from Universidad de Salamanca, whose Principal Investigator is Dra. Ana E. Carrillo del Teso.

2 On this issue, see Víctor Moreno Catena, 'El proceso penal', in VV. AA., *Derecho Procesal Penal* (10th edn, Tirant lo Blanch 2021) 37–8.

3 Along this line of thought, see Nicolás Rodríguez-García, Luis Humberto Contreras Alfaro, 'Algunas reflexiones acerca de la utilización del principio de oportunidad como instrumento de política criminal en el diseño del Derecho procesal penal del siglo XXI' (2006) 3–4 *Justicia: Revista de Derecho Procesal* 53, 55–6.

4 In this sense, the Charter of Citizens' Rights before the Judiciary made a statement in which it underlined the urgency of achieving a more open justice system, capable of offering citizens a more agile, quality and efficient service, available at https://www.abogacia.es/wp-content/uploads/2012/05/Carta-de-Derechos-de-los-Ciudadanos-ante-la-Justicia.pdf (accessed 20 December 2025).

5 See Nicolás Rodríguez-García, 'La conformidad de las personas jurídicas en el proceso penal español' (2015) 113 *La Ley Penal* 1, 1–3; and, by the same author, 'Uso y abuso del principio de oportunidad en el proceso penal del siglo XXI', in Ana Isabel Pérez Cepeda (dir), *Política criminal ante el reto de la delincuencia transnacional* (Tirant lo Blanch 2016) 272–6.

6 Vicente Gimeno Sendra, 'El principio de oportunidad y el M.F' (2016) 8746 *Diario La Ley* 1, 1–4.

7 In this sense, see Nicolás Rodríguez García and Luis Humberto Contreras Alfaro, 'Algunas reflexiones acerca de la utilización del principio de oportunidad como instrumento de política criminal en el diseño del Derecho Procesal Penal del siglo XXI' (2006) 3–4 *Justicia: Revista de Derecho Procesal* 56–8.

8 Selena Tierno Barrios, 'La revalorización de la víctima en el proceso penal y su protección a nivel transnacional: el paradigma de la orden europea de protección' (2022) 1 *Justicia: Revista de Derecho Procesal* 383, 383–91.

9 See Ana María Neira Pena, Nicolás Rodríguez-García, 'España', in Nicolás Rodríguez-García (dir); Miguel Ontiveros Alonso, Omar Gabriel Orsi, Fernando Rodríguez-López (coords), *Tratado Angloiberoamericano sobre compliance penal* (Tirant lo Blanch 2022) 433–68.

10 Adán Carrizo González-Castell, 'Reparación de la víctima y mediación penal', in Fernando Martín Diz (dir); Adán Carrizo González-Castell (coord), *Mediación en la Administración de Justicia: implantación y desarrollo* (Andavira 2017) 251–70.

11 On this issue, see Julio Banacloche Palao, 'El proceso penal. Los procedimientos especiales', in VV. AA., *Aspectos fundamentales de Derecho Procesal Penal* (5th edn, La Ley 2021) 34.

12 In this regard, see Agustín Jesús Pérez-Cruz Martín, 'El proceso penal. Los sistemas procesales penales en general: proceso inquisitivo; proceso acusatorio. El sistema procesal penal de la Ley de Enjuiciamiento Criminal: principio del juez imparcial, separación de instrucción y enjuiciamiento. Principios del proceso penal. El principio de oportunidad. La perspectiva de género en la jurisdicción penal', in Agustín Jesús Pérez-Cruz Martín (coord), *Derecho Procesal Penal* (Tirant lo Blanch 2020) 35; and Jordi Nieva Fenoll, *Fundamentos de Derecho Procesal* (Edisofer 2012) 19.

13 This is the view expressed by Javier Vecina Cifuentes, Tomás Vicente Ballestero, 'Las manifestaciones del Principio de Oportunidad en el proceso penal español' (2018) 50 *Derecho & Sociedad* 307, 314.

14 Along this line of thought, see Teresa Armenta Deu, *Lecciones de Derecho procesal penal* (9th edn, Marcial Pons 2016) 44; Nicolás Rodríguez-García, 'Hacia la maximización del principio de oportunidad en los procesos penales por hechos de corrupción', in Sonia Calaza López, José Carlos Muinelo Cobo (dirs), *Postmodernidad y proceso europeo: la oportunidad como principio informador del proceso judicial* (Dykinson 2020) 412.

15 Of this opinion is Nicolás Rodríguez-García, 'La conformidad ...' 5–6.

16 See Ana María Rodríguez Tirado, 'Los procesos por delitos leves. Manifestaciones del principio de oportunidad. Actividad instructora y principio acusatorio' (2016) 38 *Revista General de Derecho Procesal* 1, 14–15.

17 On the procedure for the trial of minor offences and the principle of discretionary prosecution, see Ana María Rodríguez Tirado, 'Los procesos por delitos leves ...' 14–15.

18 Circular 1/2015, of 19 June, of the State Attorney General's Office, on guidelines for the exercise of criminal action in relation to minor offences following the criminal reform introduced by Organic Law 1/2015 (FIS-C-2015-00001).

19 See Section 6.2.1 of Circular 1/2015 of 19 June.

20 In this regard, it can be read Section 6.2.1 of Circular 1/2015 of 19 June.

21 Adán Carrizo González-Castell, 'Reparación de la víctima ...' 265.

22 On the evolution of the criminal justice system and the deployment of restorative justice, see Silvia Barona Vilar, 'Mirada restaurativa de la justicia penal en España, una bocanada de aire en la sociedad global líquida del miedo y de la securitización', in Helena Soleto Muñoz, Ana Carrascosa Miguel (dirs), *Justicia restaurativa: una justicia para las víctimas* (Tirant lo Blanch 2019) 57–60.

23 Of this opinion are Ana Montesinos García, 'Una breve aproximación a la justicia restaurativa', in Ana Montesinos García (ed), *Tratado de Mediación. Tomo II. Mediación Penal* (Tirant lo Blanch 2017) 25–6; and Cristina Alonso Salgado, *La mediación en el proceso penal* (Tirant lo Blanch 2018) 63.

24 On this issue, see Selena Tierno Barrios, *Justicia restaurativa y mediación en el sistema penal español* (Tirant lo Blanch, 2025) 125–215.

25 Silvia Barona Vilar, 'Mirada restaurativa ...' 64–5; and Ignacio Flores Prada, 'Algunas reflexiones sobre la justicia restaurativa en el sistema español de justicia penal' (2015) 2 *Revista Internacional de Estudios de Derecho Procesal y Arbitraje* 1, 11–18.

26 Selena Tierno Barrios, 'La revalorización de la víctima en el proceso penal ...' 383–91.

27 In this regard, see Natalia Pérez Rivas, 'Evolución histórica del estatuto jurídico de la víctima: especial referencia al derecho español' (2017) 41 Revista General de Derecho Procesal 1, 22 and 29–33.

28 On this issue, see María Asunción Colás Turégano, 'Mediación juvenil: el equilibrio entre la reparación a la víctima y el interés superior del menor', in Ana Montesinos García (ed), *Tratado de Mediación. Tomo II. Mediación Penal* (Tirant lo Blanch 2017) 111–12 and 116–17; and Ana María Rodríguez Tirado, 'Los sistemas de justicia restaurativa y la mediación penal. Efectos en el sistema procesal penal español', in Ana María Rodríguez Tirado (coord), *Cuestiones actuales de Derecho Procesal. Reformas procesales. Mediación y arbitraje* (Tirant lo Blanch 2017) 312.

29 On this topic, see Selena Tierno Barrios, 'Mediación penal y justicia de menores: una manifestación del principio de oportunidad', in Lorenzo Mateo Bujosa Vadell, Fernando Martín Diz (dirs); Irene González Pulido, Walter Reifarth Muñoz (coords), *Menores y justicia juvenil* (Tirant lo Blanch 2021) 405–20.

30 This is the view expressed by Julián Carlos Ríos Martín, 'Justicia restaurativa y mediación penal' (2016) 98 ICADE: Revista cuatrimestral de las Facultades de Derecho y Ciencias Económicas y Empresariales 103, 107 and 109–10.

31 On this issue, see Adán Carrizo González-Castell, 'Reparación de la víctima ...' 253; Ana Montesinos García, 'Una breve aproximación ...' 28–9; and Helena Soleto Muñoz, 'Justicia restaurativa para la mejor reparación a la víctima', in Helena Soleto Muñoz, Ana Carrascosa Miguel (dirs), *Justicia restaurativa: una justicia para las víctimas* (Tirant lo Blanch 2019) 495–9.

32 Of this opinion are Cristina Alonso Salgado, *La mediación en el proceso penal* (Tirant lo Blanch 2018) 63–4; and Ana Montesinos García, 'Una breve aproximación ...' 29.

33 For this matter, one could also consult Mar Jimeno Bulnes, 'Sobre la mediación, justicia restaurativa y otras justicias', in Helena Soleto Muñoz, Ana Carrascosa Miguel (dirs), *Justicia restaurativa: una justicia para las víctimas* (Tirant lo Blanch 2019) 98 and 108–9; and Ana Montesinos García, 'Una breve aproximación ...' 32–3.

34 Of this opinion are Silvia Barona Vilar, *Mediación penal. Fundamento, fines y régimen jurídico* (Tirant lo Blanch 2011) 257 and 262–5; and Nicolás Rodríguez-García, 'Presente y futuro de la mediación penal', in Ana María Rodríguez Tirado (coord), *Cuestiones actuales de Derecho Procesal. Reformas procesales. Mediación y arbitraje* (Tirant lo Blanch 2017) 285–7.

35 Nicolás Rodríguez-García, 'Presente y futuro ...' 269–71.
36 Nicolás Rodríguez-García, 'La conformidad ...' 1–3.
37 Ana María Neira Pena, Nicolás Rodríguez-García, 'España ...' 450–3.
38 Selena Tierno Barrios, 'Acceso a la justicia y *compliance* ambiental frente a la responsabilidad penal de las personas jurídicas en el marco de las litigaciones climáticas', in Nicolás Rodríguez-García, Ana E. Carrillo Del Teso, Giorgio Darío María Cerina (eds), *Delincuencia corporativa*: Compliance, *canales de denuncia y persecución penal* (Tirant lo Blanch 2024) 139–48.
39 Ana María Neira Pena, Nicolás Rodríguez-García, 'España ...' 435–6.
40 See Antonio Del Moral García, 'Responsabilidad penal de personas jurídicas y presunción de inocencia', in Nicolás Rodríguez-García, Fernando Rodríguez-López (eds), *Compliance y responsabilidad de las personas jurídicas* (Tirant lo Blanch 2021) 59.
41 More broadly, see Ana María Neira Pena, 'La efectividad de los *criminal compliance programs* como objeto de prueba en el proceso penal' (2016) 11 22 *Política Criminal: Revista Electrónica Semestral de Políticas Públicas en Materias Penales* 467, 481. This 'compliance culture' implies not only compliance with legal rules by their recipients, but also the adoption of behaviour that is far removed from any fraudulent, deceitful, unsupportive or opportunistic conduct, insofar as such programmes also incorporate or are aligned with elements of business ethics, corporate social responsibility and good governance. In this sense, see José Ignacio Sánchez Macías, Fernando Rodríguez-López, 'Estudio preliminar', in Nicolás Rodríguez-García (dir); Miguel Ontiveros Alonso, Omar Gabriel Orsi, Fernando Rodríguez-López (coords), *Tratado Angloiberoamericano sobre compliance penal* (Tirant lo Blanch 2022) 28 and 30.
42 Selena Tierno Barrios, *Justicia restaurativa* ... 680–714.
43 It is in this sense that the 'compliance culture' has been defined above.
44 Ana María Neira Pena, 'La efectividad de los *criminal compliance programs* ...' 469–70.
45 Adán Carrizo González-Castell, 'Reparación de la víctima ...' 251–70.
46 On restorative justice and criminal mediation, see Adán Carrizo González-Castell, 'Justicia Restaurativa y Mediación Penal en España', in Luiz Henrique Sormani Barbugiani (coord), *Mediação e Arbitragem no Âmbito Público e Privado: Perspectivas e Limitações* (Lumen Juris 2018) 183.
47 On the subject of internal company investigations, see Nicolás Rodríguez-García, 'Las investigaciones internas como elemento esencial de los "criminal compliance programs": haciendo de la necesidad virtud' (2023) 52 *Revista Penal* 201, 201–23; and Ana Elena Carrillo Del Teso, 'El "fundido a negro" de la prueba en la persecución de la delincuencia económica', in Nicolás Rodríguez-García, Adán Carrizo González-Castell, Fernando Rodríguez-López (eds); Ana Elena Carrillo del Teso, Javier Sánchez Bernal (coords), *Corrupción: Compliance, Represión y Recuperación de Activos* (Tirant lo Blanch 2020) 472–5.

48 See Adán Nieto Martín, 'Una pieza más en la Justicia restaurativa empresarial: Programas de cumplimiento restaurativos' (2023) 15 Revista de Victimología 147, 163–4.
49 Adán Nieto Martín, 'Una pieza más ...' 164.
50 On the subject of the 'integral reparation' concept, see Selena Tierno Barrios, *Justicia restaurativa* ... 220–63.
51 Adán Nieto Martín, 'Una pieza más ...' 164.
52 Ibid 164.

References

Alonso Salgado C, *La mediación en el proceso penal* (Tirant lo Blanch 2018).
Armenta Deu T, *Lecciones de Derecho procesal penal* (9th edn, Marcial Pons 2016).
Banacloche Palao J, 'El proceso penal. Los procedimientos especiales', in VV. AA., *Aspectos fundamentales de Derecho Procesal Penal* (5th edn, La Ley 2021) 27–44.
Barona Vilar S, *Mediación penal. Fundamento, fines y régimen jurídico* (Tirant lo Blanch 2011).
Barona Vilar S, 'Mirada restaurativa de la justicia penal en España, una bocanada de aire en la sociedad global líquida del miedo y de la securitización', in Helena Soleto Muñoz, Ana Carrascosa Miguel (dirs), *Justicia restaurativa: una justicia para las víctimas* (Tirant lo Blanch 2019) 55–94.
Carrillo Del Teso AE, 'El "fundido a negro" de la prueba en la persecución de la delincuencia económica', in Nicolás Rodríguez-García, Adán Carrizo González-Castell, Fernando Rodríguez-López (eds); Ana E. Carrillo del Teso, Javier Sánchez Bernal (coords), *Corrupción: Compliance, Represión y Recuperación de Activos* (Tirant lo Blanch 2020) 449–93.
Carrizo González-Castell A, 'Justicia Restaurativa y Mediación Penal en España', in Luiz Henrique Sormani Barbugiani (coord), *Mediação e Arbitragem no Âmbito Público e Privado: Perspectivas e Limitações* (Lumen Juris 2018) 183–200.
Carrizo González-Castell A, 'Reparación de la víctima y mediación penal', in Fernando Martín Diz (dir); Adán Carrizo González-Castell (coord), *Mediación en la Administración de Justicia: implantación y desarrollo* (Andavira 2017) 251–70.
Colás Turégano MA, 'Mediación juvenil: el equilibrio entre la reparación a la víctima y el interés superior del menor', in Ana Montesinos García (ed), *Tratado de Mediación. Tomo II. Mediación Penal* (Tirant lo Blanch 2017) 109–34.
Del Moral García A, 'Responsabilidad penal de personas jurídicas y presunción de inocencia', in Nicolás Rodríguez-García, Fernando Rodríguez-López (eds), *Compliance y responsabilidad de las personas jurídicas* (Tirant lo Blanch 2021) 31–72.

Flores Prada I, 'Algunas reflexiones sobre la justicia restaurativa en el sistema español de justicia penal' (2015) 2 *Revista Internacional de Estudios de Derecho Procesal y Arbitraje* 1.
Gimeno Sendra V, 'El principio de oportunidad y el M.F.' (2016) 8746 *Diario La Ley* 1.
Jimeno Bulnes M, 'Sobre la mediación, justicia restaurativa y otras justicias', in Helena Soleto Muñoz, Ana Carrascosa Miguel (dirs), *Justicia restaurativa: una justicia para las víctimas* (Tirant lo Blanch 2019) 95–148.
Montesinos García A, 'Una breve aproximación a la justicia restaurativa', in Ana Montesinos García (ed), *Tratado de Mediación. Tomo II. Mediación Penal* (Tirant lo Blanch 2017) 21–52.
Moreno Catena V, 'El proceso penal', en VV. AA., *Derecho Procesal Penal* (10th edn, Tirant lo Blanch 2021) 37–64.
Neira Pena AM, 'La efectividad de los *criminal compliance programs* como objeto de prueba en el proceso penal' (2016) 11 (22) *Política Criminal: Revista Electrónica Semestral de Políticas Públicas en Materias Penales* 467.
Neira Pena AM and Rodríguez-García N, 'España', in Nicolás Rodríguez-García (dir); Miguel Ontiveros Alonso, Omar Gabriel Orsi, Fernando Rodríguez-López (coords), *Tratado Angloiberoamericano sobre compliance penal* (Tirant lo Blanch 2022) 433–68.
Nieto Martín A, 'Una pieza más en la Justicia restaurativa empresarial: Programas de cumplimiento restaurativos' (2023) 15 *Revista de Victimología* 147.
Nieva Fenoll J, *Fundamentos de Derecho Procesal* (Edisofer 2012).
Pérez Rivas N, 'Evolución histórica del estatuto jurídico de la víctima: especial referencia al derecho español' (2017) 41 *Revista General de Derecho Procesal* 1.
Pérez-Cruz Martín AJ, 'El proceso penal. Los sistemas procesales penales en general: proceso inquisitivo; proceso acusatorio. El sistema procesal penal de la Ley de Enjuiciamiento Criminal: principio del juez imparcial, separación de instrucción y enjuiciamiento. Principios del proceso penal. El principio de oportunidad. La perspectiva de género en la jurisdicción penal', in Agustín Jesúsn Pérez-Cruz Martín (coord), *Derecho Procesal Penal* (Tirant lo Blanch 2020) 19–38.
Ríos Martín JC, 'Justicia restaurativa y mediación penal' (2016) 98 *ICADE: Revista cuatrimestral de las Facultades de Derecho y Ciencias Económicas y Empresariales* 103.
Rodríguez-García N, Contreras Alfaro LH, 'Algunas reflexiones acerca de la utilización del principio de oportunidad como instrumento de política criminal en el diseño del Derecho procesal penal del siglo XXI' (2006) 3–4 *Justicia: Revista de Derecho Procesal* 53.
Rodríguez-García N, 'Hacia la maximización del principio de oportunidad en los procesos penales por hechos de corrupción', in Sonia Calaza López, José Carlos Muinelo Cobo (dirs), *Postmodernidad y proceso europeo: la oportunidad como principio informador del proceso judicial* (Dykinson 2020) 397–415.
Rodríguez-García N, 'La conformidad de las personas jurídicas en el proceso penal español' (2015) 113 *La Ley Penal* 1.

Rodríguez-García N, 'Las investigaciones internas como elemento esencial de los "criminal compliance programs": haciendo de la necesidad virtud' (2023) 52 *Revista Penal* 201.

Rodríguez-García N, 'Presente y futuro de la mediación penal', in Ana María Rodríguez Tirado (coord), *Cuestiones actuales de Derecho Procesal. Reformas procesales. Mediación y arbitraje* (Tirant lo Blanch 2017) 269–310.

Rodríguez-García N, 'Uso y abuso del principio de oportunidad en el proceso penal del siglo XXI', in Ana Isabel Pérez Cepeda (dir), *Política criminal ante el reto de la delincuencia transnacional* (Tirant lo Blanch 2016) 293–318.

Rodríguez Tirado AM, 'Los procesos por delitos leves. Manifestaciones del principio de oportunidad. Actividad instructora y principio acusatorio' (2016) 38 *Revista General de Derecho Procesal* 1.

Rodríguez Tirado AM, 'Los sistemas de justicia restaurativa y la mediación penal. Efectos en el sistema procesal penal español', in Ana María Rodríguez Tirado (coord), *Cuestiones actuales de Derecho Procesal. Reformas procesales. Mediación y arbitraje* (Tirant lo Blanch 2017) 311–52.

Sánchez Macías JI, Rodríguez-López F, 'Estudio preliminar', in Nicolás Rodríguez-García (dir); Miguel Ontiveros Alonso, Omar Gabriel Orsi, Fernando Rodríguez-López (coords), *Tratado Angloiberoamericano sobre compliance penal* (Tirant lo Blanch 2022) 27–58.

Soleto Muñoz H, 'Justicia restaurativa para la mejor reparación a la víctima', in Helena Soleto Muñoz, Ana Carrascosa Miguel (dirs), *Justicia restaurativa: una justicia para las víctimas* (Tirant lo Blanch 2019) 491–520.

Tierno Barrios S, 'Acceso a la justicia y *compliance* ambiental frente a la responsabilidad penal de las personas jurídicas en el marco de las litigaciones climáticas', in Nicolás Rodríguez-García, Ana E. Carrillo Del Teso. Giorgio Darío María Cerina (eds), *Delincuencia corporativa*: Compliance, *canales de denuncia y persecución penal* (Tirant lo Blanch 2024) 125–51.

Tierno Barrios S, *Justicia restaurativa y mediación en el sistema penal español* (Tirant lo Blanch 2025).

Tierno Barrios S, 'La revalorización de la víctima en el proceso penal y su protección a nivel transnacional: el paradigma de la orden europea de protección' (2022) 1 *Justicia: Revista de Derecho Procesal* 383.

Tierno Barrios S, 'Mediación penal y justicia de menores: una manifestación del principio de oportunidad', in Lorenzo Mateo Bujosa Vadell, Fernando Martín Diz (dirs); Irene González Pulido, Walter Reifarth Muñoz (coords), *Menores y justicia juvenil* (Tirant lo Blanch 2021) 405–20.

Vecina Cifuentes J and Vicente Ballestero T, 'Las manifestaciones del Principio de Oportunidad en el proceso penal español' (2018) 50 *Derecho & Sociedad* 307.

6

The republic's prosecutor and the public interest

The Turkish perspective

Rahime Erbaş, Hüseyin Şık and Çiğdem Dönmez

Introduction

> *The prosecutor, upon becoming aware of a situation that gives the impression that a crime has been committed – whether through a report or by other means – immediately begins investigating the facts to decide whether to bring a public action or not. The prosecutor is obliged to gather and preserve evidence, both for and against the suspect, through the police officers under their command, in order to reach the material truth and ensure a fair trial, while also protecting the suspect's rights.*
>
> (Art. 160)

This provision, referred to as a general regulation on the power of the prosecutors in the Turkish Penal Procedure Code of 2005 No. 5271 (hereinafter 'Procedure Code'),[1] stipulates the prosecutor's primary duties in Turkish criminal law. It, indeed, provides a great deal of insight into the structure, approach and model of Turkish criminal procedure for those who are not familiar with it. First, Turkish criminal procedure law aspires to reach 'the material truth'. Second, there is a strong hierarchical relationship between the prosecutor and the police. The prosecutor is *dominus litis* of the pre-trial which has to cover also police investigation.[2] Third, the prosecutor's role is to ensure that laws are properly enforced and to initiate prosecutions in criminal cases. As such, Turkish penal procedure law has historically been closer to the 'inquisitorial' traditions of continental European countries. Further, it embraces the due process model more than the crime control model, and private prosecution does not exist in this system. Most remarkably, Article 160 establishes that criminal investigation and prosecution are mandatory in Turkish law. These features may appear quite conventional. Indeed, on the one hand, Turkish criminal procedure presents a typical Continental European criminal procedure approach, on the one hand.[3]

On the other hand, despite this appearance, Turkish criminal procedure has developed its characteristics and a structure that significantly differ from other inquisitorial continental European criminal procedure model-oriented jurisdictions. This distinction is especially evident for the concepts like the modern roles of the public prosecutor and the public interest. In fact, Turkish criminal procedure functions within a system where the opportunity principle (principle of expediency) is rarely applied.[4] Prosecutors are neither given the authority nor the responsibility to assess the public interest, but rather are entrusted with a range of direct measures like prepayment (fine), restorative justice or serial proceeding.[5] Each measure is subject to strictly defined limits and considered in a hierarchical order of priority by prosecutors such as first restorative justice, prepayment and then serial proceeding. If one is applicable, the subsequent one is not applied. In a situation where a prosecutor is not endowed with discretionary power based on public interest, introducing a range of direct measures is inevitable because, across numerous jurisdictions, one constant remains: it is the prosecutor whose powers and duties are frequently reviewed in response to the increase in the number of criminal cases referred to the courts.

This represents the Turkish dimension, providing an alternative viewpoint on the role of prosecutors in terms of power regarding the public interest. It should, however, be noted that this does not mean that prosecutors do not owe any discretionary power in Turkish law at all. As rightly noted by Colvin, 'the discretionary power of the prosecutor is linked to the nature of the criminal law'.[6] This means prosecutors weigh significant discretionary authority in practice, which is considered as *hidden power through the discourse of a prosecuting elite*[7] at every stage of the process such as determining the nature of the charges, initiating evidence collection or directing police activities.[8]

Admittedly, the main rule in Turkish law is that criminal investigation and prosecution are mandatory. This differs from the common law tradition where even when sufficient evidence exists, a public interest test is typically applied to decide for prosecution.[9] The Turkish Constitution (1982) does not contain any explicit provision stating that criminal investigation and prosecution are mandatory as opposed to other jurisdictions such as Italy.[10] According to the

Constitution, 'Türkiye is a democratic, laic and social state governed by the rule of law' (Art. 2). It is commonly accepted that a mandatory criminal prosecution and as such a mandatory investigation stems from the rule of law. The following statements by Duff also reflect this:

> On a simple reading of the Legality Principle, [...] the prosecutor must prosecute whenever she has sufficient evidence. This might seem to be required by the rule of law, and by democratic principles. It is not the role of prosecutors, as unelected officials, to decide when the law should be enforced: once the legislature has made the law, their role is to apply it consistently.[11]

As a matter of fact, Turkish criminal law upholds the principle of mandatory prosecution that is coined as the legality principle as a fundamental component of the rule of law. In this context, Article 160 of the Procedure Code acts as the primary legal basis. Even though Article 160 states 'the public prosecutor [...] begins to investigate the facts to decide whether to bring a public action or not', this does not give the prosecutor to weigh public interest to bring a public action or not. As opposed to the common law understanding of the prosecutor's role 'that the prosecutor should not proceed if it is in "the public interest" to decide for non-prosecution',[12] the public prosecutor's discretion to weigh public interest in Turkish law is tightly constrained. As a result, over half of the cases submitted to prosecutors lead to public actions before the courts. The total number of cases brought to the prosecutor's offices in Türkiye between 2019 and 2023, along with the number of cases in which a public action was filed, a decision of non-prosecution was made, and the cases carried over to the following year are presented in Table 6.1 below:

Table 6.1 Prosecutor's office's case statistics in the first instance in Türkiye, 2019–24

Year	Total Cases	Prosecution (Pro)	No Prosecution (No-Pro)	Other Decisions	Carryover
2024	11,661,519	1,533,422	3,045,610	997,244	6,085,243
2023	11,109,462	1,387,476	2,804,133	988,864	5,928,989
2022	10,598,645	1,328,405	2,872,219	839,803	5,558,218
2021	9,857,295	1,137,386	2,702,099	720,779	5,297,031
2020	8,996,173	915,984	2,256,194	589,597	5,234,398
2019	9,343,637	1,223,745	2,511,764	629,327	4,968,801

Created by the authors using data from: Judicial Statistics, 2024; p. 17–(https://adlisicil.adalet.gov.tr/Resimler/SayfaDokuman/7042025092455Adalet_%C4%B0statistikleri_2024%20T%C3%BCrk%C3%A7e_Ingilizce.pdf accessed 2 June 2025).

The table illustrates the substantial amount of workload faced by the prosecutor's offices in Türkiye. The opportunity principle is applied only in rare cases, which leads to a high number of prosecutions and persistent court caseloads. Unlike many other jurisdictions where prosecutors weigh the public interest to decide whether to prosecute or not, this role meaning the discretionary power to balance public interest in prosecution decisions has not been historically or structurally established in Türkiye. Instead, recent reforms have introduced limited alternative (direct) measures that give prosecutors some authority to resolve cases at pre-trial, though within strict legal boundaries.

This chapter traces the evolution and current structure of criminal prosecution in Turkish law. It begins with a historical overview of the prosecution system in Türkiye, laying the groundwork for understanding its institutional transformation. It then examines the emergence and role of the modern public prosecutor, conceptualized as 'the Republic's Prosecutor'. The analysis continues with a discussion of the principle of mandatory prosecution, a core element of prosecutorial functioning, followed by an exploration of the contrasting concept of the opportunity principle. A section addresses the procedural right of the victims to request a review of non-prosecution decisions by prosecutors. The chapter concludes by critically assessing the limited role prosecutorial discretion plays in practice, highlighting the tension between rigid formalism and the potential for more nuanced, public interest-oriented decision-making within the Turkish criminal justice system.

A history of prosecution

Turkish law has its roots in the European continental law. The codification period emerging in Continental Europe especially in France and Italy particularly in the nineteenth century[13] coincided with the late of the Ottoman Empire and was profoundly influential on Turkish law as well.[14] Thus, the nineteenth century marks out a pivotal era in the transformation of Turkish law in all aspects, leading to this period being later named *the Tanzimat period*.[15] The Turkish legal historian Ahmet Mumcu identifies this era as the cornerstone of modern Turkish law; accordingly, it should be duly considered in any in-depth study of the legal transformations undertaken in the Republican period of Türkiye.[16] Indeed, the history of Turkish law prior to the establishment of the Republic of Türkiye in 1923 is commonly divided into two phases: before and after *the Tanzimat period*.[17]

It remains a disputed issue in the literature whether a prosecution authority existed before *the Tanzimat period*. One perspective holds that no such institution was present at the time[18]; while another argues that it did, in fact, exist.[19] What is certain, however, is that although a fully modern public prosecution office as we know it today did not exist, there were nevertheless some officials who served a function with limited similarity. This was because the prosecution of a crime was, historically, a matter of the victims of crime or their families in Türkiye.[20] As such, cases were traditionally brought to courts (*Sharia courts*) by individuals, much like in today's civil courts, resembling what is known as private prosecution.[21] Some officials who were assigned duties with limited similarity to those of today's prosecutor existed. However, their responsibilities were largely limited to seizing offenders and referring them to court, which covers only a narrow aspect of modern prosecution.[22] However, if the crime committed also disturbed public order, then, in addition to the sanctions imposed following a private prosecution, the ruler (Turkish: *uluemir*) would additionally acquire the authority to impose certain punishments which were enforced by a judge (Turkish: *kadı*).[23] These punishments included corporal punishment (such as beating), fines, imprisonment or even capital punishment.[24] This suggests that criminal prosecution was not merely a private matter between individuals, but assumed having a public character when public order was affected. The involvement of the ruler and the imposition of additional punishments through judicial authority indicate an early recognition of the public interest in the administration of criminal justice in Turkish law.

After *the Tanzimat period*, *Kanun-i Esasi* in 1876, the first constitution of the Ottoman Empire, in Article 91 under the section titled 'Courts' (*Mehakim*), stipulated that prosecutors responsible for safeguarding public law in criminal matters would be appointed, and that their duties and positions would be determined by law.[25] Three years after the promulgation of the Constitution, in 1879, the prosecutorial office was established for the first time through the law which was named in Turkish as *Mehakim-i Nizamiye'nin Teşkilatı Kanun-ı Muvakkatı*.[26] The Law used the term *müddeiumumi*, which corresponds to the modern concept of a prosecutor, to refer to officials appointed by the Sultan (*Padişah*) to safeguard the public interest.[27] Although the office of the prosecutor was established in the Ottoman Empire in June 1879, the institution did not gain immediate acceptance in society.[28] One of the bureaucrats of the time, Abdurrahman Şeref, made the following statements:

> What was the exact role of prosecutors? What would their role be in court? These aspects were not clearly understood by the general public. When there was already a plaintiff and a defendant, people could not make sense of a third party participating in the trial. There was no such provision or reference in the rules of Sharia law. Every new thing arouses curiosity. The students at the higher education (*mülkiye*) would ask lecturers what this new role was supposed to do. The lecturers would try to explain: for example, even if the victim in an assault case did not file a complaint, since an act prohibited by law had occurred, the law itself would be considered the plaintiff, and the prosecutor would be obliged to bring a public case on its behalf.[29]

Apart from these developments in the Ottoman period, following the declaration of the Republic of Türkiye on 29 October 1923, new laws were rapidly adopted, which included regulations regarding the modern prosecution office. For example, the 1924 Organization Law was amended to establish that the prosecution office at each court of first instance (Turkish: *Asliye Mahkemesi*) consisted of a prosecutor and assistant prosecutors. However, the distinction between prosecutors and assistant prosecutors was later abandoned in 1990, as it was not consistently applied in practice among prosecutors.[30]

The modern prosecution: The prosecutor of the republic unveiled

The modern institution of the public prosecutor in Türkiye was formally established in 1924 under the title *the Prosecutor of the Republic* (Turkish: *Cumhuriyet Savcısı*), holding a similar office to *the Procureur de la République* in the French legal system which traces its institutional roots to *the Procureur du Roi* (King's Prosecutor) of the pre-republican legal system in France, albeit now operating within a republican rather than monarchical framework. As Duff notes regarding prosecutors: 'First, as public officials, they must act in the light only of values that belong to the public realm, the *res publica*'.[31] This perspective highlights the normative foundation of prosecutorial duties, emphasizing that prosecutors are not merely legal technicians but public servants bound by the principles of justice, fairness and the common good. In this sense, their decisions must reflect the interests of society as a whole, rather than personal, political or sectional considerations. In line with this understanding, the public prosecutor who is referred to as the Prosecutor of the Republic in Türkiye acts on behalf of the state and is responsible for safeguarding the public interest. Further, today, private prosecution does not exist in Turkish law.

Today, the structure of the prosecution office in Türkiye is mainly outlined in the Law No. 5235 on the Establishment, Duties, and Powers of First Instance Courts and Regional Courts of Appeal (briefly the Code on Judicial Organization). According to Article 16 of this Code, the prosecution organization is structured as the prosecutor of the republic's office in every provincial center and district where a court is established. A prosecutor's office is composed of a chief public prosecutor and an adequate number of public prosecutors. As seen, the terminology as 'prosecutor' and 'assistant prosecutor' has changed over time; however, the understanding that assistant prosecutors perform their duties on behalf of the chief prosecutor they are assigned to has remained the same, with no changes other than the names of the positions. The Penal Procedure Code of 1929 (the former Code) in force until 2005 was inspired by the German Penal Procedure Code[32] and included a clear provision on mandatory prosecution. Article 148 of the former Code stated:

> It is the responsibility of the public prosecutor to bring a public action. In cases not otherwise specified by law, if the facts that constitute sufficient evidence for initiating criminal prosecution exist, the public prosecutor is obliged to bring a public action.

Later on, provisions incorporating the opportunity principle which served to soften the strict application of the mandatory prosecution principle were introduced into the German Penal Procedure Code. Although this development was discussed during the drafting of a law in Türkiye, it was ultimately decided not to adopt the German model of the opportunity principle.[33] The sole exception to mandatory prosecution in Turkish law was the suspect's prior conviction in that time. Article 149 of the former Code reads as: 'If the punishment resulting from the prosecution has no impact because the suspect is already convicted of another offence or will not affect the sentence for another offence, the public action may be dismissed'.

In 2005, the new Penal Procedure Code No. 5271 (Procedure Code), along with the Penal Code No. 5237 and the Execution Code No.5275, came into effect. Further, Article 20 of the Code on Judicial Organization outlines the duties of the prosecutor as 'carrying out judicial and administrative tasks assigned by the chief public prosecutor'. In addition, carrying out judicial procedures, attending trials and appealing to higher courts are also included in the responsibilities of prosecutors in the Article.

What's more, the duty and authority to conduct investigations which are considered the main responsibility of a modern prosecutor are clearly defined in Turkish law. Article 170 of Procedure Code states, 'it is the responsibility of the public prosecutor to bring a public action'. This provision mirrors the language of the former code, which similarly assigned this duty under Article 148. However, the Code of 2005 did not include the provision of the former Code requiring the Public Prosecutor to bring public action when sufficient evidence exists, unless specified otherwise by law. Further, Article 17 of the Code on Judicial Organization No. 5235 stipulates that conducting or supervising investigations is listed not as a duty of the 'prosecutor', but as a responsibility of the 'Republic's Prosecution Office'. Therefore, although Turkish law grants prosecutors the authority to conduct investigations, decide whether to press charges, and either prepare an indictment or issue a decision of non-prosecution, in practice, they do not carry out these tasks entirely on their own. That is to say, individualized enforcement actions are limited and as such a prosecutor often faces oversight or scrutiny in their role by the chief public prosecutor. In fact, the chief public prosecutor's office is an integrated organization, and prosecutors do not carry out investigations on their own, but rather on behalf of the chief public prosecutor's office to which they are affiliated.[34] Accordingly, prosecutors are allowed to replace one another in performing their duties, as the office of the chief public prosecutor is considered an indivisible whole, and the role is not tied to the individuality of any specific officeholder.[35]

The structure of the chief public prosecutor's office has raised the question of whether the prosecution office is affiliated with the executive branch or the judiciary.[36] This determination is crucial as it directly relates to the issue of whether a prosecutor, like a judge, should be impartial and independent. What's more, the Turkish Constitution provides for prosecutors and judges in an equivalent manner, granting them equal rights and safeguards in terms of professional status (Arts.138–40). It is also significant because it helps to define the prosecutor's position within criminal processes. Although the main duties and powers of prosecutors, such as conducting investigations and preparing indictments, are judicial in nature, it can be argued that prosecutors carry out both judicial and executive functions,[37] considering that the prosecution organization follows a hierarchical structure.

This observation, however, does not lead to the conclusion that the prosecution office is included in both the judiciary and the executive branches. According to *the principle of separation of powers*, it is not possible for an institution to be part of both branches at the same time in Turkish law. The prevailing view is that prosecutors are part of the judiciary, not the administrative branch. However, their activities are not considered judicial in the strict sense, as they do not perform adjudicative functions like judges. Although it is possible for the prosecutor to conclude some criminal conflicts at the pre-trial phase through direct measures such as prepayment/fine (original in Italian, *oblazione*; Turkish: *önödeme*) or restorative justice programmes (Turkish: *uzlaştırma*), it should be emphasized that even in these measures (alternatives), the prosecutor does not resolve criminal conflicts as it is resolved through judicial proceedings.[38]

Today, criminal investigation and prosecution, as a rule, are carried out *ex officio* by the prosecutors. The prosecution of crime in Türkiye is a public matter, and as such the victims of crime or their families are not a compulsory, but supportive part of the process. Criminal procedure, as a rule, operates under the legality principle and as such mandatory prosecution is applied in cases in which there was sufficient admissible evidence.[39] Although in some cases, the individuals directly harmed by the crime may be identifiable, Turkish law holds that the state is the party harmed by the crime in all cases, due to the disturbance of social peace.[40] As such, prosecutors take a more prominent role during the pre-trial phase as opposed to the former Penal Code period.

This has led to expressions such as 'the emperor of the pre-trial phase', 'the boss of the pre-trial phase' and 'the master of the pre-trial phase' being used in the literature when discussing the role of the prosecutor in Turkish law.[41] While it is obvious that all of these expressions are meant to convey that the prosecutor is the dominant actor in the pre-trial phase. However, in Turkish law, prosecutors are subjects who are hierarchically linked to the chief public prosecutor's office, carry out all their actions on behalf of the chief public prosecutor's office, and make decisions on behalf of the chief public prosecutor.

Private prosecution was only available for certain offences that required a complaint to initiate legal proceedings.[42] However, the concept of private prosecution was strongly opposed – on various grounds – by Nurullah Kunter, one of the most influential scholars in the shaping of modern Turkish criminal procedure. According to Kunter, regardless of whether the system adopts the principle of mandatory prosecution or the opportunity principle, private prosecution is unnecessary, as the duty to prosecute ultimately belongs to the state and the enforcement of criminal laws represents a public function.[43] As a matter of fact, private prosecution was completely excluded as the new Penal Procedure Code came into force in 2005. With the abolition of private prosecution in Turkish criminal law, the responsibility for investigation, evidence collection and filing public charges has been given exclusively to the prosecution office

Mandatory prosecution

In Turkish law, as a rule, criminal actions must be pursued by the state, regardless of the victim's wishes. This principle ensures that criminal acts are addressed in the public interest, maintaining the rule of law and public order.[44] There is no definitive answer as to which principle – the mandatory principle (the legality principle) or the opportunity principle – provides a more appropriate or effective foundation for the criminal process.[45] However, Kunter considered that the principle of mandatory prosecution is more suitable for Türkiye, as it is less susceptible to arbitrary use.[46] He further suggested that the potential disadvantages of not adopting the opportunity principle could be mitigated through other ways of solutions such as the implementation of direct measures by prosecutors[47] – a view that was later confirmed in practice. Indeed, today's widespread use and variety of direct (alternative) measures implemented by public prosecutors can be attributed to the limited application of the opportunity principle in Turkish criminal procedure.

Overall, today, in Turkish law, mandatory prosecution is the main rule, and the opportunity principle is only used in exceptional cases.[48] Mandatory prosecution is understood to comprise three sub-principles: the duty to investigate (1), the duty to bring a public action (2) and the duty to pursue the prosecution during the trial phase (3).[49] These duties are not separate sub-principles, but practical reflections of the mandatory prosecution principle. Each of them is respectively set out in Articles 160, 170 and 188 of the Procedure Code.[50]

The Turkish Constitution does not contain any explicit provision stating that criminal investigation and prosecution are mandatory as opposed to the other jurisdictions such as Italy. But, there is also no provision in Turkish criminal law that would negate or severely undermine the obligation to prosecute. However, a mandatory criminal prosecution – and, by extension, a mandatory investigation – stems from the principle of the rule of law, which is enshrined in Article 2 of the Constitution declaring that Türkiye is a democratic, secular and social state governed by the rule of law. Articles 160 and 170 of the Procedure Code serve as the main provisions on the matter. Even though Article 160 states 'the public prosecutor […] begins investigating the facts to decide whether to bring a public action or not', this does not give the prosecutor the power to weigh public interest to bring a public action or not. Likewise, Article 170 of the Procedure Code reflects on mandatory prosecutions as 'the duty to bring a public action' as: 'If the evidence gathered during the pre-trial phase establishes a sufficient level of suspicion that a crime has occurred, the public prosecutor is required to prepare an indictment'. As such, Article 170 may suggest that mandatory prosecutions are without any exception in Turkish law,[51] but there are a few exceptions to the principle of mandatory prosecution which we will discuss in the following part.

The 'opportunity principle'

Apart from *ex parte* offences and complaint-based offences, there are a few exceptional instances that soften the strict application of the mandatory prosecution principle. These are regarded by some scholars as limitations or exceptions to mandatory prosecution.[52] The inclusion of these exceptions has been regarded as essential to avoid delays in the administration of criminal justice, according to Council of Europe Recommendation No. R (87) 18 on the Simplification of Criminal Justice.[53] The discretionary power of the prosecutor (the opportunity principle) set out in Article 171 of the Procedure Code, titled as *discretion in bringing a public action*, as:

1. Should the conditions requiring the application of *effective remorse* provisions as a personal ground for eliminating punishment exist, or if there is a *personal ground for impunity*, the public prosecutor may decide to dismiss the case.
2. Excluding offences that are subject to restorative justice and prepayment, the public prosecutor may decide to suspend the initiation of a public prosecution for five years for offences punishable by a maximum prison sentence of three years or less, even where sufficient suspicion has been established. The victim or the suspect may appeal this decision under the provisions of Article 173.

The title of Article 171 of the Procedure Code, '*discretion in bringing a public action*', gives the impression that, as a rule, a public prosecutor has a discretion in initiating a public case. This, in turn, suggests that the principle of opportunity/expediency also has a place in Turkish criminal law. This does not constitute a general discretionary power, however. First, because these cases in which the prosecutor exercises discretion by issuing a decision of non-prosecution are, in fact, subject to strict conditions. Second, the prosecutor can still decide to bring a public action even if one of these situations exists, and this decision cannot be challenged (Art. 173/5).[54]

To begin an analysis of these conditions, it is important to first consider their legal basis and scope. First, in the first paragraph of Article 171, the public prosecutor is granted the authority to conclude the criminal case from the outset as follows: Primarily, the prosecutor must establish sufficient suspicion that the crime has been committed in order to file a public case. As emphasized by the Court of Cassation (Yargıtay), the Criminal Procedure Code requires that a decision not to prosecute can only be made after the investigation is fully completed. Regardless of whether the decision is based on a lack of suspicion, missing legal elements, or public interest considerations, the investigation must be carried out thoroughly, without leaving anything out.[55]

Despite the existence of sufficient suspicion to file a public prosecution, if there is *effective remorse* as a personal ground for eliminating punishment or *any personal grounds for impunity*, the public prosecutor may decide not to proceed with the case by issuing a decision of non-prosecution, thereby terminating the criminal conflict at the pre-trial. This authority is facultative; the prosecutor is not obligated to exercise it. Further, it is suggested that, in case of doubt, the public prosecutor should exercise their authority in favour of initiating a public action by submitting the indictment to the court. Since the legal reason pertains to an obstacle to punishment, the authority to terminate the criminal conflict at the pre-trial is granted outright, or *in limine*, as expressed in Latin.

At this stage, it is crucial to determine what constitutes effective remorse (the offender's sincere regret for the offence) and personal grounds for impunity, as both are provided for in the Penal Code only in relation to specific types of offences – these mechanisms are not granted for offences in general.[56] Both effective remorse and personal grounds for impunity as legal institutions reflect the penal policy.[57]

As for effective remorse, there are two forms of effective remorse under the Turkish law: one leads to a reduction of the sentence, while the other eliminates punishment entirely. This distinction is made based on the nature of the offence and the point in time at which the offender expresses remorse. Where effective remorse leads only to a reduction in punishment, as opposed to full exemption, the public prosecutor is still required to initiate public action, without having discretionary power.[58] Indeed, the prosecutor exercises discretionary power on effective remorse that eliminates punishment entirely. The offences for which the concept of effective remorse is applicable under the Turkish Penal Code include, for example, the following: trafficking in human organs (Art. 93), zoning pollution (Art. 184), drug-related offences (Art. 192), bribery (Art. 254), perjury (false testimony) (Art. 274), false swearing (Art. 275), money laundering (Art. 282), conspiring to commit an offence (Art. 316) and some organized crime (Art. 221)

To illustrate, 'in cases of founding a criminal organization with the purpose of committing a crime, no conviction shall be issued against the founders or leaders who dissolve the organization or ensure its dissolution by providing information [*effective remorse*], before an investigation has been initiated and before a crime is committed in line with the organization's purpose' (Turkish Penal Code, Article 221/1). Similarly: 'if a member of the criminal organization voluntarily informs the relevant authorities that they are leaving the organization without participating in any criminal activity within the framework of the organization's operations, no conviction shall be issued against them [*effective remorse*]' (Turkish Penal Code, Article 221/2). In both cases, should the suspect show effective remorse and as such fulfil the criteria in these provisions, the prosecutor may decide for non-prosecution.[59]

As for the discretionary power of the prosecutor in cases of *personal grounds for impunity*, the Turkish Penal Code limits their applicability to certain specific offences.[60] As such, in cases where offences against property – such as theft, fraud, breach of trust or damage to property – are committed to the detriment of: a) a spouse from whom the offender is not legally separated, b) an ascendant or descendant, an affine in the same degree, an adoptive parent or an adopted child, c) a sibling living in the same household, no punishment shall be imposed on the offender with respect to the aggrieved relative (Art. 167). These offences, when committed by family members against each other, are considered personal grounds for impunity under Turkish law.[61] Like effective remorse, there are two forms of personal grounds for impunity under Turkish law: one leads to a reduction of the sentence, while the other eliminates punishment entirely. The prosecutor exercises discretionary power on the one that eliminates punishment entirely.

A significant example of *personal grounds for impunity* is regulated in Article 22/6 of the Penal Code for an offence committed by a negligent act as disobeying due care (like a car accident). According to this provision, if the consequences of such an act by an offender have already caused the offender to suffer profoundly – taking into account their personal and familial circumstances – the imposition of a criminal penalty may be deemed unnecessary. The prosecutor may exercise discretionary power and decide for non-prosecution. However, this form of personal impunity is narrowly construed. It applies only where the harm is limited to the offender and their immediate family. If the negligent act results in harm to third parties as well, this exception is not applicable. The inclusion of the phrase 'personal and familial circumstances' serves to confine the scope of the provision and prevent its overly broad application.[62]

Further examples include certain offences committed within the context of family relations, which may fall under personal grounds for impunity. As such, when theft is committed by a person to the detriment of their ascendant or descendant, or a relative of the same degree in law or an adoptive parent or adopted child, no conviction shall be issued against the perpetrator (Turkish Penal Code, Article 167). This is a *personal ground for impunity.* The prosecutor may decide for non-prosecution.

In the second paragraph of Article 171, the public prosecutor is given the authority to terminate the criminal conflicts from the outset in the following manner: instead of making such a decision outright, the prosecutor opts to suspend the bringing of a public action. This legal mechanism was introduced into Turkish criminal procedure law in 2006.[63]

In this context, the severity of the penalty is taken into account – specifically, offences punishable by a maximum prison sentence of three years or less (Art. 171(2) of the Procedure Code). However, for children involved in criminal conduct and under the age of fifteen, the upper limit is five years (Art. 19 of the Law on Child Protection). The relatively minor nature of the penalty – limited to offences carrying a maximum prison sentence of three years or less – requires a more nuanced evaluation of all circumstances related to both the suspect and the offence. As a result, the authority to terminate the criminal conflict is made subject to a gradual process (*per gradus*, in Latin). The suspension period is five years for adult suspects (Art. 171(2) of the Criminal Procedure Code) and three years for children involved in crime (Art. 19 of the Law on Child Protection).

As can be seen, under Turkish law, unlike in common law jurisdictions, prosecutors are not granted discretionary authority to refrain from initiating a public prosecution based on general factors such as the seriousness of the offence or its impact on the victim. In Türkiye, although the legal framework allows prosecutors to exercise discretionary powers in very specific cases – such as decisions not to prosecute based on effective remorse or personal grounds for impunity – these powers are rarely used in practice. Prosecutors tend to adopt a strict interpretation of the principle of mandatory prosecution, often avoiding any subjective evaluation of the offender's personal circumstances or the public interest. This rigid approach results in a highly formalistic application of criminal law, where legal discretion exists in theory but remains largely dormant in actual prosecutorial decision-making. As a result, there is a tendency to over-rely on alternatives such as prepayment, serial proceeding and restorative justice mechanisms.

The right to review

As a rule, in cases where the prosecutor issues a decision of non-prosecution, victims are entitled to challenge this decision through an objection procedure. As we noted above, private prosecution does not exist in Turkish law. For this reason, the right to a review has been thoroughly regulated under the Turkish Code of Criminal Procedure to protect the victim's interests. However, the victim's right to review the no-pro decision of the prosecutor depends on whether the prosecutor decided not to prosecute because of a lack of sufficient evidence or by exercising their discretion. As such, if the public prosecutor decides not to prosecute because there is not sufficient evidence or because prosecution is not legally possible, the victim has the right to object to this decision within seven days of its notification (Art. 173/1). The notification must include information on the right to review, the time limit and the competent authority for such review (Art.172/1). One important amendment regarding reviewing the prosecutor's decision of no-prosecution in the procedure code reads as: 'Where the European Court of Human Rights (ECHR) finds in a final judgment that the non-prosecution decision was made without an effective investigation, or if the case is struck out due to a friendly settlement or a unilateral declaration by the government, the investigation may be reopened upon request within three months of the judgment becoming final' (Art.172/3). This represents the general rule.

However, in cases where the public prosecutor exercises their discretionary power because of effective remorse or personal grounds for impunity not to bring a public action (no-pro), the decision of no-prosecution shall not be subject to review.[64] As for the cases where the public prosecutor decides to suspend the bringing a public action, pursuant to Article 171 of the Turkish Criminal Procedure Code, both the victim and the suspect have the right to object to this decision under Article 173. In such instances, either party may appeal the decision before the competent criminal court of peace. This appeal mechanism introduces judicial oversight into the exercise of prosecutorial discretion and reinforces the participatory rights of both the victim and the suspect within the criminal justice process.

Conclusion

Turkish criminal procedure is firmly rooted in the principle of mandatory prosecution, which reflects the broader commitment to the rule of law under Article 2 of the Constitution. Despite the absence of an explicit constitutional provision, both legislative practice and prosecutorial conduct adhere closely to this principle. Articles 160 and 170 of the Criminal Procedure Code further reinforce this obligation by framing prosecution as a duty once sufficient evidence has been gathered.

Today's prosecutors are expected to do more with less – take on bigger roles, make tougher calls and show more flexibility than ever before. As their responsibilities grow, so does the need for smart, fair and well-judged decisions. However, the Turkish legal framework does provide limited and exceptional grounds for discretionary decision-making, most notably through Article 171. These include cases involving effective remorse, personal grounds for impunity and certain minor offences subject to deferred prosecution. Yet, in practice, prosecutors rarely utilize these mechanisms. Rather than exercising discretion in the interest of justice and public interest, they often adopt a rigid and formalistic interpretation of the legal requirements, treating prosecutorial discretion as a theoretical tool rather than a practical one.

This overly cautious approach has led to an over-reliance on procedural shortcuts, such as prepayment, restorative justice and serial proceeding, which serve more as caseload-management tools than as meaningful alternatives to prosecution. In this context, Turkish law appears to recognize the value of discretion in limited terms but falls short of integrating it into prosecutorial practice. Future reforms may be necessary to align the law's potential for flexibility with its actual implementation in practice.

As Colvin aptly notes, the discretionary power of prosecutors is closely linked to the structure of criminal law. This power often operates behind the scenes, allowing prosecutors to influence many aspects of the process – from selecting charges to shaping the collection of evidence and directing law enforcement efforts. This highlights the need for a deeper examination of how prosecutors assess the 'public interest' in their decisions. Rather than being viewed as arbitrary or unchecked power, prosecutorial discretion should be understood as a complex legal and ethical responsibility that requires transparency, accountability and clear guiding principles.[65]

Legislations

Council of Europe Recommendation No. R (87) 18 on the Simplification of Criminal Justice.Mehakim-i Nizamiye'nin Teşkilatı Kanun-ı Muvakkatı.

Kanun-i Esasi in 1876

German Penal Procedure Code.

Code on the Establishment, Duties, and Powers of First Instance Courts and Regional Courts of Appeal in 2004 No. 5235

Execution and Security Measures Code in 2005 No.5275.

Child Protection Code in 2005 No. 5395

Turkish Constitution (1982).Execution and Security Measures Code in 2005 No.5275 (Execution Code)

Turkish Penal Code in 2005, No. 5237

Turkish Penal Procedure Code in 1929 No. 1412 (The former)

Turkish Penal Procedure Code in 2005 No. 5271.

Case

Yargıtay, 16.C.D., Date. 29.11.2017, E. 2016/7553, K. 2017/5508 (UYAP, 29.04.2018).

Notes

1 Cumhur Şahin and Neslihan Göktürk, *Ceza Muhakemesi Hukuku* (15th edn, Seçkin, 2024) 120.

2 See particularly Bahri Öztürk and others, *Nazari ve Uygulamalı Ceza Muhakemesi Hukuku* (18th edn, Seçkin, 2024) 131 and 219.

3 For an in-depth analysis, see Rahime Erbaş, 'Pre-trial Procedure in Turkey: Post-Salduz', in Edward Johnston, Rahime Erbaş and Dan Jasinski (eds), *A Comparative*

Analysis of Pre-Trial Procedure in Europe: The Search for an Ideal Model (İstanbul University Press, 2020) 209 ff.

4 Cf. Uriel Moeller, 'Pre-trial Procedure in Germany', in Edward Johnston, Rahime Erbaş and Dan Jasinski (eds), *A Comparative Analysis of Pre-Trial Procedure in Europe: The Search for an Ideal Model* (İstanbul University Press, 2020) 87 ff; Raquel Borges Blázquez, 'Pre-trial Procedure in Spain', in Edward Johnston, Rahime Erbaş and Dan Jasinski (eds), *A Comparative Analysis of Pre-Trial Procedure in Europe: The Search for an Ideal Model* (İstanbul University Press, 2020) 177 ff. See Edward Johnston, Rahime Erbaş, Dan Jasinski, 'Concluding Thoughts', in Edward Johnston, Rahime Erbaş and Dan Jasinski (eds), *A Comparative Analysis of Pre-Trial Procedure in Europe: The Search for an Ideal Model* (İstanbul University Press, 2020) 229 ff.

5 See for critics Melik Kartal, *Karşılaştırmalı Hukuk Işığında Kamu Davasının Açılmasında Cumhuriyet Savcısının Takdir Yetkisi* (On İki Levha, 2015) 210.

6 Victoria Colvin, 'The Riddle of Prosecutorial Discretion', in Victoria Colvin and Philip Stenning (eds), *The Evolving Role of the Public Prosecutor: Challenges and Innovations* (Routledge, 2019) 146.

7 Robyn Holder, 'Decoding Hegemony: Exploring the Discourse of a Prosecuting Elite', in Victoria Colvin and Philip Stenning (eds), *The Evolving Role of the Public Prosecutor: Challenges and Innovations* (Routledge 2019) 15.

8 See Colvin (n 6) 139. For example, for the discretionary power of the public prosecutor to assess whether the evidence is sufficient for proving a crime has also been discussed in Turkish criminal law doctrine, see Hasan Tahsin Gökcan, 'Cumhuriyet Savcısının Delilleri Değerlendirme Yetkisi ve Yargıtay Uygulaması' (2012) 1 *Ankara Barosu Dergisi* 195, 204.

9 See Colvin (n 6) 140.

10 Cf. Article 112 of the Italian Constitution, see Francesco Rossi, Giulia Ducoli and Giuseppe Schena, 'Pre-trial Procedure in Italy', in Edward Johnston, Rahime Erbaş and Dan Jasinski (eds), *A Comparative Analysis of Pre-Trial Procedure in Europe: The Search for an Ideal Model* (İstanbul University Press 2020) 111 ff.

11 Antony Duff, 'Discretion and Accountability in a Democratic Criminal Law', in Ma´ximo Langer and David Alan Sklansky (eds), *Prosecutors and Democracy: A Cross-national Study* (Cambridge University Press, 2017) 19.

12 Ibid 22 and 24.

13 Andreas B. Schwarz, 'İngiliz Hukuku ve Kontinental Hukuk' (tr Hıfzı Veldet, 1937) 3 İstanbul Üniversitesi Hukuk Fakültesi Mecmuası 215, 223.

14 See Tahir Taner, 'Tanzimat Devrinde Ceza Hukuku', in *Tanzimat I: Yüzüncü Yıldönümü Münasebetile* (Maarif Matbaası, 1940) 12; Doğan Soyaslan, *Ceza Muhakemesi Hukuku* (4th edn Yetkin, 2010) 175–6.

15 See Ahmet Mumcu, 'Tanzimat Döneminde Türk Hukuku', in Halil İnalcık, Bülent Arı and Selim Aslantaş, (eds) *Adâlet Kitabı* (Kadim, 2012) 207 ff.

16 Ibid. 228.

17 For more detail, see Taner (n 14) 1.

18 Nurullah Kunter, *Ceza Muhakemesi Hukuku* (9th edn, Yaylacık Matbaası, 1989) 207; Soyaslan (n 14) 176–7.

19 Hüseyin Şık, *Türk Adli Yargı Sisteminde Savcılık Kurumu* (Adalet Yayınevi, 2018) 44.

20 Kunter (n 18) 207–8.

21 Taner (n 14) 1; Kunter (n 18) 207; Nur Centel and Hamide Zafer, *Ceza Muhakemesi Hukuku* (22nd edn, Beta, 2024) 128.

22 Şık (n 19) 44–5.

23 Taner (n 14) 1.

24 Ibid.

25 Şık (n 19) 46–7.

26 Kunter (n 18) 208; Centel and Zafer (n 18) 128; Şık (n 19) 47.

27 Şık (n 19) 47.

28 Ibid. 47, n.154.

29 Ekrem Buğra Ekinci, *Osmanlı Mahkemeleri (Tanzimat ve Sonrası)* (Arı Sanat Yayınevi 2004) 230.

30 Centel and Zafer (n 21) 128.

31 Duff (n 11) 27.

32 See further information Erbaş (n 3) 209 ff.

33 Öztekin Tosun, 'Ceza Davasının Açılmasında Sistemler' (2011) 34 (1–4) *İstanbul Üniversitesi Hukuk Fakültesi Mecmuası* 42, 53. Cf. Kunter (n 18) 204.

34 Şahin and Göktürk (n 1) 113; Hakan Karakehya, *Ceza Muhakemesi Hukuku* (Adalet 2024) 124.

35 Soyaslan (n 14) 181.

36 Şahin and Göktürk (n 1) 113–16; Ahmet Gökcen, Mehmet Emin Alşahin and Kerim Çakır, *Ceza Muhakemesi Hukuku* (8th edn, Adalet, 2024) 221; Karakehya (n 34) 126–8; Tuba Kelep Pekmez, 'Ceza Muhakemesinde Objektif Bir Taraf Olarak Savcılık Makamı' (2021) 7 (2) *Anadolu Üniversitesi Hukuk Fakültesi Dergisi* 275, 276–80.

37 Karakehya (n 34) 126.

38 Ibid.

39 Centel and Zafer (n 21) 123–4.

40 Kunter (n 18) 210.

41 See particularly Öztürk and others (n 2) 131, 219 and 251.

42 Kunter (n 18) 210–11.

43 Ibid. 215 ff.
44 Kunter (n 18) 200 ff.
45 Ibid. 201. Cf. Feridun Yenisey and Ayşe Nuhoğlu, *Ceza Muhakemesi Hukuku* (12th edn, Seçkin 2024) 741.
46 Kunter (n 18) 202.Cf. Yenisey and Nuhoğlu (n 45) 741.
47 Kunter (n 18) 202.
48 Ibid. 202–3; Öztürk and others (n 2) 149–50; see further Mustafa Özen, 'Kamu Davası Açma Konusunda Benimsenen İlkeler, Cumhuriyet Savcısının Takdir Yetkisi ve İddianamenin İadesi' (2009) 67 (3) *Ankara Barosu Dergisi* 18, 19 ff.; Gökcan (n 8) 196.
49 Öztürk and others (n 2) 150. Cf. Yenisey and Nuhoğlu (n 45) 740–1; Serkan Meraklı, *Cumhuriyet Savcısının Kamu Davasını Açmada Takdir Yetkisi* (Seçkin 2014) 48.
50 Meraklı (n 49) 50.
51 See ibid. 52.
52 Özen (n 48) 20; Kartal (n 5) 59; Gökcen, Alşahin and Çakır (n 36) 606; Şık (n 19) 331.
53 Council of Europe, *Recommendation No R (87) 18 of the Committee of Ministers to Member States concerning the simplification of criminal justice* (Strasbourg, 17 September 1987) https://search.coe.int/cm?i=09000016804e19f8 accessed 14 June 2025; Cf. Şık (n 19) 332.
54 Şahin and Göktürk (n 19) 134; Kartal (n 5) 60.
55 Yargıtay, 16.C.D., Date. 29 November 2017, E. 2016/7553, K. 2017/5508 (UYAP, 29.04.2018), retrieved from Şık (n 19) 333, n.412.
56 Şık (n 19) 333–4 and 337.
57 Ibid. 333.
58 Ibid. 337.
59 See further ibid. 334–5.
60 See further Büşra Demiral Bakırman, *Şahsi Cezasızlık Sebepleri ve Cezada İndirim Yapılmasını Gerektiren Şahsi Sebepler* (On İki Levha 2023) 5ff.
61 Ibid. 159 ff.
62 Şık (n 19) 338.
63 See Özen (n 48) 21.
64 Şık (n 19) 344.
65 Colvin (n 6) 146.

References

Blázquez RB, 'Pre-trial Procedure in Spain', in Edward Johnston, Rahime Erbaş and Dan Jasinski (eds), *A Comparative Analysis of Pre-Trial Procedure in Europe: The Search for an Ideal Model* (İstanbul University Press 2020) 177.

Centel N and Zafer H, *Ceza Muhakemesi Hukuku* (22nd edn, Beta 2024).

Colvin V, 'The Riddle of Prosecutorial Discretion', in Victoria Colvin and Philip Stenning (eds), *The Evolving Role of the Public Prosecutor: Challenges and Innovations* (Routledge 2019) 139.

Demiral Bakırman B, *Şahsi Cezasızlık Sebepleri ve Cezada İndirim Yapılmasını Gerektiren Şahsi Sebepler* (On İki Levha 2023).

Duff A, 'Discretion and Accountability in a Democratic Criminal Law', in Ma´ximo Langer and David Alan Sklansky (eds), *Prosecutors and Democracy- A Cross-national Study* (Cambridge University Press 2017) 9.

Ekinci EB, *Osmanlı Mahkemeleri (Tanzimat ve Sonrası)* (Arı Sanat Yayınevi 2004).

Erbaş R, 'Pre-trial Procedure in Turkey: Post-Salduz', in Edward Johnston, Rahime Erbaş and Dan Jasinski (eds), *A Comparative Analysis of Pre-Trial Procedure in Europe: The Search for an Ideal Model* (İstanbul University Press 2020) 209 ff.

Gökcan HT, 'Cumhuriyet Savcısının Delilleri Değerlendirme Yetkisi ve Yargıtay Uygulaması' (2012) 1 *Ankara Barosu Dergisi* 195.

Gökcen A, Alşahin ME and Çakır K, *Ceza Muhakemesi Hukuku* (8th edn, Adalet 2024).

Holder R, 'Decoding Hegemony- Exploring the Discourse of a Prosecuting Elite', in Victoria Colvin and Philip Stenning (eds), *The Evolving Role of the Public Prosecutor: Challenges and Innovations* (Routledge 2019) 15.

Johnston E, Erbaş R and Jasinski D, 'Concluding Thoughts', in Edward Johnston, Rahime Erbaş and Dan Jasinski (eds), *A Comparative Analysis of Pre-Trial Procedure in Europe: The Search for an Ideal Model* (İstanbul University Press 2020) 229.

Judicial Statistics, 2024, https://adlisicil.adalet.gov.tr/Resimler/SayfaDokuman/7042025092455Adalet_%C4%B0statistikleri_2024%20T%C3%BCrk%C3%A7e_Ingilizce.pdf accessed 2 June 2025.

Karakehya H, *Ceza Muhakemesi Hukuku* (Adalet 2024).

Kartal M, *Karşılaştırmalı Hukuk Işığında Kamu Davasının Açılmasında Cumhuriyet Savcısının Takdir Yetkisi* (On İki Levha 2015).

Kelep Pekmez T, 'Ceza Muhakemesinde Objektif Bir Taraf Olarak Savcılık Makamı' (2021) 7 (2) *Anadolu Üniversitesi Hukuk Fakültesi Dergisi* 275.

Kunter N, *Ceza Muhakemesi Hukuku* (9th edn, Yaylacık Matbaası 1989).

Meraklı S, *Cumhuriyet Savcısının Kamu Davasını Açmada Takdir Yetkisi* (Seçkin 2014).

Moeller U, 'Pre-trial Procedure in Germany', in Edward Johnston, Rahime Erbaş and Dan Jasinski (eds), *A Comparative Analysis of Pre-Trial Procedure in Europe: The Search for an Ideal Model* (İstanbul University Press 2020) 87.

Mumcu A, 'Tanzimat Döneminde Türk Hukuku', in Halil İnalcık, Bülent Arı and Selim Aslantaş (eds) *Adâlet Kitabı* (Kadim 2012) 207.

Mustafa Özen, 'Kamu Davası Açma Konusunda Benimsenen İlkeler, Cumhuriyet Savcısının Takdir Yetkisi ve İddianamenin İadesi' (2009) 67 (3) *Ankara Barosu Dergisi* 18.

Öztürk B and others, *Nazari ve Uygulamalı Ceza Muhakemesi Hukuku* (18th edn, Seçkin 2024).

Rossi F, Ducoli G and Schena G, 'Pre-trial Procedure in Italy', in Edward Johnston, Rahime Erbaş and Dan Jasinski (eds), *A Comparative Analysis of Pre-Trial Procedure in Europe: The Search for an Ideal Model* (İstanbul University Press 2020) 109.

Şahin C and Göktürk N, *Ceza Muhakemesi Hukuku* (15th edn, Seçkin 2024).

Schwarz AB, 'İngiliz Hukuku ve Kontinental Hukuk' (tr Hıfzı Veldet, 1937) 3 *İstanbul Üniversitesi Hukuk Fakültesi Mecmuası* 215.

Şık H, *Türk Adli Yargı Sisteminde Savcılık Kurumu* (Adalet Yayınevi 2018).

Soyaslan D, *Ceza Muhakemesi Hukuku* (4th edn Yetkin 2010).

Taner T, 'Tanzimat Devrinde Ceza Hukuku', in *Tanzimat I: Yüzüncü Yıldönümü Münasebetile* (Maarif Matbaası 1940) 1.

Tosun Ö, 'Ceza Davasının Açılmasında Sistemler' (2011) 34 (1–4) *İstanbul Üniversitesi Hukuk Fakültesi Mecmuası* 42.

Turhan F, *Ceza Muhakemesi Hukuku* (Asil 2006).

Yenisey F and Nuhoğlu A, *Ceza Muhakemesi Hukuku* (12th edn, Seçkin 2024).

7

The constant reform of the criminal procedure in Romania

The exercising of public interest by the prosecutor

Mihail Udroiu and Cristian Dumitru Miheș

Introduction

The Romanian Code of Criminal Procedure, which entered into force in 2014, under Article 7 of the Code of Criminal Procedure (CPC), named 'obligation to initiate and prosecute criminal proceedings'.[1,2] The structure of this article is quite significant to be understood, since it encompasses directly or indirectly several principles of the criminal procedure in Romania. In the first place, the rule established by this first paragraph refers to the ex officio principle with regard to the official duty of the public prosecutor, who is obliged to initiate and pursue criminal proceedings when there is evidence of the commission of a criminal offence and there is no legal ground for impediment other than those provided for in the other paragraphs of Article 7 of the CPC. This provision is in line with the principle of 'separation of judicial functions' laid down in Article 3 of the CPC, in particular the provisions of paragraph 2: 'Judicial functions shall be exercised ex officio, unless otherwise provided by law'.

In fact, the main purpose of Article 3 is to regulate the separation of judicial functions: 'a) the function of criminal prosecution; b) the function of deciding on the fundamental rights and freedoms of the person during criminal prosecution; c) the function of reviewing the legality of detention or non-detention; d) the function of trial'. In addition, specialized literature also mentions the function of enforcement, which is not provided for in the CPC but corresponds to the last stage of the criminal process, which is of a judicial nature.[3] As a new matter introduced in the Code.[4]

This is a new approach and perspective, since the former provisions of the CPC did not regulate before, *expressis verbis*, any possibility as regards the materialization of the principle of opportunity. However, it must be mentioned that in the former Code of Criminal Law, there was a provision that was very important in materializing the right of the prosecutor to decide on pursuing criminal charges. This right belonged both to the prosecutor and to the court under certain conditions, and the incursion into the content of this institution of penal law is important for understanding the evolution of regulations that affect the exercise of the public interest in the Romanian legal system. Article 18, index 1 of the former Criminal Code of Romania, regulated the situations in which an act, although criminalized by the Criminal Code or a special law – did not have the degree of social danger of a crime. This meant that if an act or omission caused minimal damage to a value protected by law and was manifestly insignificant, it could not be considered a crime.

In order to determine whether an act falls within the scope of this (former) provision, the judicial authorities had to take into account a number of factors which were expressly provided for in the rules: the manner and means of committing the act, the purpose of the act, the circumstances in which the act was committed, the consequences produced or which might have been produced, and the person and conduct of the perpetrator, if known. In this situation, the public prosecutor or the court may also apply one of the administrative sanctions provided for in Article 91 of the former Criminal Code. This provision of the former Criminal Code of Romania indicated that the prosecutor or the court could decide on the application of administrative sanctions for offences that did not present a sufficient degree of social danger to justify a criminal sanction. These sanctions, provided for in Article 91 of the former Criminal Code, offered an alternative to criminal liability in the strict sense, allowing a proportionate response to minor offences.

In practice, the former provision established an attribute for verifying the appropriateness and a solution for concretizing the application of the principle of public interest both by the prosecutor and by the court. The role of this provision was to avoid overburdening the criminal justice system with less serious cases and instead to offer more flexible measures such as warnings, administrative fines, educational or disciplinary measures. We can therefore say that this provision prepared the ground for the future principle of proportionality, which was introduced in later legislation. Moreover, although at first glance the application of Article 18, index 1 of the former Criminal Code seems quite simple and within the reach of the prosecutor or the court, there were still a series of problems and controversies, some of which we will mention below.

One of these controversies was the subject of an appeal in the interest of the law, resolved by its admission by the High Court of Cassation and Justice of Bucharest. Specifically, the Prosecutor General declared an appeal in the interest of the law in order to establish the manner of applying administrative sanctions to concurrent acts for which the provisions of Article 18, index 1 of the Criminal Code are applicable, given that the jurisprudence existing at that time does not result in a unified point of view regarding the application of administrative sanctions in the case of concurrent offences. This non-uniformity was presented as follows:

> 1. Some courts have assessed that if it is found that the concurrent acts do not present the degree of social danger of an offense, a single administrative sanction is applied; respectively 2. In the same matter, other courts have decided that an administrative sanction must be applied for each act, operating the rule of arithmetic accumulation, as in the matter of contraventions.[5]

Following this approach, the High Court of Cassation and Justice of Bucharest admitted the appeal in the interest of the law, and by Decision no. 35 of 6 November 2006 regarding the application of administrative sanctions to concurrent acts in cases where the provisions of Article 18, index 1 of the Criminal Code are[6] applicable, it established that 'in the case of the same person committing concurrent acts which, within the meaning of the aforementioned legal text, do not present the degree of social danger of certain crimes, a single administrative sanction shall be applied, in accordance with the provisions of Article 91 of the Criminal Code'. In order to decide in this way, it was taken into account that among the administrative sanctions provided for by Article 91 of the Criminal Code, which may be applied in accordance with Article 18, index 1 para. 3 of the Criminal Code, are both 'reprimand' and 'reprimand with warning', sanctions that cannot be mathematically cumulated, but also, especially, the circumstance that the legal nature of the act that does not present the degree of social danger of a crime attracts the continuation (solution) of the criminal process in accordance with criminal and not administrative norms – specifically the rules regarding legal cumulation regulated, in the case of fines, in Article 34 para. 1 letter c) of the former Criminal Code.[7]

Later, with the reform of criminal legislation and criminal procedure,[8] controversies arise between the article concepts (from the former Criminal

Code) and the newer legal concepts/institutions, which are gradually starting to be introduced into the Romanian legal system. Such a 'novelty' was the simplified procedure, which essentially allows the trial to take place only on the basis of the evidence administered during the criminal investigation phase, only when the defendant declares that he fully acknowledges the facts contained in the court notification act and does not request the administration of evidence, except for the circumstantial documents that he can administer at this trial term.[9]

Thus, a jurisprudential controversy arose as to whether the provisions of Article 18, index 1 of the former Criminal Code can still be applied in the situation where the defendant opts for this simplified procedure under the conditions in which the procedure involves the recognition of the act. It was argued that the provisions of Article 18, index 1 of the former Criminal Code cannot be applied because the defendant (against whom the accusation has already been formulated) recognizes the commission of the crime (qualified as such by the court's notification act), or the application of Article 18, index 1 of the former Criminal Code involves the assessment of the lack of social danger of the act – as an essential feature of the crime (in the former regulation).[10] In the former Criminal Code, there was another institution that could be similar – the replacement of criminal liability from the system of the 1968 Criminal Procedure Code, but this was within the jurisdiction of the court and not the prosecutor.[11]

The New Criminal Procedure Code, *de iure*, introduced the principle of opportunity as a subsidiary principle of Romanian Criminal procedure that could be incident in certain limited cases.[12] In this respect, consequently, the new code expressly provided for the possibility for the prosecutor to order two solutions for not prosecuting the case: case dismissal and dropping criminal prosecution. Thus, dropping criminal prosecution was regulated under Article 318 of the CPC as a solution to be applied in adherence to the principle of opportunity.

Specialized literature[13] has observed that 'the mandatory exercise of criminal action has been mitigated by the introduction of rules regarding the opportunity of criminal prosecution' [the tempered legality regime of criminal prosecution, in accordance with point I(a) and (b) of the Recommendation of the Committee of Ministers of the Council of Europe No. (87) 18 of 17 September 1987 concerning the simplification of criminal justice]. Further, it was mentioned that the renunciation of criminal prosecution aims to find a balance between the principles of officialdom and opportunity and aims at an efficient management of state resources intended to combat and prevent crime.[14] From another perspective, but in the same vein, there is rightly talk of the efficient management of the mechanism for bringing criminal responsibility.[15]

Under these rules, the prosecutor can, with justification, decide to drop criminal prosecution in certain cases and under the strict and limiting conditions provided for in Article 318 of the Criminal Procedure Code. The enforcement of conditions for applying 'opportunistic dismissal' aims to ensure transparency and eliminate any arbitrariness in taking decisions that effectively represent policy options for the Public Prosecutor's Office, ensure effective judicial control of prosecutor decisions based on the principle of opportunity, and prevent an excessive increase in the powers of prosecutors, who might otherwise become the principal actors in the state's criminal policy.

Similarly, the doctrine[16] has emphasized that 'the prosecutor's discretion applies to those situations where the act constitutes an offence, and the person is responsible, with the prerogative to select among similar cases those that, for various reasons, do not present public interest being distinct from the prerogative to determine whether the act is criminally reprehensible or not'. The power of discretion of the prosecutor seems to be very significant, because of the decision to drop the criminal charges: the deeds are no longer prosecuted, the perpetrator is not subject to any criminal procedure and his criminal record will be clear of this offence.

Concluding, it has rightly been shown that the waiver of criminal prosecution is similar, to a certain extent, to the removal from criminal prosecution based on the provisions of Article 18, index 1 Criminal Code (1968), but the theoretical foundation is different because the waiver of criminal prosecution does not have a substantial legal basis, given that social danger is no longer a feature of the crime under the new regulation, so there is no legal impediment to the investigation of the act.[17]

Unconstitutionality of procedural provisions regarding 'public interest'

In the original form of the text of Article 318 of the Code of Criminal Procedure, this was likely to contribute to relieving the courts of a significant number of cases, as the solution was ordered by the prosecutor without the intervention of the judge (unlike the replacement of criminal liability in the system of the CPC of 1968, which was within the jurisdiction of the court).

In Decision no. 23/2016, the Constitutional Court ruled that the provisions of Article 318 of the CPC are unconstitutional because, by regulating the institution of dropping criminal prosecution, the legislature failed to achieve an adequate balance between the principle of legality, specific to the continental legal system in Romania, and the principle of opportunity, specific to the Anglo-Saxon legal system, giving precedence to the latter to the detriment of the former by assigning prosecutors tasks specific to the judiciary.

Within the grounds for the exception of unconstitutionality, the author of the exception of unconstitutionality stated that the phrase 'public interest' in the text under criticism is ambiguous, generates corruption, leads to the commission of crimes for which the law provides for penalties of up to seven years, favours offenders in the conditions in which the prosecution authorities do not act seriously in order to gather evidence on the existence of crimes, to identify the perpetrators and to determine the other elements of the crime, and does not allow the defence or guarantee of property.[18]

The Court also notes that the plea bargain, regulated by Articles 478–488 of the Code of Criminal Procedure, which, like the waiver of prosecution, is also a form of negotiated justice, based on the principle of expediency/opportunity. In justifying this solution, the Constitutional Court noted the following:

> Regarding the term 'public interest', contested by the author of the exception, the Court notes that the enumeration in Article 318(1) of the Criminal Procedure Code of elements related to the content of the act, the manner and means of commission, the intended purpose, the specific circumstances of the act's commission, and the consequences produced or that could have been produced does not clarify the meaning of the contested term.[19]

Furthermore, Article 318(2) states that when the perpetrator is known, considerations of public interest also include the suspect's or defendant's identity, prior conduct and efforts made to mitigate or eliminate the consequences of the crime.[20] Thus, the Court finds that the term 'public interest' is not defined by the legislature through the provisions of Article 318(1) and (2) of the Criminal Procedure Code, and the elements listed therein as criteria for determining 'public interest' are not sufficient to define the term. These elements instead serve as criteria for individualizing penalties if a court determines the commission of offences. In this regard, the Constitutional Court previously held in Decision no. 390 of 2 July 2014, that 'a legal term may have an autonomous content and meaning differing from one law to another, provided the law using the term also defines it. Otherwise, the recipient of the norm is left to determine its meaning on a case-by-case basis, a process which cannot but be subjective and, consequently, discretionary'.[21]

'The Court held that one of the requirements of the principle of respect for the law concerns the quality of normative acts and that, in principle, any normative act must meet certain qualitative conditions, including predictability, which implies that it must be sufficiently clear and precise to be applied'.[22]

At the same time, the arguments from the cases resolved by the European Convention of Human Rights (ECHR) were also retained: *Rotaru v. Romania* (paragraph 52), *Sissanis v. Romania* (paragraph 66), *Dragotoniu and Militaru-Pidhorni v. Romania* (paragraph 34) and *Beyeler v. Italy* (paragraph 109). The considerations of these decisions result in the obligation of standards of quality of the law, not only the formal adoption of a legal provision with the force of law. It was said that 'the European court held that the phrase "provided for by law" requires that the measure in question have a basis in domestic law, but also aims at the quality of the law in question: it must, indeed, be accessible to the litigant and foreseeable as to its effects'. Moreover, it has been held that only a rule which is sufficiently precise to enable the individual to control his conduct can be regarded as 'law'; he must be able to foresee, if necessary by seeking expert advice on the matter, the consequences which might result from a given act, within a reasonable degree of precision in the circumstances of the case.[23]

As regards the phrase 'public interest', criticized by the author of the exception, the Court held that the enumeration in Article 318(1) of the CPC of the elements relating to the content of the act, the manner and means of commission, the purpose pursued, the specific circumstances of the commission of the act and the consequences produced or which might have been produced by the commission of the offence, in addition to which Article 318(2) of the CPC states that, where the perpetrator is known, the assessment of the public interest shall also take into account the person of the suspect or defendant, his conduct prior to the commission of the offence and the efforts made to eliminate or mitigate the consequences of the offence is not such as to clarify the meaning of the phrase under criticism. Thus, the Court finds that the term 'public interest' is not determined by the legislator by the provisions of Article 318, paragraphs (1) and (2), of the CPC, and the elements listed therein as criteria for determining the 'public interest' are not such as to define the above-mentioned concept, as they constitute criteria for individualizing the penalties in the event of a finding by a court of law that a crime has been committed.

In this regard, the Constitutional Court previously held in Decision no. 390 of 2 July 2014, that a legal term may have an autonomous content and meaning differing from one law to another, provided the law using the term also defines it. Otherwise, the recipient of the norm is left to determine its meaning on a case-by-case basis, a process which cannot but be subjective and, consequently, discretionary.[24]

In this sense, the Court finds that the legislature must normatively regulate both the framework for conducting criminal proceedings and the competence of judicial bodies, as well as the specific implementation of each stage of the criminal proceedings. The Court further notes that in the continental system, jurisprudence is not a source of law that could clarify the meaning of the contested term, as, in such a case, the judge would become a legislator. Accordingly, the institution of dropping criminal prosecution under Article 318 of the Criminal Procedure Code differs from the institution regulated by Article 18, index 1 of the 1969 Criminal Code, which provided for the possibility of applying an administrative sanction in cases where the harm caused was minimal and clearly of low significance. This distinction is based on the fact that 'public interest in criminal prosecution', as used in Article 318 of the current Criminal Procedure Code, is different from the 'social danger' of the offence under Article 181 of the 1969 Criminal Code.

From the perspective of complying with the analysis of the incidence of the principle of separation of judicial functions, the Court also considers that the prosecutor's renunciation of criminal prosecution, without it being subject to the control and approval of the court, is equivalent to the exercise by him of powers that belong to the sphere of competence of the courts, regulated by Article 126 paragraph (1) of the Constitution, according to which justice is administered through the High Court of Cassation and Justice and through the other courts established by law.[25]

Consequently, the Court finds that the criticized text does not meet the standards of clarity, precision and predictability of the criminal law, violating the principle of legality of the criminal process, regulated in Article 2 of the Criminal Procedure Code and, consequently, the provisions of Article 1 paragraph (5) of the Constitution, which provide that the Constitution, its supremacy and the laws must be respected in Romania.

New regulation on dropping criminal prosecution

Following the decision of the Constitutional Court of Romania no. 23 of 2016, through Government Emergency Ordinance No. 18/2016, the regulation of the institution of dropping criminal prosecution was entirely restructured, and Article 318 of the CPC was essentially rewritten. Thus, the prosecutor *may* resort to the mechanisms of prosecutorial discretion and decide to drop prosecution only when the following four conditions are met[26]:

A. Positive conditions – For a prosecution to proceed in accordance with these criteria, several essential conditions must be met: (a) A formal prosecution process must have been initiated, which means that the authorities have started to investigate the case and gather evidence. The evidence collected must be sufficient to establish that the alleged crime has taken place, proving its existence by factual, legal and procedural elements. The material supporting the case must provide clarity and certainty, ensuring that the basis of the prosecution is complete. (b) The criminal offence in question must be one that carries a legal sanction, either a monetary fine or imprisonment of up to seven years. This categorization ensures that only cases falling in the low-to-medium range of seriousness are considered under these provisions. In addition, prosecution cannot be linked to incidents resulting in the death of a victim, as such cases require a higher level of judicial scrutiny and often have stricter legal consequences.

B. Negative conditions – There are several restrictive conditions that prevent the prosecution from moving forward: (a) The evidence obtained during the investigation must not indicate any legal impediment to the initiation or continuation of criminal proceedings. If any element of the case reveals procedural errors, lack of key requirements or legal obstacles which render prosecution unjustified, the case cannot proceed under these provisions. The absence of obstacles ensures that the judicial process remains fair and well-founded. (b) Where a decision to waive prosecution in the same case has been taken previously and has subsequently been quashed by a pretrial chamber judge on the grounds of lack of justification, the case cannot be re-examined. In other words, any previous decision to discontinue the prosecution must remain valid unless it is found to have been duly justified. This prevents unnecessary re-examination of cases that have already been assessed and dismissed on reasonable grounds. (c) There must be no indications of a strong public interest in securing prosecution. If elements of the case suggest that prosecution is crucial because of wider societal concerns – such as risks to public safety, legal precedents or ethical considerations – the case may be excluded from these conditions. Authorities need to assess whether allowing prosecutions to be discontinued would have a negative impact on public confidence in justice.

According to Article 318(2) of the Code of Criminal Procedure,[27] in evaluating the lack of public interest, the following criteria must be considered, which essentially pertain to the offence, the perpetrator or the procedural conduct[28]:

- The content of the act and the specific circumstances in which it was committed: In order to determine the impact and seriousness of a crime, it is essential to consider both its content and the context in which it was committed. Among the defining elements are the degree of damage to social values protected by law, such as public security, physical integrity or patrimony. An act that causes minimal damage may be assessed differently from one that generates major prejudice; the time and place of the act (for example, a crime committed in a crowded public space may have greater social implications than one committed in a private setting); and the real danger that the act presents, analysing whether it directly endangered the life, health or safety of other people or whether it had a limited impact on the community.
- The manner and means of committing the act[29]: The assessment of the manner in which the crime was committed allows for a deeper understanding of the intention and degree of premeditation of the perpetrator. In this case, the following will be taken into account: existence or lack of premeditation – if the act was the result of a spur-of-the-moment impulse, without prior planning, it can be analysed differently from a meticulously thought-out and executed action; the preparatory acts carried out for the commission of the act, including the use of special means or the involvement of third parties in organizing or facilitating the action.
- The purpose pursued by committing the act[30]: That is, what the perpetrator of the act seeks to achieve by committing the act. The purpose is different from the reason that led the perpetrator to act and can influence both the legal qualification of the act and the degree and mode of incidence of the criminal law norms. For example, if the crime was committed to help other people in critical situations, such as providing food or medicine for individuals suffering from an acute lack of resources; or if the action had a beneficial or morally justifiable purpose, even if it is not covered by the law.

- The consequences produced or that could have been produced by committing the crime[31]: When analysing an act, it is crucial to evaluate its results. If the damage caused is insignificant or of low value, the sanction must be calibrated according to this aspect; if the act had a negligible impact on the victims or society, this may influence the authorities' decision regarding the need to continue the criminal process.
- The efforts of the criminal investigation bodies are necessary for carrying out the criminal process by referring to the seriousness of the act and the time elapsed since its commission.[32, 33] Depending on the seriousness of the act and the time elapsed since its commission, it is important to analyse: the complexity of the investigation and the difficulty of the evidence collection process; the frequency of criminal prosecutions and the speed with which the authorities intervened in the investigation of the case; and the problems encountered in international judicial cooperation, if the investigation involves multiple jurisdictions.
- The victim's procedural attitude[34]: If the person affected by the crime wishes to terminate the criminal proceedings, the authorities must analyse this request: statements by the victim indicating that the damage has been repaired or that he or she no longer wishes to continue the process; reconciliation between the parties; and direct redress of the consequences of the crime.
- The existence of a clear disproportion between the expenses that the criminal trial would entail and the seriousness of the consequences produced or that could have been produced by the commission of the crime[35]: An essential aspect in the decision-making process is the balance between the resources invested in the investigation and the real impact of the act committed. If the conduct of judicial proceedings involves significant costs, and the crime has minimal consequences, the need to continue the criminal process may be reconsidered; authorities must avoid disproportionate expenses for cases that do not pose a significant social risk.
- Profile of the suspect or defendant and the public interest[36]: In assessing the public interest in continuing the criminal prosecution, the profile of the perpetrator must be analysed: his or her age, education and professional experience; degree of social integration and compliance with community norms; any criminal record, either in the country or abroad; and the health status of the suspect or defendant.

These criteria must be assessed holistically, taking into account the unique circumstances of each case, rather than being applied rigidly or in isolation. Since no individual criterion article has a predetermined weight in the legislative framework, the decision-making process remains flexible and adaptable to the specifics of the situation. Additionally, the sequence in which the criteria are listed does not denote their relative importance – each factor may gain or lose relevance depending on the details of the case.

Moreover, while certain elements might appear more influential in certain scenarios, it's entirely possible for just one or a few of these considerations to be decisive in determining whether prosecution should proceed or be dropped. This approach allows for a nuanced and case-sensitive analysis, ensuring fairness and proportionality in the application of criminal law.

The position of victims in this procedure

The protection of the victim in the procedure for waiving criminal prosecution, regulated by Article 318 of the Code of Criminal Procedure, is ensured through a series of procedural guarantees and reparative measures, intended to balance the public interest with the rights of the injured person.

In the context of analysing the victim's position in this procedure, it must be emphasized, however, that one of the criteria that the prosecutor must take into account is precisely the consequences produced or that could have been produced by the commission of the crime, as well as the procedural attitude of the injured person (Article 318 paragraph 2 letters d and f). From this, we can conclude that the position of the victim (injured person) is indirectly contributory to the decision-making.[37]

The prosecutor may order, after consulting the suspect or defendant, that he or she fulfil one or more of the following obligations: (a) to eliminate the consequences of the criminal act or to repair the damage caused or to agree with the civil party on a way to repair it; (b) to publicly apologize to the injured person; (c) to perform unpaid community service for a period of between thirty and sixty days, unless the person is unable to perform this work due to his or her health condition; (d) to attend a counselling programme.[38]

In the procedure for dropping criminal prosecution, one of the obligations that may be imposed on the suspect or defendant, whether a natural or legal person, is to eliminate the consequences of the criminal act or to repair the damage caused. This obligation may include not only the actual repair of the damage but also the initiation of mediation or negotiation procedures to establish a method of compensation. It is not necessary that the injured party was a civil party in the criminal proceedings, but only that the damage was not fully covered prior to the decision to waive the prosecution.

The Constitutional Court's Decision no. 125/2021 emphasizes that, although Article 318 of the CPC does not expressly regulate the manner of resolving the civil action, the legislator has provided guarantees for the reparation of the damage, including the possibility for the prosecutor to condition the waiving of criminal prosecution on the achievement of this reparation. If the damage is not covered by the procedural means provided, the injured person may notify the civil court, according to Article 27 of the Code of Criminal Procedure, using the evidence administered in the criminal trial.

Other complementary obligations include presenting a public apology to the victim, imposing unpaid community service (for individuals able to work, including minors over sixteen years of age, according to Decision no. 15/RIL/2019) and participating in a counselling programme, applicable only to individuals. These measures aim not only to repair the damage but also to hold the perpetrator accountable and reintegrate him into society.

Although it was emphasized that the imposition of these obligations 'must be conditional on the consent of the suspect or defendant in order to avoid situations of injustice',[39] from our point of view, consent is not necessary; the law obliges the prosecutor to consult with the suspect or defendant and in no way to ask for his consent. However, the issue of consent is more sensitive, and it must be given in advance when community service is imposed as a measure, because otherwise we would be in the presence of a situation of forced labour, which contravenes human rights. The situation would be somewhat similar, in the sense that the consent of the person concerned (suspect or defendant) would be required in the case of the measure to attend a counselling programme.[40]

These measures have a reparative and educational character, contributing to restoring social balance and recognizing the victim's suffering. In addition, if these obligations are not fulfilled in good faith, the prosecutor may revoke the waiver order (paragraph 9, Article 318, Criminal Procedure Code), which provides the victim with an additional guarantee that his or her rights will not be ignored.

The order to drop off criminal prosecution is also subject to hierarchical control and verification of legality and merits by the preliminary chamber judge (paragraph 10, Article 318, Code of Criminal Procedure), who may reject the solution if he considers it unjustified. In this case, the case is sent back for the continuation of the criminal investigation or for the initiation of criminal prosecution.

Researching judicial practice, we have exemplified a few situations below:
In this regard, the court finds that the injured party requested compensation in the amount of 600 lei and the criminal liability of the perpetrators, according to his statement recorded in tab 16 of the criminal investigation file. It is considered that the material damage of 600 lei is significant for the injured party AA, a pensioner, as evidenced by the statement in tab X of the criminal investigation file. Given these considerations, pursuant to Article 318, paragraphs 14 and 15 of the Code of Criminal Procedure, the request for confirmation of the decision to abandon criminal prosecution, ordered in file no. J of the Prosecutor's Office attached to Court Z will be rejected.[41]

In another case, the court considers that, in relation to the manner of committing the act – intentional omission to scan a number of five postal items in order to wrongfully appropriate the amounts of money – the act poses a social danger. On the other hand, the court finds that the damage caused is very high, 6004.27 lei, an amount with which the injured person constitutes a civil party in the criminal proceedings. Consequently, the court will reject the request of the Prosecutor's Office attached to the A. Court to confirm the solution of waiving the criminal prosecution ordered by the prosecutor.[42]

A final jurisprudential argument is another decision rejecting the request for confirmation of the decision to drop the criminal prosecution, in a case in which the prosecutor had ordered the drop of the criminal prosecution, considering that the defendant, although she personally collected the amount of 30,000 lei from the victim, subsequently collaborated with the authorities and was in her first offence. The preliminary chamber judge rejected this solution, considering that the acts committed by the defendant do not fall under complicity but co-authorship in the crime of fraud, because she actively participated in misleading the victim, claiming to be the secretary of a fictitious prosecutor and thus facilitating the obtaining of the money. The court emphasized the seriousness of the act, the significant damage caused to an elderly person and the lack of scruples of the defendant. It was also noted that no order was made to repair the damage, which would have left the victim without the possibility of obtaining compensation. Consequently, the case was sent back to the prosecutor's office for the initiation of criminal prosecution on charges of fraud.[43]

From the examination of the case law regarding the positioning of victims in the procedure for waiving criminal prosecution, we note the attention that the court pays to the injury caused by the crime.

Some statistical data

Analysing the latest activity report of the prosecutors,[44] we note several interesting aspects:

Thus, in 2024, the decision to drop criminal prosecution against 22,643 suspects and defendants was adopted. This number must be seen in the context of the total number of 541,671 cases resolved during this year.

At the same time, if we analyse the data from the Superior Council of Magistracy – Report on the State of Justice for 2023 (for 2024 report has not yet been published), we find that the provisions for waiving criminal prosecution were applied to 23,230 accused and defendants (2 per cent less than in 2022 when their number was 23,713).[45]

On the other hand, if we look at the effects of the change in legislation in 2016, we observe that before the Criminal Procedure Code was amended in 2016 (due to decision 23/2016 of the Constitutional Court, presented above), the number of cases resolved by waiving criminal prosecution decreased significantly from 134,436 in 2015 to 89,725 in 2016.

From this point of view, by referring to the provisions invoked by the Court when it admitted the exception of unconstitutionality and also invoking the provisions of the ECHR (Article 6), the solution appears to be fair – judicial review being essential and normal in ensuring respect for human rights. However, from the perspective of the workload of the courts, it was shown that these files having as their object the confirmation of the renunciation of criminal prosecution doubled the number of files that a judge had to resolve.[46]

Moreover, in recent times, there has been an increase in cases resolved by waiving criminal prosecution, their number fluctuating (ascending) from 57,044 in 2020 to 60,153 in 2024. But, as a share of total suspects and defendants, individuals in resolved cases, we observe a certain decrease from 20.3 in 2020 to 18.5 in 2024.

Comparative presentation in relation to the legislation of other states in this matter

Comparing Article 318 of Romania's CPC with similar legal provisions in other countries reveals both common principles and distinct approaches to prosecutorial discretion. While Romania's regulation broadly aligns with international practices, different jurisdictions adopt unique criteria for determining whether a case should proceed. These legal frameworks share a fundamental goal: ensuring that prosecution serves a legitimate legal and societal interest rather than being pursued mechanically. The comparison was made within the finding of the dissenting opinion of the decision, Decision no. 23/2016 of the Constitutional Court,[47] mentioned above, and we will try to summarize and present it as follows[48]:

In the United States, prosecutorial discretion is heavily influenced by the absence of a substantial federal interest. The US Attorneys' Manual provides guiding factors for dismissing charges, including law enforcement priorities, the severity of the crime, deterrent effects and the accused's criminal history. Prosecutors assess whether pursuing a case aligns with broader federal interests while balancing resource allocation and case significance. Notably, this evaluation is flexible – none of the criteria listed are mandatory, meaning decisions rely on the overall assessment rather than rigid rules.

Similarly, Canada applies a structured two-tier test in federal prosecutions. Crown prosecutors first determine whether there is a reasonable prospect of conviction based on available evidence. If this threshold is met, they then assess whether prosecution serves the public interest. This approach reflects a measured balance between legal certainty and discretionary power, allowing for objective and case-sensitive decision-making.

The UK follows a comparable model, requiring prosecutors to consider both the strength of evidence and the broader public interest. Law enforcement agencies collaborate closely in these assessments, ensuring that prosecution aligns with societal needs and legal priorities. This structure allows a pragmatic approach to case evaluation, reducing unnecessary prosecutions.

In France, prosecutorial discretion is exercised through mechanisms of negotiated justice, such as penal composition and transactional agreements. These procedures offer alternatives to formal prosecution in cases where offenders acknowledge guilt and agree to remedial actions. Prosecutors may impose fines or alternative sanctions – such as surrendering items used in the crime, temporary license revocation or rehabilitation programmes – without the need for court trials. While the French system does not explicitly reference 'public interest', it incorporates elements that define this concept in a succinct and practical manner.

Germany similarly allows for non-prosecution in minor offences where guilt is minimal and the public interest does not justify legal proceedings. Cases may be discontinued with judicial approval, ensuring oversight of discretionary decisions. Additionally, Germany's procedural framework includes options for dismissing cases based on political considerations, reinforcing the flexibility of prosecutorial discretion.

Other European nations, including Belgium, Finland, Sweden and Austria, emphasize proportionality – prosecution may be waived when its benefits are negligible compared to associated costs. Sweden, for instance, allows preliminary investigations to be halted if the financial burden is deemed unreasonable in relation to the severity of the offence. The Netherlands explicitly acknowledges public interest considerations in prosecution decisions, providing clear legislative grounds for case dismissal.

Austria follows a structured approach when deciding not to prosecute minor offences. Prosecutors may drop charges if specific conditions are met: the harm caused is relatively low, the offender's culpability is minimal and the individual has made efforts to remedy damages. This ensures that prosecutions remain focused on cases warranting legal intervention while reducing unnecessary litigation.

Despite differences in terminology and implementation, all these systems converge on the principle of proportionality and efficiency in criminal justice. Each legal framework acknowledges that prosecution should be pursued only when justified by broader legal or societal needs. Romania's Article 318 aligns with these international norms, ensuring that legal action is proportionate to the gravity of offences.

While some countries rely on explicit statutory provisions, others grant prosecutorial discretion through broader legal principles. Romania's approach ensures that decisions are based on a collective assessment of relevant factors, rather than on a rigid hierarchy of considerations. This flexibility allows prosecutors to evaluate cases holistically, weighing both objective and subjective elements.

Ultimately, prosecutorial discretion remains a vital tool for maintaining balance in criminal justice. By allowing case-by-case evaluation, legal systems across the world ensure that prosecution aligns with public interest, legal resources are efficiently allocated and judicial processes remain fair and proportional. Romania's framework, although refined through legislative adjustments and constitutional review, stands as part of a broader international trend aimed at maintaining judicial efficiency while respecting the nuances of each case.

Conclusion

Such a possibility for the prosecutor to assess to what extent, with respect to certain aspects concerning the act and the perpetrator, there is proportionality between the public interest, satisfied by the exercise of criminal action, and the 'costs' of such an approach, does not contradict the practice of the ECHR and is not an original creation of the Romanian legislator.[49]

The evolution of Romania's approach to defining public interest in criminal prosecution reflects a deliberate effort to create a framework that balances legal certainty with judicial flexibility. The initial legislative hesitation, later addressed by the Constitutional Court, highlights the complexity of establishing clear yet adaptable criteria that allow prosecutors to make reasoned decisions while upholding principles of fairness and proportionality.

By incorporating both objective and subjective elements into the evaluation process, the Romanian legislature has aimed to equip prosecutors with a well-structured methodology for determining whether a case warrants pursuit. Objective criteria ensure that decisions are grounded in concrete legal and factual considerations, such as the gravity of the offence, its societal impact and procedural efficiency. Meanwhile, subjective criteria allow room for discretion, factoring in aspects like the offender's personal circumstances, potential for rehabilitation and the broader implications of prosecution. This measured approach is essential in preventing arbitrary decisions while acknowledging that each case must be assessed in its unique context. The underlying concern is to avoid mechanical legal interpretations that disregard nuances critical to ensuring that justice is not only served but also appropriately tailored to the realities of each individual case.

Case-Law

Alexandria City Court, Criminal Sentence 110 of 23.01.2018 https://www.jurisprudenta.com/jurisprudenta/speta-163cazwf/ accessed 1 June 2025.

Bacău City Court - Criminal Section, Sentence no. 1262 of 28.09.2016 http://legeaz.net/spete-penal/confirmare-renuntare-urmarire-penala-jurisprudenta-1262-2016 accessed 1 June 2025.

Constitutional Court Decision no. 23 of 2016, published in the Official Gazette no. 240 of 31.03.2016 https://www.ccr.ro/wp-content/uploads/2020/07/Decizie_23_2016.pdf accessed 1 June 2025.

Constitutional Court Decision no. 390 of July 2, 2014 published in the Official Gazette of Romania, Part I, no. 532 of July 17, 2014 DECIZIE 390 02/07/2014 - Portal Legislativ accessed 1 June 2025.

High Court of Cassation and Justice of Bucharest, Decision no. XXXV of November 6, 2006 in File no. 25/2006, Published in the Official Gazette, Part I no. 368 of 05/30/2007 https://www.iccj.ro/2006/11/06/decizia-nr-35-din-06-noiembrie-2006-cu-privire-la-aplicarea-sanctiunilor-cu-caracter-administrativ-faptelor-concurente-in-cazul-cand-sunt-incidente-dispozitiile-art-18-indice-1-din-codul-penal/ accessed 1 June 2025.

Iaşi City Court, Criminal Sentence no. 534 of 18.05.2017 https://legeaz.net/spete-penal/confirmare-renuntare-urmarire-penala-cerere-534-2017 accessed 1 June 2025.

Others

Report on the activity carried out by the Public Ministry (2024) raport_activitate_2024.pdf accessed 1 June 2025.

Notes

1 Article 7 from the CPC reads as: '(1) The public prosecutor shall be obliged to initiate and prosecute criminal proceedings ex officio when there is evidence of the commission of an offence and there is no legal ground for impediment other than those provided for in paragraphs. (2) and (3); (2) In the cases and under the conditions expressly provided by law, the public prosecutor may waive the prosecution if, in relation to the concrete elements of the case, there is no public interest in the realization of the object of the prosecution; (3) In the cases expressly provided by law, the public prosecutor shall initiate and prosecute the criminal

proceedings after the injured party has lodged a prior complaint or after the authorization or referral to the competent body has been obtained or after another condition provided by law has been fulfilled'.

2 Some of the concepts explored in this chapter were also previously published by the chapter's co-author, Mihail Udroiu, in his earlier work *Sinteze de procedură penală. Partea Specială* [Syntheses of Criminal Procedure, Special Part], vol I (5th edn, C.H. Beck Publishing House, Bucharest 2024), particularly on pages 192–5.

3 Mihail Udroiu, *Sinteze de procedură penală. Partea generală [Syntheses of criminal procedure. General part]*, 1st volume (5th edn, C.H. Beck Publishing House, Bucharest 2024) 10.

4 Gheorghita Mateuţ, *Procedură penală [Criminal Procedure, General Part]* (Universul Juridic Publishing House 2023) 69.

5 Alina Matei, 'Aplicarea unei singure sancţiuni administrative în cazul săvârşirii unor fapte *concurente [Application of a single administrative sanction in the case of committing concurrent acts]*' (30 November 1999) https://www.juridice.ro/46796/aplicare-unei-singure-sanciuni-administrative-savarsirii-fapte.html accessed 1 June 2025.

6 High Court of Cassation and Justice of Bucharest, Decision no. XXXV of 6 November 2006 in File no. 25/2006, published in the Official Gazette, Part I no. 368 of 05/30/2007 https://www.iccj.ro/2006/11/06/decizia-nr-35-din-06-noiembrie-2006-cu-privire-la-aplicarea-sanctiunilor-cu-caracter-administrativ-faptelor-concurente-in-cazul-cand-sunt-incidente-dispozitiile-art-18-indice-1-din-codul-penal/ accessed 1 June 2025.

7 High Court of Cassation and Justice of Bucharest, Decision no. XXXV of 6 November 2006 in File no. 25/2006, published in the Official Gazette, Part I no. 368 of 05/30/2007 https://www.iccj.ro/2006/11/06/decizia-nr-35-din-06-noiembrie-2006-cu-privire-la-aplicarea-sanctiunilor-cu-caracter-administrativ-faptelor-concurente-in-cazul-cand-sunt-incidente-dispozitiile-art-18-indice-1-din-codul-penal/ accessed 1 June 2025.

8 'Law no. 202/2010 on some measures to accelerate the resolution of trials 1, was called by its initiator, the Ministry of Justice, since the public debate phase, the "small reform" to delimit it from the "big reform" of criminal legislation and criminal procedure that is to take place through the entry into force of the new codes' – for developments on this topic, please see Mihail Udroiu, '*Mica Reformă în procesul penal [The Small Reform of Criminal Trial]*' [2011] 1 Dreptul 598.

9 Article 320, index 1 – Judgement in the event of recognition, Criminal Procedure Code, https:// s intact.ro / legislation/monitorul-oficial/codul-de-procedura-penala-din-1968-codul-de-procedura-penala-16804068/art-320-1 accessed 1 June 2025.

10 Marius-Gabriel Săndulescu, 'Controversa privind aplicarea art. 18 indice 1 din Codul penal atunci când instanța recurge la procedura simplificată de recunoaștere a vinovăției conform art. 320 indice 1 din Codul penal *[Controversy of the application of art. 18 index 1 of the Criminal Code when the court resorts to the simplified procedure of recognition of guilt according to art. 320 index 1 of the Criminal Code]*' (28 February 2014) https://www.juridice.ro/245872/controversa-aplicarii-art-18-indice-1-cp-cand-instanta-recurge-la-procedura-simplificata-a-recunoasterii-vinovatiei-conform-art-320-indice-1-cpp.html accessed 01 June 2025. We do not entirely agree – but it is not the subject of this chapter, but we must show that the provisions of Article 320 paragraph 4 of the Criminal Procedure Code expressly states that the Court resolves the criminal aspect when 'the evidence administered during the criminal investigation shows that the act exists (s.n.), constitutes a crime and was committed by the defendants' – therefore, it makes an assessment of the act, and on this occasion it can decide on the merits of the problem.

11 Radu Slăvoiu, *Renunțarea la urmărire penală [Dropping of Criminal Prosecution Part]* (Hamangiu Publishing House, Bucharest 2023) 223.

12 Mateuț (n 3) 69–70.

13 Udroiu (n 2) 186.

14 Vasile Pavil, '*Considerations Regarding Withdrawal of Criminal Prosecution*' [2023] 1–2 Themis 1.

15 Slăvoiu (n 10) 20.

16 John H. Langbein, 'Controlling Prosecutorial Discretion in Germany' (1974) 41 (3) *University of Chicago Law Review* 439, 440.

17 Marius Bogdan Bulancea and Alexandra Mihaela Șinc, 'Renunțarea la urmărire penală' [Dropping of Criminal Prosecution] in Mihail Udroiu (ed.), 'Codul de procedură penală. Comentariu pe articole' [*Criminal Procedure Code. Commentary on Articles]* (3rd ed., Ed. C.H. Beck, Bucharest, 2020) 1745.

18 Paragraph 4 of the reasoning of the Constitutional Court Decision no. 23 of 2016, published in the Official Gazette no. 240 of 31 March 2016 https://www.ccr.ro/wp-content/uploads/2020/07/Decizie_23_2016.pdf accessed 1 June 2025.

19 Paragraph 15 of the reasoning of the Constitutional Court Decision no. 23 of 2016, published in the Official Gazette no. 240 of 31 March 2016 https://www.ccr.ro/wp-content/uploads/2020/07/Decizie_23_2016.pdf accessed 1 June 2025.

20 This matter is very sensitive and it should be analysed very carefully also from the perspective of observing the suspect's rights – Cristian Miheș, Mihaela Pătrăuș, Radu Dacin, 'Reflection on the Procedural Right of Suspect and Defendants, with Special Reference to the Witness's Right not to Self-incriminate – the Romanian Perspective', in Akos Farkas, Gerhard Dannecker and Judit Jacso (eds), *External, Internal and Criminal Investigations of Criminal Offenses Affecting the Financial*

Interests of the European Union (Wolters Kluwer, Budapest, Hungary 2022).

21 Paragraph 15 of the reasoning of the Constitutional Court Decision no. 23 of 2016, published in the Official Gazette no. 240 of 31 March 2016 https://www.ccr.ro/wp-content/uploads/2020/07/Decizie_23_2016.pdf accessed 1 June 2025.

22 Paragraph 13 had invoked in this regard the jurisprudence of the Constitutional Court: Decision no. 903 of 6 July 2010, published in the Official Gazette of Romania, Part I, no. 584 of 17 August 2010, Decision no. 743 of 2 June 2011, published in the Official Gazette of Romania, Part I, no. 579 of 16 August 2011, Decision no. 1 of 11 January 2012, published in the Official Gazette of Romania, Part I, no. 53 of 23 January 2012, or Decision no. 447 of 29 October 2013, published in the Official Gazette of Romania, Part I, no. 674 of 1 November 2013 – Constitutional Court Decision no. 23 of 2016, published in the Official Gazette no. 240 of 31 March 2016 https://www.ccr.ro/wp-content/uploads/2020/07/Decizie_23_2016.pdf accessed 1 June 2025.

23 Paragraph 14 of the reasoning of the Constitutional Court Decision no. 23 of 2016, published in the Official Gazette no. 240 of 31 March 2016 https://www.ccr.ro/wp-content/uploads/2020/07/Decizie_23_2016.pdf accessed 1 June 2025.

24 Constitutional Court Decision no. 390 of 2 July 2014 published in the Official Gazette of Romania, Part I, no.532 of 17 July 2014 DECIZIE 390 02/07/2014 – Portal Legislativ accessed 1 June 2025.

25 Paragraphs: 18, 21, 33 of the reasoning of the Constitutional Court Decision no. 23 of 2016, published in the Official Gazette no. 240 of 31 March 2016 https://www.ccr.ro/wp-content/uploads/2020/07/Decizie_23_2016.pdf accessed 01 June 2025.

26 Mihail Udroiu, 'Fişe de Procedură penală' *[Factsheets of Criminal Procedure. Special Part]* (5th edition, 1st volume, C.H. Beck Publishing House, Bucharest 2024) 87–8.

27 Letter 'a' from Article 318(2) of the Code of Criminal Procedure.

28 Mihail Udroiu, 'Sinteze de procedura penală Partea Specială' *[Syntheses of Criminal Procedure, Special Part]* (5th edition, 1st volume, C.H. Beck Publishing House, Bucharest 2024) 192–5.

29 Letter 'b' from Article 318(2) of the Code of Criminal Procedure.

30 Letter 'c' from Article 318(2) of the Code of Criminal Procedure.

31 Letter 'd' from Article 318(2) of the Code of Criminal Procedure.

32 Letter 'e' from Article 318(2) of the Code of Criminal Procedure.

33 Letter 'e' from Article 318(2) of the Code of Criminal Procedure.

34 Letter 'f' from Article 318(2) of the Code of Criminal Procedure.

35 Letter 'g' from Article 318(2) of the Code of Criminal Procedure.

36 Article 318(3) of the Code of Criminal Procedure.

37 Pavil (n 13) 6.

38 Udroiu (n 25) 89.

39 Pavil (n 13) 7.

40 Udroiu (n 25) 87–8.

41 Bacău City Court – Criminal Section, Sentence no. 1262 of 28 September 2016 http://legeaz.net/spete-penal/confirmare-renuntare-urmarire-penala-jurisprudenta-1262-2016 accessed 1 June 2025.

42 Alexandria City Court, Criminal Sentence 110 of 23.01.2018 https://www.jurisprudenta.com/jurisprudenta/speta-163cazwf/ accessed 1 June 2025.

43 Iaşi City Court, Criminal Sentence no. 534 of 18.05.2017 https://legeaz.net/spete-penal/confirmare-renuntare-urmarire-penala-cerere-534-2017 accessed 1 June 2025.

44 Report on the activity carried out by the Public Ministry (2024) raport_activitate_2024.pdf accessed 1 June 2025.

45 The report: SCM – Reports on the state of justice accessed 1 June 2025.

46 Slăvoiu (n 10) 223–4.

47 Decision no. 23/2016 of the Constitutional Court was taken with a majority of votes (6 to 3).

48 Findings of the dissenting opinion to the Decision no. 23/2016 of the Constitutional Court.

49 See, in this regard, the ECHR judgements *Calvelli and Ciglio v. Italy,* App. no. 32967/96 (ECHR, 17 January 2002), *Kilic v. Turkey,* App. no. 22492/93 (ECHR 28 March 2000), *Mahmut Kaya v. Turkey,* App. no. 22535/93 (ECHR 28 March 2000), *Trocellier v. France,* App. no. 75725/01 (ECHR 5 October 2006), *Benderskiy v. Ukraine,* App. no. 22750/02 (ECHR 15 November 2007) – Vasile Nester and Dragoş-Cătălin Borcea, '*Renunţarea la urmărire penală. Consecinţele juridice ale unei instituţii (ne)constituţionale [Dropping of criminal prosecution. The legal consequences of an (un)constitutional institution]*' (28 June 2019) https://www.juridice.ro/644883/renuntarea-la-urmarire-penala-consecintele-juridice-ale-unei-institutii-neconstitutionale.html accessed 1 June 2025.

References

Bulancea MB and Şinc AM, 'Renunţarea la urmărire penală' [Dropping of Criminal Prosecution], in Mihail Udroiu (ed), *Codul de procedură penală. Comentariu pe articole [Criminal Procedure Code. Commentary on Articles]* (3rd ed., Ed. C.H. Beck, Bucharest 2020) 1745 ff.

Langbein JH, 'Controlling Prosecutorial Discretion in Germany' (1974) 41 (3) *University of Chicago Law Review* 439.

Matei A, 'Aplicarea unei singure sancţiuni administrative în cazul săvârşirii unor fapte *concurente [Application of a Single Administrative Sanction in the Case of Committing Concurrent Acts]*' (30 November 1999) https://www.juridice.ro/46796/aplicare-unei-singure-sanciuni-administrative-savarsirii-fapte.html accessed 1 June 2025.

Mateuț G, *Procedură penală [Criminal Procedure, General Part]* ('Universul Juridic' Publishing House 2023).

Miheş C, Pătrăuş M and Dacin R, 'Reflection on the Procedural Right of Suspect and Defendants, with Special Reference to the Witness`s Right Not to Self-incriminate – the Romanian Perspective', in Akos Farkas, Gerhard Dannecker and Judit Jacso (eds), *External, Internal and Criminal Investigations of Criminal Offenses Affecting the Financial Interests of the European Union* (Wolters Kluwer, Budapest, Hungary 2022) 314–27.

Nester V and Borcea D-C, '*Renunțarea la urmărire penală. Consecințele juridice ale unei instituții (ne)constituționale [Dropping of Criminal Prosecution. The Legal Consequences of an (Un)constitutional Institution]*' (28 June 2019) https://www.juridice.ro/644883/renuntarea-la-urmarire-penala-consecintele-juridice-ale-unei-institutii-neconstitutionale.html accessed 1 June 2025.

Săndulescu M-G, 'Controversa privind aplicarea art. 18 indice 1 din Codul penal atunci când instanța recurge la procedura simplificată de recunoaştere a vinovăției conform art. 320 indice 1 din Codul penal [*Controversy of the Application of Art. 18 Index 1 of the Criminal Code When the Court Resorts to the Simplified Procedure of Recognition of Guilt according to Art. 320 Index 1 of the Criminal Code]*' (28 February 2014) https://www.juridice.ro/245872/controversa-aplicarii-art-18-indice-1-cp-cand-instanta-recurge-la-procedura-simplificata-a-recunoasterii-vinovatiei-conform-art-320-indice-1-cpp.html accessed 1 June 2025.

Slăvoiu R, *Renunțarea la urmărire penală [Dropping of Criminal Prosecution Part]* ('Hamangiu' Publishing House, Bucharest 2023).

Udroiu M, *Fişe de Procedură penală [Factsheets of Criminal Procedure. Special Part]*, 1st volume (5th edn, 'C.H. Beck' Publishing House, Bucharest 2024).

Udroiu M, '*Mica Reformă în procesul penal [The Small Reform of Criminal Trial]*' (2011) 1 Dreptul.

Udroiu M, *Sinteze de procedură penală. Partea generală [Syntheses of Criminal Procedure. General Part]*, 1st volume (5th edn, 'C.H. Beck' Publishing House, Bucharest 2024).

Udroiu M, *Sinteze de procedura penală Partea Specială [Syntheses of Criminal Procedure, Special Part]*, 1st volume (5th edn, 'C.H. Beck' Publishing House, Bucharest 2024).

Vasile P, '*Considerations Regarding Withdrawal of Criminal Prosecution*' (2023) 1–2 Themis 1.

The impact of the public interest on the legislative and judicial penal policy

The case of the Republic of North Macedonia

Aleksandra Gruevska Drakulevski and
Aleksandra Deanoska Trendafilova

Introduction

The public interest is a complex category that is difficult to define. As stated in the Dictionary on Media Literacy, public interest is 'that, which is of interest or benefit to the greatest number of people or the protection of values for which there is a broad social consensus; a common good that is above the interests and preferences of individual political or economic centers'.[1]

A huge number of laws in North Macedonia mention the concept of public interest, but no strict or sufficiently descriptive definition can be found. The Law on Prevention of Corruption and Conflict of Interests has a more substantive definition, stipulating that

> The term 'public interest' means the protection of fundamental freedoms and rights of man and citizen recognized by international law and established by the Constitution of the Republic of Macedonia, prevention of risks to health, defence and security, protection of the environment and nature, protection of property and freedom of the market and entrepreneurship, rule of law and prevention of crime and corruption.[2]

Therefore, one of the main challenges the penal policy creators face is how society should react to those who break the law. Taking into account the steady increase in rates of criminality, especially certain serious types, this is an issue that has been attracting attention for years.[3]

The appropriate fight against crime, as the main goal of penal policy, requires greater advocacy in studying the aetiology of crime in society and the application of new, suitable and better measures than the existing ones in order to achieve the objectives of penal policy – the suppression of crime.

The first issue that is usually examined when exploring the subject of crime and public interest is the question of the public prosecution's discretion in determining whether to prosecute or not in a certain case. The Macedonian procedural legislation accepts the principle of legality, meaning that the public prosecutor has a duty to prosecute no matter his or her personal belief on the necessity and purposefulness of prosecuting in the respective case. There is an exception in the cases stipulated in Articles 43 and 44 of the Law on Criminal Procedure.[4] Namely, in a very strict number of cases and conditions entailed by the law, the public prosecutor may apply the principle of opportunity and conditionally postpone the criminal prosecution for less serious criminal offences, i.e. offences punishable with imprisonment sentences of up to three years.[5]

The right to waive the criminal procedure is regulated in Article 44 of the Law on Criminal Procedure stipulating that the public prosecutor may not undertake criminal prosecution in case: the Criminal Code provides for the possibility for the accused to be convicted but acquitted from punishment and the prosecutor considers that a conviction without punishment is not necessary in the respective case; the crime is punishable with fine or imprisonment of up to three years and the suspect already has shown regret and prevented or repaired the damages; and in case the suspect is a member or organized criminal group and willingly cooperates with the authorities and his or her cooperation and statement are of utmost importance for the procedure.[6]

The two basic types of anti-crime are preventive and repressive action. There is no doubt that the usual reaction to crime in many legislations is punishment. But the issue is complicated in terms of choosing the type of criminal sanction from the many available, whether the perpetrator of a crime should be punished with a prison sentence, a fine, one of the secondary sentences, or with today's increasingly popular alternative measures.

The problem, however, does not end with the type of criminal sanction that shall be imposed; to satisfy justice and equity, attention should be paid to the amount/length of the criminal sanction, which is determined by the set objective of punishment. There are several objectives, such as prevention, rehabilitation, neutralization, etc.[7] In fact, in a democratic society, the whole circle of 'paying the debt' ultimately fulfils the public interest when the perpetrator's sanction is executed, and in a matter of time, he or she again gets the *praesumtio boni viri* status as a fully rehabilitated citizen.[8]

In determining the purpose of the punishment in the Republic of North Macedonia, the starting point is the Macedonian Criminal Code (CCM),[9] according to which the purpose of the punishment, besides serving justice, is (1) to prevent the offender from committing crimes and his correction and (2) educational influence on others, so as not to perform crimes.[10]

In setting the basic purpose of execution of the sentence of imprisonment, the Law on Execution of Sanctions[11] (LES) starts from the principle of special prevention and re-socialization – empowering convicts to engage in a society with the best prospects for independent life in accordance with the law. In order to achieve the goal of imprisonment, the convicted person develops a sense of responsibility and is encouraged to accept and actively participate in the treatment during the execution of the sentence, motivated and directed towards re-education and development of the positive character traits and abilities that speed up successful return to society.[12]

The purpose of the alternative measures is not to sentence a principal offender for a less serious crime when that is not absolutely necessary in the specific case and when it can be expected that the purpose of the punishment may be achieved by a warning with a threat of punishment (probation), only a warning (court reprimand) or measures of assistance and supervision of the behaviour of the released offender.[13] The purpose of the safety measures is to remove situations or conditions that may influence the offender to commit crimes in the future.[14]

The system of criminal sanctions in the Republic of North Macedonia

The system of criminal sanctions in the Republic of North Macedonia is determined by the Criminal Code of the Republic of North Macedonia (CCM). The following sentences may be imposed on the criminally liable offenders for the crimes they have committed:

1. imprisonment;
2. fine;
3. prohibition on practicing a profession or performing an activity or duty;
4. prohibition on operating a motor vehicle;

5. expulsion of a foreigner from the country; and
6. prohibition on attending sports competitions.[15]

Alternative measures that may be imposed on the perpetrators of criminal acts are:

1. suspended sentence;
2. suspended sentence with protective supervision (probation);
3. probationary suspension of the criminal procedure;
4. community service;
5. court reprimand; and
6. house arrest.[16]

Offenders may be imposed the following safety measures:

1. compulsory psychiatric treatment and custody in a health institution;
2. compulsory psychiatric treatment in freedom;
3. compulsory treatment of alcoholics and drug addicts; and
4. medical-pharmacological treatment.[17]

The CCM also provides sentences for legal entities. A fine shall be imposed as the main sentence for crimes of legal entities.[18] Under the conditions determined by this Code, the court, as soon as it assesses that the legal entity has abused its activity and that there is a risk for it to repeat the crime in the future, can impose one or more secondary sentences.[19]

In compliance with the principle that 'no one may retain the indirect or direct property benefit obtained through a crime', the CCM provides confiscation of property and property benefit and seizure of objects.[20]

Judicial penal policy in the Republic of North Macedonia (2017–23)

As a next step in this chapter, in brief, the judicial penal policy in the Republic of North Macedonia in the period 2017–23 is analysed.[21] As such, in general, the question that arises is why such an analysis is needed when we know that punishment in large part is a subjective category. Namely, during the judicial process of meting out a sentence, the principle of individualization is dominated, according to which the judge determines a sentence that, in both the type and the height, is most suitable for the concrete case, so that the perpetrator of the sentence fulfils the purpose of the sentence.[22]

It is worth mentioning one specific solution in our penal system, which was that the court shall mete out the sentence in accordance with the Rulebook for the Manner of Meting the Sentences adopted by the president of the Supreme Court of the Republic of Macedonia, upon previous opinion of the Public Prosecutor of the Republic of Macedonia and the Bar Chamber of the Republic of Macedonia.[23] The introduction of such a solution was expected to ensure efficient and successful functioning of the new concept of criminal procedure in practice and a secure basis for the promotion and harmonization of the penal policy of domestic criminal courts.[24] Later, the Law on Amending the Criminal Code (Official Gazette of the Republic of Macedonia No. 199/2014) provides that the court shall mete out the sentence in accordance with the Law on the Determination of the Type and the Length of the Sentence.[25] Namely, the meting out of sentence was regulated by a law rather than by a Rulebook. This decision followed as a result of numerous criticisms and debates by experts that this matter cannot be regulated by a bylaw.[26]

The question still remained whether the proposed guidelines do not violate or abandon the essence of free judicial assurance and the individualization of the criminal sanction. Hence, in 2017, this law was abolished by a decision of the Constitutional Court of the Republic of Macedonia.

Criminal sanctions imposed by courts in North Macedonia in the period 2017–23

The subject of the analysis of this chapter is the judicial penal policy in the Republic of North Macedonia in the period 2017–23, while not maintaining the legal penal policy, that is, the legally prescribed sanctions by type and amount.[27]

For the analysis of the penal policy in the Republic of North Macedonia, official statistical data from the State Statistical Office of the Republic of Macedonia were used in the period from 2017 to 2023.

According to the analyses in the period 2017–23, on average, there were 6,446 convicted adults. 50.39 per cent of the total convicted persons were punished and 49.42 per cent of the convicted adults were imposed alternative measures.

Of those who were punished, 37.65 per cent on average were imprisoned and 55.57 per cent were fined.

Regarding the alternative measures, a high 92.87 per cent were suspended sentences of imprisonment, 4.54 per cent were suspended sentences of fine, 1.40 per cent were court reprimands, 0.64 per cent were community service and 0.56 per cent were probation with protective supervision.

The other alternative measures – probationary suspension of the criminal procedure and house arrest – were not imposed at all.

We are confronted with a situation in which these alternative measures remain merely theoretical, lacking practical implementation. This raises the question of why such a discrepancy exists. Given the fact that the penal policy in relation to the imposed effective sentences of imprisonment is lenient, namely, the short prison sentences are dominant: those lasting up to six months (30.14 per cent), from six months to one year (27.40 per cent) and from one to two years (19.72 per cent), there is no reason why judges should not impose more often alternative measures, of course, if the formal and material conditions for their imposition are fulfilled. It is questionable why judges in North Macedonia do not impose, for example, the alternative measure of probationary suspension of the criminal procedure, for which there is no need to create additional conditions for its execution. Alternatively, one might question why the alternative measure of suspended sentences with protective supervision has not been utilized at all, particularly when considering the presence of probation officers.

Regardless, the more frequent application of alternative measures will contribute to resolving some of the problems that our penitentiary system faces, above all, the problem of overcrowding of penitentiary institutions; furthermore, the alternative measures are a way to annul the problem of criminal infection, which is important for reducing the rates of recidivism in North Macedonia.

Next, on average, 0.02 per cent of the convicted persons were found guilty, but no penal sanction was imposed.

In the analysed period, in North Macedonia, on average, the total number of convicted persons who were imposed security measures is only 1.52 per cent. Only 0.76 per cent of the convicted were imposed confiscation of property and 10.21 per cent – confiscation of objects.

The data are summarized in Tables 8.1, 8.2, 8.3 and 8.4.

Table 8.1 Convicted adult perpetrators by type of sentence and sex (2017–23)

	2017	2018	2019	2020	2021	2022	2023	Average	%
Total convicted persons	6273	5857	4712	6351	7634	7769	6528	6446	
Convicted persons – Women	550	419	410	558	664	758	568	561	8.70
Convicted persons – Men	5723	5438	4302	5793	6970	7011	5960	5885	91.30
Punishments – Total	2739	2403	2186	3416	4287	4360	3347	3248	50.39
Total imprisonment	1255	1246	1181	914	1176	1372	1417	1223	37.65
Total fine	1381	1052	871	2455	2742	2515	1622	1805	55.57
Alternative measures – Total	3534	3454	2526	2927	3323	3383	3152	3186	49.42
Convicted but no penal sentence	–	–	–	8	–	–	–	1	0.02
Imposed security measure without imposing a punishment	–	–	–	–	24	26	29	11	0.18

Source: State Statistical Office of the Republic of North Macedonia

Table 8.2 Convicted adult perpetrators by applied main sentence – imprisonment and fine (2017–23)

	2017	2018	2019	2020	2021	2022	2023	Average	%
Total imprisonment	1255	1246	1181	914	1176	1372	1417	1223	
Life imprisonment	1	1	3	2	2	9	-	3	0.21
Imprisonment over 20 years	5	2	6	5	2	10	8	5	0.44
Imprisonment 10–15 years	14	14	21	5	14	17	16	14	1.18
Imprisonment 5–10 years	63	27	37	54	56	75	81	56	4.59
Imprisonment 3–5 years	119	81	70	75	111	135	112	100	8.21
Imprisonment 2–3 years	142	94	65	66	97	116	114	99	8.11
Imprisonment 1–2 years	290	231	210	138	210	303	306	241	19.72
Imprisonment 6–12 months	307	360	362	258	347	366	346	335	27.40
Imprisonment up to 6 months	314	436	407	311	337	341	434	369	30.14
Total fine	1381	1052	871	2455	2742	2515	1622	1805	
Fine up to 5000 denars	35	42	4	23	12	10	5	19	1.04
Fine 5001–10000	46	30	33	104	117	72	72	68	3.75
Fine 10001–30000	587	691	521	927	1445	1269	897	905	50.14
Fine over 30001 denars	713	289	313	1401	1168	1164	648	814	45.07

Source: State Statistical Office of the Republic of North Macedonia

Table 8.3 Convicted adult perpetrators by types of applied alternative measures (2017–23)

	2017	2018	2019	2020	2021	2022	2023	Average	%
Alternative measures – Total	3534	3454	2526	2927	3323	3383	3152	3186	
Suspended sentence – Imprisonment	3350	3307	2412	2676	2990	3050	2923	2958	92.87
Suspended sentence Fine	138	108	72	215	218	146	115	145	4.54
Probation with protective supervision	–	–	–	4	14	46	60	18	0.56
Probationary suspension of the criminal procedure	–	–	–	–	–	–	–	0	0.00
Community service	–	–	–	2	42	91	7	20	0.64
Court reprimand	46	39	42	30	59	50	47	45	1.40
House arrest	–	–	–	–	–	–	–	0	0.00

Source: State Statistical Office of the Republic of North Macedonia

Table 8.4 Convicted adult perpetrators by total applied security measures, confiscation of property and confiscation of objects (2017–23)

	2017	2018	2019	2020	2021	2022	2023	Average	%
Security measures	86	83	199	133	74	61	50	98	1.52
Confiscation of property	44	48	49	67	49	51	37	49	0.76
Confiscation of objects	508	581	608	490	682	880	860	658	10.21

Source: State Statistical Office of the Republic of North Macedonia

To sum up, this research is particularly important because the analysis of judicial penal policy is important to assess the effectiveness of the various sanctions. The relationship between the judicial practice of punishment and the rates of crime may be important to draw conclusions about the effectiveness of the various sanctions and to show to what extent certain sanctions are applied.

It is not uncommon for the public to point out that the penal policy in the Republic of Macedonia is lenient, and hence, more and more often the public demands that the penalties in the Criminal Code should be increased, and that the perpetrators of criminal acts should be given more severe punishments in order to reduce the crime rates, and at the same time, according to the public's perceptions, harsher penalties are proportionate to the crimes committed. In practice, the impact was confirmed in particular crimes, such as paedophilia, crimes against traffic, etc. However, as a result of numerous studies carried out, it can be concluded that not the severity of the sentence, but the urgency of the pronounced sentence and the certainty of the sentence, deter the persons from committing criminal acts.

The definition of harshness or leniency of sanctions is complex and relative. Sanctions vary according to their nature and duration and are imposed in order to achieve different goals. The harshness/leniency of the penal policy cannot be judged merely by the number of imposed prison sentences, but other sanctions (the fine, other minor penalties, alternative measures, etc.) should be taken into account, which additionally complicates the issue, since people differently perceive and understand individual values such as freedom, money, reputation, etc. On the other hand, not only the imposed prison sentences should be taken into account, but also the length of its duration and the type of penitentiary-correctional institution where it is served.

Hence, further research on the penal policy of the courts in North Macedonia is needed. A question that also deserves particular attention is the (in)equality of penal policy. Namely, an effective criminal policy for the suppression of crime is largely an expression of a uniform policy of punishment, which will be fundamentally ensured by creating optimal conditions for uniqueness in the application of the leading principles – legality and individualization – as basic elements for judicial determination of the sentence.[28]

Moreover, the recommendations of the Council of Europe should be taken into account for the limitation of the imposition of prison sentences and a wider application of alternative sanctions and measures. The public should be convinced that the penal repression of the system should be reduced. Then, the alternative sanctions and measures do not put in question the system of criminal justice at all, since they take into account the victim, and the convict is subject to treatment and supervision by professional and authorized persons in the community, and that these punishments have a greater effect in the direction of reducing the rates of recidivism.[29]

Public interest in criminal law reform and sentencing: Insights from Macedonian case law

Case No. 1 – The public interest and the amendments of the Criminal Code for sexual/paedophilia provisions

Quite often, certain criminal events in the country have a serious public impact. This largely depends on how the information is conveyed from the media to the citizens in terms of intensity and content. Media reports very often shape the opinion and perception of the public. This, in turn, affects the professional public, as well as policymakers in the country, but also the judicial system.

In January 2008, amendments to the Criminal Code were adopted, and among other provisions, those for sexual abuse of children were also subject to changes.[30] Several new crimes were introduced and the prescribed punishments were elevated.

However, in 2008, the Macedonian media began to report more frequently on cases of sexual offences, especially acts of paedophilia. The narrative was that the number of such acts had increased, and especially that paedophilia, i.e. the sexual abuse of children, had become more frequent.[31] This was also visible in the public statements of many civil society organizations dealing with the rights and protection of children.[32]

As a result, after the January amendments, once again in 2008, the Ministry of Justice constituted a working group for preparing amendments to the Criminal Code in order to prescribe more severe punishments for sexual offences against children. By the end of the year, i.e. in November 2008, these amendments had been adopted.

The increase in the length of the prescribed imprisonment was not symbolic at all. Namely, for the basic form of the offence 'sexual assault of a child under the age of 14', an imprisonment of a minimum of four years was envisaged before amendments. But with the amendments, this minimum was raised to eight years. As a result, the perpetrators of the basic form of paedophilia that could be previously sentenced from four to fifteen years of imprisonment, after the amendments, could get from eight to fifteen years of imprisonment. For the aggravated form (if the victim is a special needs child or if the perpetrator is a relative), previously sentenced to a minimum of eight years, the minimum was raised to at least twelve years of imprisonment.[33]

The minimums were raised also for other sexual crimes involving children; for example, for the offence 'Pimping children and enabling sexual acts', the prescribed sentence of three months to five years was elevated to a minimum of eight years (and up to fifteen years at the time).[34] The incest with a child up to fourteen years was envisaged to be punishable with at least ten years (up to fifteen) of imprisonment.

After the amendments of November 2008, the media continued to inform the public on the increased number of paedophilia cases. In December 2008, BBC Macedonian published an article stating that, according to the Ministry of Interior Affairs, every week new cases of paedophilia had been registered.[35]

The Minister of Justice, at a press conference in 2009, announced a new proposal for amendments, additionally stating that the number of pronounced prison sentences for sexual abuse of children increased as a result of the Criminal Code novelties of 2008.[36] In 2009, once again amendments to the Criminal Code took place with interventions in the sexual offences provisions and provisions on other offences against children.[37] Thus, in less than two years, the Criminal Code was subject to interventions three times on the matters of the provisions on crimes against children (mostly crimes of a sexual nature). Some of the interventions were justified, but some prescribed sentences have raised so much, even going over those prescribed for intentional murder. For example, in cases of child neglect where the consequence is serious bodily injury or serious damage to the health of the child, or where the child, as a result of the neglect, has engaged in begging, prostitution or other forms of antisocial behaviour, the prescribed imprisonment has been raised from three months to five years, to at least ten years and up to fifteen years. The imprisonment of at least ten years, for comparison, is prescribed for the aggravated (most serious) forms of murder.

It still remained unanswered whether all these claims in the media and in the public discussions have been a reason for the so-called panic legislation or whether they were really based on specific relevant facts.

Official statistical data, however, suggests a different reality. For the purpose of this research, we have taken into consideration data from a period of ten years (the relevant years of 2008 and 2009 as well as the years preceding and following).

The numbers of reported, accused and convicted persons in the period 2003–12 are presented in Table 8.5 and Figure 8.1.

As can be observed, the number of reported sexual offences not only failed to increase during the period 2006–8 (prior to the legislative changes), but in fact showed a decline. Even the trend of convicted persons in the period 2006–8 was quite stable. A rise in the number of reported persons took place in 2009 (after these crimes had been quite present in the media and caused amendments to the Criminal Code twice in 2008), but the number of convictions in 2009 decreased by almost 30 per cent and continued its fall in 2010 by an additional 18 per cent. Even the gap between the reported and convicted in the period directly preceding the legislative amendments was not as big as it became after the CCM interventions.

The data presented in Table 8.6 and Figure 8.2 show that the sentencing policy of the courts in general did not change as a result of the legislative amendments.

Table 8.5 Total number of reported, accused and convicted adult perpetrators for sexual offences (2003–12)

	2003	**2004**	**2005**	**2006**	**2007**	**2008**	**2009**	**2010**	**2011**	**2012**
Total reported	126	148	107	109	92	86	123	109	83	109
Total accused	67	85	109	103	93	99	78	63	66	54
Total convicted	59	76	84	91	89	92	65	54	54	47

Source: State Statistical Office of the Republic of North Macedonia

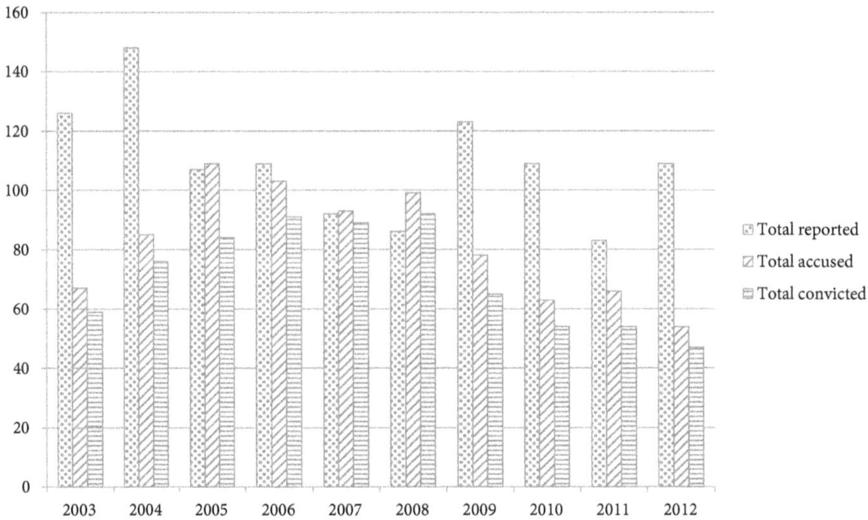

Figure 8.1 Reported, accused and convicted adult perpetrators for sexual offences (2003–12, trends).

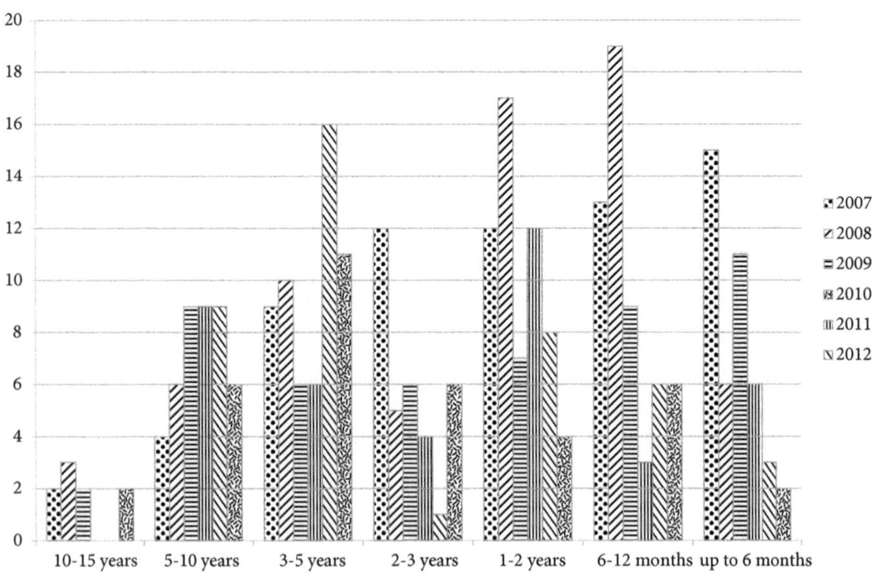

Figure 8.2 The imprisonment sentencing trends for sexual crimes (2007–12).

Table 8.6 Sentencing policy for the criminal offences against sexual freedom and sexual morals (2007–12)

	Convicted total	Total punishments	Life imprisonment	i. of 20 years	10–15 years	5–10 years	3–5 years	2–3 years	1–2 years	6–12 months	up to 6 months
2007	89	67	/	/	2	4	9	12	12	13	15
2008	92	66	/	/	3	6	10	5	17	19	6
2009	65	50	/	/	2	9	6	6	7	9	11
2010	54	40	/	/	/	9	6	4	12	3	6
2011	54	43	/	/	/	9	16	1	8	6	3
2012	47	37	/	/	2	6	11	6	4	6	2

Source: State Statistical Office of the Republic of North Macedonia

Given the fact that the number of convicts for sexual offences did not increase but in fact fell by almost 50 per cent from 2008 to 2012, we assume that the judges were not influenced by the public opinion and media coverage. But these data are about the sexual offences in general.

In addition, we will take into consideration the most relevant sexual crime in respect of paedophilia: sexual assault of a child under the age of fourteen.

Even after the legislative changes for prescribing more severe punishments, especially for the provision relevant for this crime, the reality did not end with higher numbers of imprisonment sentences of over ten years. An increase has been detected in the number of imprisonment sentences from five to ten years, with a sharp rise in 2009.

Taking into consideration the length of the sentences (Table 8.7 and Figure 8.3), one can assume that although paedophilia is a serious phenomenon, most of the cases might not consist of sexual intercourse with a child but most probably of other sexual acts that, when it comes to children, may constitute touching not only intimate body parts but even caressing the hair and the head of the child, if the perpetrator was driven by sexual instinct.

This example is one of the least explained, and in Macedonian criminal law science it is still discussed as not being the most adequate public policy response

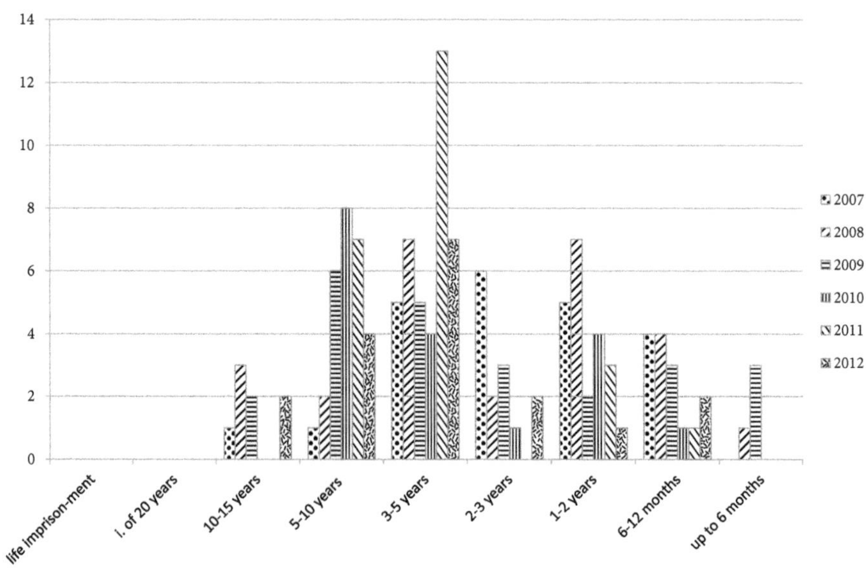

Figure 8.3 The imprisonment sentencing trends on sexual assault of a child under the age of fourteen (2007–12).

Table 8.7 Sentencing policy for the criminal offence sexual assault of a child under the age of fourteen (2007–12)

Year	Convicted, total	Punishments, total	life imprison-ment	i. of 20 years	10–15 years	5–10 years	3–5 years	2–3 years	1–2 years	6–12 months	up to 6 months
2007	30	25	/	/	1	1	5	6	5	4	/
2008	38	26	/	/	3	2	7	2	7	4	1
2009	26	24	/	/	2	6	5	3	2	3	3
2010	20	18	/	/	/	8	4	1	4	1	/
2011	26	24	/	/	/	7	13	/	3	1	/
2012	21	18	/	/	2	4	7	2	1	2	/

Source: State Statistical Office of the Republic of North Macedonia

to a public interest that, while not strongly fact-founded, was indisputably raised.

As a result, many actions against children, at least in the legislation, have been treated as more severe than murders, even though in the specific cases the legally protected value or good was not of the same level of importance.

Case No. 2: Traffic crimes and change of the sentencing policy of the courts

In 2020, the public interest in North Macedonia was directed to the problem of traffic misdemeanours and crimes. In view of the fact that whenever a traffic accident results in a bodily injury to a person or significant material damages, it constitutes a crime, the citizens and civil society turned their attention to the sentencing policy of the courts.

However, taking into consideration the available statistical data for ten years presented in Table 8.8 and graphically presented below the table (see Figure 8.4), one can notice that the number of reports declined continuously until 2019, when a sharp fall occurred, followed by a sharp rise from 2020 to 2021, and then again followed by a decline in the figures. Nevertheless, these sharp fluctuations from 2020 to 2023 have not been the case with respect to the numbers of accused and convicts.

Table 8.8 Total number of reported, accused and convicted adult perpetrators for crimes against traffic safety (2014–23)

	Reported	Accused	Convicted
2014	2849	1858	1708
2015	2710	1538	1432
2016	2679	1373	1322
2017	2628	1215	1165
2018	2573	1009	975
2019	2597	815	799
2020	2106	798	770
2021	2465	1098	1056
2022	3030	1204	1171
2023	2582	1300	1253

Source: State Statistical Office of the Republic of North Macedonia

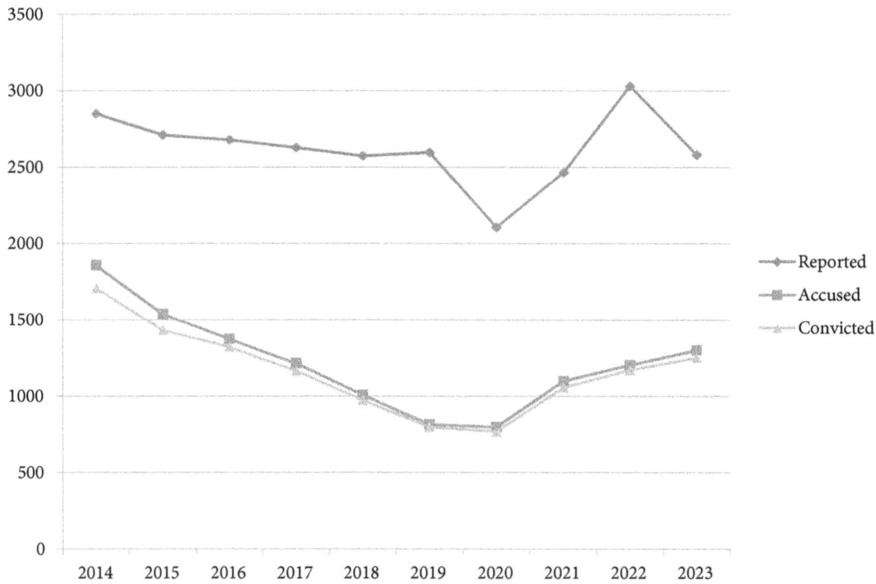

Figure 8.4 Traffic crimes perpetrators trends (2014–23).

As mentioned above, intensified reactions in public and media regarding traffic accidents with casualties arouse in North Macedonia in 2020.

According to the Coalition All for Fair Trials, in just a year the number of traffic accidents rose by about 50 per cent and about half of the perpetrators got suspended sentences or have been released.[38] NGOs are alarmed that the perpetrators usually have been getting suspended sentences, which did not serve the aim of general and special prevention.

Several protests of citizens took place in recent years as a result of young people's lives lost.[39] In a car accident, a young motorcycle rider lost his life; his pregnant wife was severely injured, and she lost the baby. The perpetrator ruthlessly violated the traffic rules and was found guilty but got a suspended sentence for imprisonment. Several protests took place due to this sentence of the court. Citizens were seeking real justice and responsibility.[40]

The media coverage and the reactions of the public seemed to have an influence on the sentencing policy of the judges. In the following table, we have presented the data from the MAKSTAT base.[41]

To conclude, there are changes in the sentencing policy. The judges previously tended to impose alternative measures to the percentage of almost up to 40 per cent, which was a really lenient sentencing policy; however, the trend changed

Table 8.9 Pronounced punishments and alternative measures for crimes against traffic safety and endangering traffic safety (2017–23)

	Total convicted persons	**Punishments – Total**	**Alternative measures – Total**	**Total convicted persons**	**Punishments – Total**	**Alternative measures – Total**
Year	Crimes against traffic safety	Crimes against traffic safety	Crimes against traffic safety	Endangering traffic safety	Endangering traffic safety	Endangering traffic safety
2017	1165	814 (69.8%)	351 (30.1%)	1159	809 (69.8%)	350 (30.2%)
2018	975	621 (63.7%)	354 (36.3%)	973	620 (63.7%)	353 (36.3%)
2019	799	493 (61.7%)	306 (38.3%)	783	484 (61.8%)	299 (38.2%)
2020	770	477 (61.9%)	293 (38%)	766	475 (62%)	291(38%)
2021	1056	748 (71%)	308 (29%)	1045	742 (71%)	303 (29%)
2022	1171	900 (77%)	271 (23%)	1162	894 (77%)	268 (23%)
2023	1253	972 (77.6%)	281 (22.4%)	1244	965 (77.6%)	279 (22.4%)

Source: State Statistical Office of the Republic of North Macedonia

from 2020 to 2023, and the proportion of pronounced punishments raised constantly from 2020 to 2023; namely, it raised from about 62 per cent in 2020 to 77.6 per cent in 2023, and the percentage of alternative measures dropped from 38 per cent in 2020 to 22.4 per cent in 2023 (see Table 8.9).

Table 8.10 Convicted adult perpetrators by types of criminal offences and applied main sentence – imprisonment and fine (2017–23)

		Total imprisonment	Total fine
2017	Crimes against traffic safety	71	676
	Endangering traffic safety	70	672
	Other crimes against traffic safety	1	4
2018	Crimes against traffic safety	52	515
	Endangering traffic safety	52	514
	Other crimes against traffic safety	-	1
2019	Crimes against traffic safety	45	400
	Endangering traffic safety	45	392
	Other crimes against traffic safety	-	8
2020	Crimes against traffic safety	31	417
	Endangering traffic safety	31	416
	Other crimes against traffic safety	-	1
2021	Crimes against traffic safety	50	642
	Endangering traffic safety	49	637
	Other crimes against traffic safety	1	5
2022	Crimes against traffic safety	48	785
	Endangering traffic safety	47	781
	Other crimes against traffic safety	1	4
2023	Crimes against traffic safety	43	834
	Endangering traffic safety	42	828
	Other crimes against traffic safety	1	6

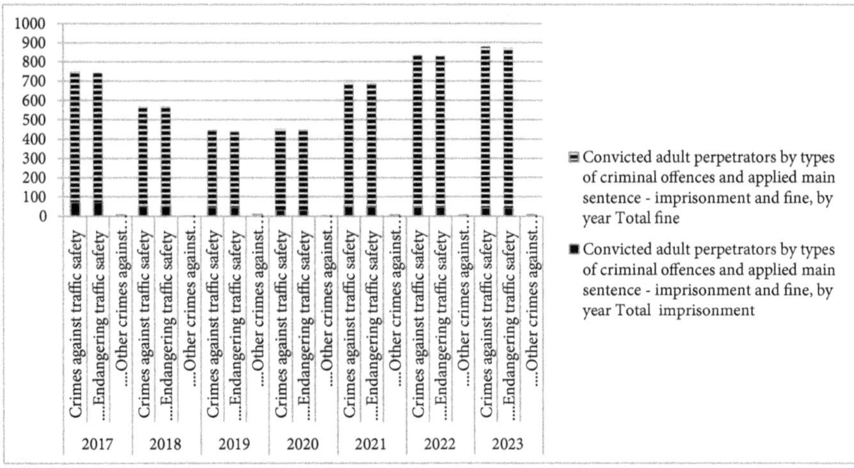

Figure 8.5 Imposed imprisonment and fine for traffic crimes (2017–23).

Table 8.11 Sentencing imprisonment policy of the courts for the criminal offence endangering traffic safety (2017–23)

	i. 10–15 years	i. 5–10 years	i. 3–5 years	i. 2–3 years	i. 1–2 years	i. 6–12 months	i.up to 6 months
2017	–	–	1	2	10	25	32
2018	–	–	–	5	9	11	27
2019	–	–	1	1	4	22	17
2020	–	2	1	3	2	11	11
2021	1	1	4	1	8	18	16
2022	1	3	6	3	12	6	16
2023	–	3	6	–	7	5	21

Regarding the punishments, the fine is still the dominant punishment for these crimes. A high 90–5 per cent of the imposed punishments for this type of crime are fines, and only up to 10 per cent are imprisonment sentences Figure 8.5.

Since the criminal offence 'Endangering traffic safety' is the dominant crime of the traffic crimes group (evident from Table 8.10), we will present data on the length of the imprisonment sentence pronounced for this specific crime.

The figure presents an insight into the rise of imprisonment sentences of longer duration in the last three years. The rise is mostly seen in the imprisonment

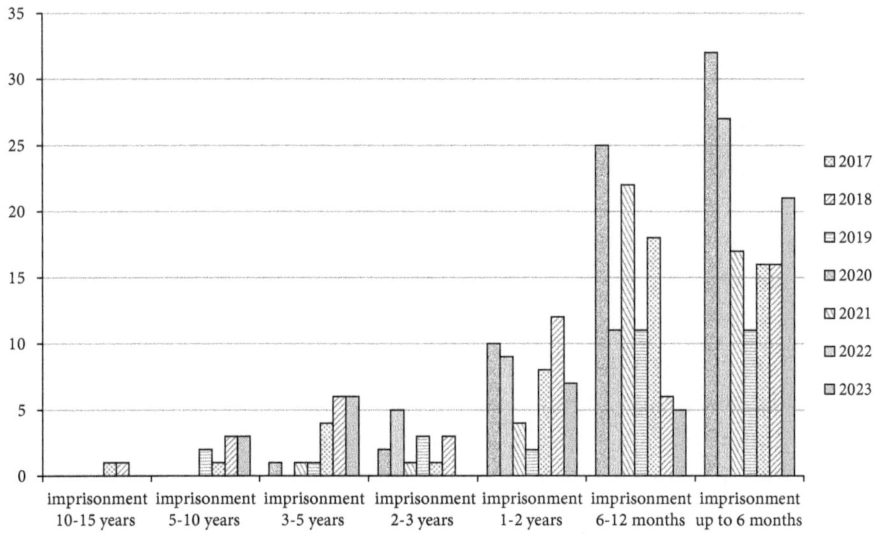

Figure 8.6 Imposed imprisonment sentence according to the length (2017–23).

ranges of five to ten years and three to five years, as well as in the pronounced sentences of more than ten years, which had not been present in the years before 2021 covered by the analysis (see Table 8.11 and Figure 8.6).

Taking into consideration the rise of the perpetrated serious traffic misdemeanours,[42] several of these actions have been 'elevated' to the level of a crime by the introduction of a new criminal offence in the CCM with the amendments of September 2023 – reckless motor vehicle driving.[43]

Conclusion

Public interest is a complex category that is related to the well-being of citizens and society as a whole, so values that are common must be preserved and protected by all and for all. The protection of citizens from criminal acts and the efficiency of the suppression of crime are two of the main goals of punishment, but also of every government.

Although preventing and fighting crime today represents a serious challenge that needs to be carefully planned in the area of public policies, which requires great knowledge and expertise, the general and lay public cannot be completely excluded from it, and their influence can be enormous, and often directional.

Indeed, the media often play a role in creating public opinion with the manner and intensity of reporting on certain events. This, in turn, causes reactions among the public and the civil sector, which then influences relevant creators of public policies to act in a certain manner. It is not excluded that sometimes the policymakers themselves have their own hidden influence on the media, and thus on the public, and consequently force reactions with which they justify their intentions and actions.

The two cases presented for the Republic of North Macedonia show that the public can have a great influence on legislation and penal policy. In this regard, the reaction of citizens to the mild sanctioning of perpetrators of traffic crimes (especially with serious consequences) seems to have led to harsher sentencing of perpetrators of such crimes, while in the case of acts of paedophilia in the distant 2008, it seems that the public and the media caused an avalanche of legal changes that did not have a significant impact on the sentencing policy.

It may be inferred that, in the eyes of the public, the severity of punishment – particularly the length of imprisonment – is not always the primary concern in cases involving grave offences. Rather, the emphasis lies on ensuring that offenders are held accountable and do not benefit from suspended sentences, which are often interpreted by the public as indicators of impunity and a lack of justice.

Notes

1 Institute for Communication Studies, Dictionary on Media Literacy, https://recnik.medium.edu.mk/termin/javen-interes/ accessed 30 December 2024.

2 Law on Prevention of Corruption and Conflict of Interests, Official Gazette of Republic of Macedonia, 12/2019, art. 8, para. 8.

3 Aleksandra Gruevska-Drakulevski, 'Criminal Policy of the Courts in the Republic of Macedonia in the Period 2007–2011' (2012) 18, 19 (1–2) *Macedonian Journal for Criminal Law and Criminology*, 157, 158; Aleksandra Gruevska, 'Judicial Determination of Sanction: From Theory to Practice – Comparative Review' (2005) 12 (1) *Macedonian Journal for Criminal Law and Criminology* 105, 107.

4 Law on Criminal Procedure, Official Gazette of the Republic of Macedonia 150/10, 100/12, 142/16, 198/18.

5 For example, the damaged party (victim) agrees with the conditional postponement of the criminal procedure, and the suspect is ready to act according to the

directions of the public prosecutor and to return the illegally obtained objects or to repair the damages etc. See art. 43 of the Law on Criminal Procedure.

6 For more details see art. 44 of the Law on Criminal Procedure.

7 Andrew von Hirsch and Andrew Ashworth (eds.), *Principled Sentencing: Readings on Theory and Policy* (Hart Publishing, Oxford and Portland, Oregon 1998) 24; Eugene McLaughlin and John Muncie (eds.), *The Sage Dictionary of Criminology* (Sage Publications, London 2001) 1, 186, 242.

8 Aleksandra Deanoska Trendafilova, 'Rehabilitated from the conviction or forgotten in the criminal records? (On the need to establish a new concept of rehabilitation of convicted persons in the Macedonian criminal legislation)' (2021) 28 (1) *Macedonian Journal of Criminal Law and Criminology* 5, 25.

9 Criminal Code of the Republic of Macedonia – CCM, Official Gazette of the Republic of Macedonia 37/96, 80/99, 4/02, 43/03, 19/04, 81/05, 60/06, 73/06, 7/08, 139/08, 114/09, 51/11, 135/11, 185/11, 142/12, 166/12, 55/13, 82/13, 14/14, 27/14, 28/14, 41/14, 115/14, 132/14, 160/14, 199/14, 196/15, 226/15, 97/17, 248/18 Official Gazette of the Republic of North Macedonia No. 36/23, 188/23.

10 Article 32 of the CCM.

11 Law on Execution of Sanctions, Official Gazette of the Republic of North Macedonia 99/19, 220/19, 236/22, 74/24.

12 Article 37 of the CCM.

13 Article 48 of the CCM.

14 Article 60 of the CCM.

15 Article 33 para. 1 of the CCM.

16 Article 48-a of the CCM.

17 Article 61 of the CCM.

18 Article 96-a of the CCM.

19 Article 96-b of the CCM: '1) prohibition to obtain a permit, license, concession, authorization or other right determined by separate law; 2) prohibition to participate in procedure for open calls, awarding public procurement agreements and agreements for public and private partnership; 3) prohibition to founding new legal entities; 4) prohibition to use subventions and other favourable loans; 5) prohibition to use the funds from the Budget of the Republic of Macedonia for financing political parties; 6) revoking of a permit, license, concession, authorization or other right determined by separate law; 7) temporary prohibition to perform certain activity; 8) permanent prohibition to perform certain activity and 9) termination of the legal entity'.

20 Article 97, Article 97-a, Article 98, Article 98-a.

21 For more, see: Nikola Tupanceski, Dzemali Saiti, Aleksandra Deanoska Trendafilova and Andrej Bozinovski, *Practical Application of the Law on the*

Determination of the Type of Sentence and the Determination of the Length of the Sentence – Legal Analysis (Association of Criminal law and Criminology and OSCE Mission to Skopje, Skopje 2017) 1, 18; Nikola Tupanceski and Aleksandra Deanoska Trendafilova, 'One Year of the Implementation of the Law on the Determination of the Type of Sentence and the Determination of the Length of the Sentence – Issues and Challenges' (2017) 24 (1) *Macedonian Journal of Criminal Law and Criminology* 1, 15; Aleksandra Gruevska-Drakulevski, 'Criminal Policy of the Courts in the Republic of Macedonia in the Period 2007–2011' (2012) 18, 19 (1–2) *Macedonian Journal for Criminal Law and Criminology* 157, 167.

22 See Kambovski, Vlado, *Criminal Law – general part* (UKIM Skopje 2011) 476–8.

23 See Article 1 of the Law on Amending the Law on Criminal Procedure, Official Gazette of the Republic of Macedonia 28/2014.

24 See in detail Aleksandra Gruevska Drakulevski, 'Criminal Policy of the Courts in the Republic of Macedonia in the Period 2007–2011' (2012) 18, 19 (1–2) *Macedonian Journal for Criminal Law and Criminology* 157.

25 Law on the determination of the type of sentence and the determination of the length of the sentence, Official Gazette of the Republic of Macedonia 199/2014.

26 See: Criminal Code of North Macedonia art. 39–43-a; Vlado Kambovski, *Criminal Law – general part* (UKIM Skopje 2011) 473–93; Gjorgji Marjanovic and Metodija Kanevchev, *Macedonian Criminal Law – general part* (Prosvetno delo 2010) 341–79; Jovan Proevski, *Criminal Code – Explanations, Comments, Case-Law* (Agency Academic 1998); Zoran Sulejmanov, *Criminal Law – General Part* (Grafohartija, 2001).

27 Imprisonment cannot be shorter than thirty days or longer than twenty years. For the crimes for which the law prescribes life imprisonment, long-lasting imprisonment of up to forty years may be imposed. If a sentence of twenty years of imprisonment is prescribed for a premeditated crime, a sentence of life imprisonment may be prescribed for severe forms of this crime. The sentence of life imprisonment may not be prescribed as the only main sentence. The sentence of life imprisonment may not be pronounced for an offender, who at the time the crime was committed, has not turned the age of twenty-one years. Imprisonment shall be pronounced with full years and months, and up to six months, also with full days. When imprisonment is prescribed for crimes without appointing a minimal measure, and when the maximum measure is no longer than three years, it is compulsory to also impose a fine besides the imprisonment. The imprisonment shall be served within facilities for serving punishment, specified by law. The convicted person may be released from serving imprisonment under the condition that until the expiration of the period for which the sentence was pronounced, he does not commit a new crime if he has corrected himself so that it is justifiably

expected for the offender to behave well in freedom and particularly that he would not commit crimes. During the evaluation of whether the convicted person shall be released on probation, one shall consider his conduct during the serving of the imprisonment, fulfilment of the assignments in line with his work ability, and other circumstances which show that the aim of the punishment has been achieved. The convicted person, having served half of the imprisonment, can be released on probation. As an exception, a convicted person who has served one-third of an imprisonment may also be released on probation, under the conditions referred to in paragraph 1, and if special circumstances concerning the personality of the convicted person evidently show that the aim of the sentence has been achieved. The convicted person sentenced to life imprisonment cannot be released on probation before he serves at least twenty-five years of the imprisonment. See Articles 35–37 of the CCM.
The fine shall be imposed as daily fines, whereas the number of the daily fines may not be less than 5 or more than 360 daily fines. The court shall specify the number of daily fines in accordance with the general rules for specifying the fine. The court shall determine the level of the daily fine considering the material and personal circumstances of the offender, starting, as a rule, from the net daily income the offender makes or might make, as well as the family and other obligations of the offender and his property at the time of adopting the court decision. The lowest amount of a daily fine shall be one euro in Denar counter-value, and the highest amount shall be euro 5.000 in Denar counter-value. See Articles 38–38-a of the CCM.

28 Jovan Proevski, *Criminal Code – Explanations, Comments, Case-Law* (Agency Academic, Skopje 1998) 137.

29 For more details see: Aleksandra Gruevska-Drakulevski, *Imprisonment and Recidivism* (Studiorum, Skopje 2016) 186.

30 Law on Amendments of the Criminal Code, Official Gazette of the Republic of North Macedonia 7/2008, art. 5–11.

31 See details in: Nikola Tupancheski, Gordana Lazhetikj, Aleksandra Gruevska Drakulevski and Aleksandra Deanoska Trendafilova 'Sexual Offences in the Republic of North Macedonia', in Rahime Erbaş (ed.) *Global Problems in Sexual Offenses* (Rowmann & Littlefield 2022) 45.

32 In the 'Reaction on the frequent cases of pedophilia in Macedonia', published by the NGO Megjasi in 2008, they stated, 'Until when will judges give pedophiles the mildest sentences? Does the most terrible thing have to happen, for a pedophile to be sentenced to the harshest sentence? How much are our children a priority for the institutions of the system? Convictions will not yield results as long as pedophiles are given minimum sentences!' http://www.childrensembassy.org.

mk/2008-ns_article-reakcija-po-povod-zacestenite-slucai-na-pedofilija-vo-makedonija.nspx accessed 30 December 2024.

33 See: Law on Amendments of the Criminal Code, Official Gazette of the Republic of Macedonia 139/2008, art. 3.

34 Article 6 of the Law on Amendments to the Criminal Code No. 139/2008.

35 BBC Macedonian, Increased paedophilia in Macedonia https://www.bbc.co.uk/macedonian/news/story/2008/12/081212_mac_paedophils.shtml accessed 30 December 2024.

36 Press conference of Minister Manevski: Number of prison sentences for child sexual abuse increased https://www.pravda.gov.mk/vest/315 Macedonia Information Agency (MIA), – In Macedonia, forty-four prison sentences were pronounced in connection with criminal acts of sexual abuse of children and paedophilia from July 2008 to July 2009. This increase in the number of prison sentences pronounced is primarily due to the application of a stricter sentencing policy envisaged by the amendments to the Criminal Code from November 2008. – During this period, prison sentences of over eight years were pronounced on eleven people, prison sentences of three to eight years were pronounced on seven people, prison sentences of one to three years were pronounced on sixteen people, prison sentences of up to one year were pronounced on ten people, and a suspended sentence was pronounced on three people, informed the Minister of Justice Mihajlo Manevski at today's press conference. He reminded that in the previous three years, five prison sentences of over eight years and twenty-two suspended sentences were pronounced for sexual abuse of children and paedophilia. – In this period, as in the previous one, the most common crime is 'sexual assault on a minor under 14 years of age'. The age of the perpetrators is from thirty to fifty-five years, and previously it ranged from twenty-one to seventy-eight years, said Manevski. The age of the victims, as the minister added, is from ten to fourteen years, while in the previous period a victim was identified as being seven years old. Manevski pointed out that the duration of proceedings before the basic courts has also been significantly reduced. – A good part of the cases or 24 per cent are completed within one to three months before the basic courts, while previously the proceedings before the first instance courts lasted up to two years and six months, added the Minister of Justice. Of the prison sentences imposed, 25 per cent are over eight years, of which one sentence is fifteen years, two are thirteen years, six are ten years and two are nine years. In the penal and correctional institutions in Macedonia, 150 people are currently serving prison sentences for sexual abuse of children and paedophilia. Manevski added that the Draft Law on Amendments to the Criminal Code, which is currently in parliamentary procedure, proposes imposing a ban on performing a profession, activity or duty when a prison sentence of at least six months has been imposed, if the crime was committed by a teacher, educator, doctor or other

person abusing their position. The proposed amendments provide for the liability of legal entities for the crime of 'mediation in prostitution'. – Coercion of a minor to commit the crime is punishable by imprisonment for three to eight years, or at least four if it concerns a minor who has not reached the age of fourteen, added Manevski. The minister pointed out that with the proposed amendments for the production and distribution of child pornography through a computer system, the prison sentence of three to five years is increased to at least five years, and for the purchase or possession, the sentence of six months to three years in prison is increased to five to eight years in prison. The proposed amendments to the Criminal Code introduce a new criminal offense of 'enticing a minor under the age of 14 to engage in sexual intercourse or other sexual activity', which is punishable by a prison sentence of one to five years. accessed 30 December 2024.

37 Law on amendments of the Criminal Code No. 114/2009.

38 Lider 'Increased number of traffic accidents in a period of one year' https://lider.mk/zgolemen-brojot-na-soobrakjajni-nezgodi-vo-period-od-edna-godina/ accessed 30 December 2024.

39 MIA, 'Peaceful protest at City Mall for the deceased Viktoria Nikolova' https://kanal5.com.mk/miren-protest-kaj-siti-mol-za-zaginata-vitorija-nikolova/a514117 accessed 30 December 2024.

40 4NEWS 'Justice for Goce and Natasha: motorcycle protests in Skopje' https://4news.mk/pravda-za-gotse-i-natasha-protest-so-motori-vo-skopje accessed 30 December 2024.

41 The data in this new base (MAKSTAT) in a more detailed manner are available for the period 2017–23.

42 Source: Ministry of Interior, Analysis, Traffic, 2010–2023 https://mvr.gov.mk/analiza/soobrakjaj/72 accessed 30 December 2024.

43 Article 297-a of the CCM.

References

BBC Macedonian, 'Increased Paedophilia in Macedonia' https://www.bbc.co.uk/macedonian/news/story/2008/12/081212_mac_paedophils.shtml accessed 30 December 2024.

Criminal Code of the Republic of Macedonia – CCM, Official Gazette of the Republic of Macedonia 37/96, 80/99, 4/02, 43/03, 19/04, 81/05, 60/06, 73/06, 7/08, 139/08, 114/09, 51/11, 135/11, 185/11, 142/12, 166/12, 55/13, 82/13, 14/14, 27/14, 28/14, 41/14, 115/14, 132/14, 160/14, 199/14, 196/15, 226/15, 97/17, 248/18 and Official Gazette of the Republic of North Macedonia No. 36/23, 188/23.

Deanoska TA, 'Rehabilitated from the Conviction or Forgotten in the Criminal Records? (On the Need to Establish a New Concept of Rehabilitation of Convicted Persons in the Macedonian Criminal Legislation)' (2021) 28 (1–2) *Macedonian Journal of Criminal Law and Criminology* 8–37.

Gruevska-Drakulevski A, 'Criminal Policy of the Courts in the Republic of Macedonia in the Period 2007–2011' (2012) 18, 19 (1–2) *Macedonian Journal for Criminal Law and Criminology* 157.

Gruevska-Drakulevski A, *Imprisonment and Recidivism* (Studiorum 2016).

Hirsch von Andrew and Ashworth Andrew (eds.), *Principled Sentencing: Readings on Theory and Policy* (Hart Publishing, Oxford and Portland 1998).

Institute for Communication Studies, Dictionary on Media Literacy https://recnik.medium.edu.mk/termin/javen-interes/ accessed 30 December 2024.

Kambovski V, *Criminal Law - General Part* (UKIM Skopje 2011).

Law on Amending the Law on Criminal Procedure, Official Gazette of the Republic of Macedonia 28/2014.

Law on Amendments of the Criminal Code, Official Gazette of Republic of Macedonia 139/2008.

Law on Criminal Procedure, Official Gazette of the Republic of Macedonia 150/10, 100/12, 142/16, 198/18.

Law on the Determination of the Type of Sentence and the Determination of the Length of the Sentence, Official Gazette of the Republic of Macedonia 199/2014.

Law on Execution of Sanctions, Official Gazette of the Republic of North Macedonia 99/19, 220/19, 236/22, 74/24.

Law on Prevention of Corruption and Conflict of interests, Official Gazette of Republic of Macedonia 12/2019. Law on Amendments of the Criminal Code, Official Gazette of Republic of North Macedonia 7/2008.

Lider, 'Increased Number of Traffic Accidents in a Period of One Year' https://lider.mk/zgolemen-brojot-na-soobrakjajni-nezgodi-vo-period-od-edna-godina/ accessed 30 December 2024.

Macedonia Information Agency (MIA), Ministry of Justice, Press conference of Minister Manevski: Number of prison sentences for child sexual abuse increased https://www.pravda.gov.mk/vest/315 accessed 30 December 2024.

Marjanovic G and Kanevchev M, *Macedonian Criminal Law - General Part* (Prosvetno delo 2010).

McLaughlin E and Muncie J (eds), *The Sage Dictionary of Criminology* (Sage Publications 2001).

MIA, 'Peaceful Protest at City Mall for the Deceased Viktoria Nikolova' https://kanal5.com.mk/miren-protest-kaj-siti-mol-za-zaginata-vitorija-nikolova/a514117 accessed 30 December 2024.

Ministry of Interior, Analysis, Traffic, 2010–2023 https://mvr.gov.mk/analiza/soobrakjaj/72, accessed 30 December 2024.

4News, Justice accessed 30 December 2024.

NGO Megjashi, 'Reaction on the Frequent Cases of Pedophilia in Macedonia' http://www.childrensembassy.org.mk/2008-ns_article-reakcija-po-povod-zacestenite-slucai-na-pedofilija-vo-makedonija.nspx accessed 30 December 2024.

Proevski J, *Criminal Code - Explanations, Comments, Case-Law* (Agency Academic 1998).

Sulejmanov Z, *Criminal Law - General Part* (Grafohartija 2001).

Tupanceski N and Deanoska TA, 'One Year of the Implementation of the Law on the Determination of the Type of Sentence and the Determination of the Length of the Sentence - Issues and Challenges' (2017) 24 (1) *Macedonian Journal of Criminal Law and Criminology* 57–74.

Tupanceski N, Saiti D, Deanoska TA and Bozinovski A, *Practical Application of the Law on the Determination of the Type of Sentence and the Determination of the Length of the Sentence – Legal Analysis* (Association of Criminal Law and Criminology and OSCE Mission to Skopje, Skopje 2017).

9

Public interest at the intersection of criminal law and constitutional oversight in Ukraine

Larysa Zhdankina

Introduction

Ukraine's national interests and priorities determine the vector of formulation of its strategic tasks and foreign policy goals, which can undoubtedly be considered the development of Ukraine as an independent sovereign state, preserving national values and cultural identity, and ensuring economic security and territorial integrity. The security, well-being and social and cultural progress of Ukraine and Ukrainians depend on how the public interest and aspirations of the Ukrainian people are realized.[1]

The category of public/state/social interest in the understanding of the Ukrainian legislator is an indefinite and, therefore, evaluative concept that covers an extensive and unclear range of legal and moral interests. Through specific aspirations of individual participants in relations, these interests are embodied through a particular set of (1) private interests or (2) important needs for many individuals and legal entities. Ukraine guarantees this by the legally established competence.

The 'state interest' concept is not subject to an unambiguous qualification (definition). Therefore, such interests should be subject to autonomous assessment by the court in each criminal case. As a result, within the scope of its judicial discretion, the court shall check whether the decision is consistent (non-contradictory) with the principles of national security, public (state) interest and protection of human rights. The main document of Ukrainian legislation does not precisely determine 'public interest', but we find the word 'interest' in the Constitution of Ukraine[2] (hereinafter also Fundamental Law).

Some of the provisions on interest relate to the guarantee of the right to freedom of thought and speech,[3] freedom of ideology and religion,[4] satisfaction of political, economic, social, cultural and other interests by forming political parties,[5] the right to strike,[6] use of property[7] and protection of intellectual property.[8] The constitutional provisions also include general regulations on the judiciary and safeguarding the interests of individuals,[9] judges[10] and territorial communities.[11] However, the legislator's main idea was to emphasize the importance of public interests in the criminal hearings by understanding national interests.

First of all, it is worth noting that Article 18(1) of the Constitution of Ukraine stipulates that Ukraine's foreign policy activity is aimed at ensuring its national interests and security by maintaining peaceful and mutually beneficial cooperation with members of the international community, by the generally recognized principles and norms of international law. In addition, while guaranteeing the inviolability of personal and family life,[12] the right to form political parties, public organizations and participation in trade unions,[13] and the right to peaceful assembly,[14] the legislator notes that the primary condition is the observance of public interests and national security interests.

Moreover, it should be emphasized that the Constitution of Ukraine obliges MPs and the newly appointed President of Ukraine to promise allegiance to the interests of all compatriots.[15] The Parliament of Ukraine, in turn, is empowered to form temporary investigative commissions to conduct investigations into matters of public interest,[16] and the Prosecutor's Office of Ukraine represents the state's interests in court.[17] Explicit constitutional provisions demonstrate the crucial importance of the public interest for the life of the state and society.

What is the public interest in the context of the Constitution of Ukraine, and how does this concept relate to criminal law? How does constitutional control ensure the public interest is respected in state-building and court actions? How do criminal proceedings in Ukraine consider the public interest, and is there a balance between the protection of public interests and the rights of participants in the process? These questions will allow us to explore the essence of the legislative understanding of the concepts of 'public interest', 'national security interests', 'state interests' and 'social interest' to compare them with each other and to identify the key aspects of their application for proper state-building and human rights protection, that are the main areas of this chapter and the objectives of this paper.

Public interest through an understanding of national security

The fundamentals of national security and defence of Ukraine, as well as goals and basic principles of state policy that guarantee the protection of society and every citizen from threats, are established by the Law of Ukraine On National Security of Ukraine[18] (hereinafter Law No 2469-VIII).

While the national security of Ukraine is the protection of state sovereignty, territorial integrity, democratic constitutional order and other national interests of Ukraine from actual and potential threats, the national interests of Ukraine are vital interests of a person, society and the state, the realization of which ensures state sovereignty of Ukraine, its progressive democratic development and its people's safe living conditions and well-being.[19] By providing separate definitions for these concepts, the legislator also emphasizes that national security should contribute to the interests of the individual, society and the state. Phenomena, trends and factors that make it impossible or difficult to realize national interests and preserve the national values of Ukraine pose a threat to the national security of Ukraine.[20] Here, the foundations are laid, covered by the national security interest.

To prevent these reflections from becoming too rhetorical and declarative, it is necessary to understand clearly what national security guarantees. The fundamental national interests of Ukraine[21] are:

1. State sovereignty and territorial integrity, democratic constitutional order and non-interference in the internal affairs of Ukraine;
2. Sustainable development of the national economy, civil society and the state to ensure an increase in the standard of living and quality of life;
3. Ukraine's integration into the European political, economic, security and legal space, membership in the European Union and the North Atlantic Treaty Organization, and development of equal and mutually beneficial relations with other states.

If we set a goal to determine what these theses mean for a particular person within the framework of guaranteeing national security, then, firstly, they most likely form the basis for personal security, social protection and quality development of each citizen, as they ensure security, stability and protection from external threats, which allow, for example, citizens to participate in the political life of the country through elections, access to justice, freedom of speech and religion, as well as guarantee the preservation of national values and avoid destabilization. Secondly, it means improving living standards through access to quality services, jobs, income growth and social guarantees. As a result, fundamental human rights include active participation in decision-making, transparency in the activities of state institutions and control over the authorities. Third, access to European standards of living, education, healthcare, justice, the labour market and membership in security organizations strengthens the guarantees of protection of every person's life.

To realize national interests, the state policy of Ukraine in the areas of national security and defence is aimed at protecting: (1) a person and a citizen – their life and dignity, constitutional rights and freedoms, and safe living conditions; (2) society – its democratic values, welfare and conditions for sustainable development; (3) the state – its constitutional order, sovereignty, territorial integrity and inviolability; (4) territory and the environment – from emergencies.[22]

The analysis of this provision illustrates that protecting human life, dignity, and constitutional rights is a priority of state policy in the field of national security and a cornerstone of understanding the state's public interest. Simultaneously, while the state protects its public interest (the constitutional order, sovereignty and territorial integrity), human rights and freedoms, creating conditions for the harmonious development of the individual, society and the environment, remains the central value. Consequently, national interests are shaped through the prism of human dignity, which becomes the basis for determining the priorities of Ukraine's national security, defence and sustainable development.

By scanning the activities of the prosecutor's office through the prism of Ukraine's national security framework, we can admit a powerful connection between public interest prosecutions and fundamental societal values. Fulfilling their duties, they directly affect victims' rights and public safety by determining which threats to state sovereignty, territorial integrity and constitutional order receive priority attention from the justice. What makes this approach distinctive is how the Ukrainian legal system accommodates human dignity at the centre of its national security concept, explicitly asserting that the protection of human life, dignity and constitutional rights is a priority of state policy in national security.

This human-centred approach flows from the constitutional provisions[23] and paves the bridges to alternative sanctions[24] and restorative justice.[25] Since national interests are defined as helping to maintain legally protected interests of an individual, society and the state, prosecutors have the instruments for pursuing justice that genuinely restore harm rather than merely punish offenders.[26] Furthermore, as the law emphasizes the necessity of creating conditions for sustainable development and improving living standards through access to quality services, the role of prosecutor events should ultimately augment social welfare rather than simply securing convictions.

Similarly, media and public opinion are influential because national security prosecutions inherently involve high-stakes issues that generate significant public attention. When cases relate to state sovereignty or constitutional order, they attract intense scrutiny. However, by recognizing that national security contributes to the interests of the individual, society and state, the law provides prosecutors with a standard against which public pressure can be evaluated. This helps maintain the independence of prosecutors while acknowledging that prosecutors ultimately serve the public, whose safety and rights they are charged with protecting.

State interests and the role of the prosecutor's office

The role of the prosecutor's office in representing the state's interests in court is essential to protecting Ukraine's national interests. The activities of the prosecutor's office in this area are regulated in Ukraine both at the level of the Constitution of Ukraine and at the level of a special law.

One of the most significant consequences of the June 2016 constitutional reform[27] on the organization of state power in Ukraine is that the Prosecutor's Office has lost its separate status in the state power structure. Instead, according to the new Ukrainian constitutional legal order, the prosecutor's office as an institution performing the function of criminal prosecution is structurally integrated into the general system of justice.

According to Article 129(2)(4) of the Constitution of Ukraine, the basic principle of judicial proceedings is the prosecutor's support of public prosecution in court. This provision is also duplicated in the first paragraph of Article 131–1 of the Fundamental Law, which declares that a public prosecutor's office in Ukraine maintains prosecution in court. This function of the prosecutor's office is significant because the legislator declares it through the principles of judicial proceedings and, therefore, through the administration of justice with all its principles. In this regard, the Venice Commission noted: 'It is evident that a system where both prosecutor and judge act to the highest standards of integrity and impartiality presents a greater protection for human rights than a system which relies on the judge alone'.[28]

However, it is not only the structural provision of Article 131–1 of the Constitution of Ukraine that defines the new place of the prosecutor's office in the system of state power of Ukraine. The fact that the prosecutor's office belongs to the Ukrainian justice system is also indirectly derived from the provision of the Constitution of Ukraine,[29] according to which in the justice system bodies and institutions are established and operate following the law, which deals with equivalent activities about judges and prosecutors – their selection, professional training, evaluation and consideration of cases of their disciplinary responsibility.[30]

The peculiarities of the functioning of the prosecutor's office are regulated by the special law No 1697-VII 'On the Prosecutor's Office'[31] (hereinafter Law No 1697-VII), which defines the legal basis for the organization and activities of the prosecutor's office of Ukraine, the status of prosecutors, the procedure for exercising prosecutorial self-government, as well as the system of the prosecutor's office of Ukraine.[32] The prosecutor's office of Ukraine constitutes a unified system that, in the manner prescribed by this Law, performs the functions established by the Constitution of Ukraine to protect human rights and freedoms, as well as the general interests of society and the state.[33]

Whereas the prosecutor's office supports the state[34] prosecution in court, a key question is whether 'state' or 'public' interests prosecutors do support in exercising their primary function. The Constitution of Ukraine, as amended by Law No. 1401-VIII, was supplemented with Article 131–1(1)(3), which stipulates that the prosecutor's office shall represent the state's interests in court only in exceptional cases and in accordance with the procedure established by law. Additionally, Article 2(2)(1) of Law No 1697-VII provides that the function of the prosecutor's office is to represent the interests of a citizen or the state in court in cases determined by this Law and Chapter 12 of Section III of the Civil Procedure Code of Ukraine.[35] These roles of the prosecutor concern the public interest, but with particular limits on interfering in private and business activities, allowing it only in exceptional cases.

Following this law, a prosecutor may represent the public or state interest in court only if (1) there is a violation or threat to those interests, and if (2) no competent authority is properly protecting them or such authority is absent. The prosecutor must prove the existence of grounds for intervention, and representation is permitted only after the court has confirmed these grounds. The main purpose is to ensure compliance with the principles of proportionality and legal certainty. Prosecutors are also restricted from intervening in spheres such as electoral processes, the activities of Parliament, media operations and political parties to safeguard democratic values. Furthermore, when maintaining public prosecution in court, the prosecutor acts in accordance with the Criminal Procedure Code of Ukraine,[36] exercising procedural rights and obligations to guarantee that prosecution serves the public interest and respects the rights of all participants.[37]

This regulation manifests a balanced approach to protecting the public interest, which involves ensuring parties' rights to legal relations and avoiding abuse of power by public authorities. At the same time, the effectiveness of this model raises several questions about its practical application and impact on the implementation of constitutional principles, including the rule of law, proportionality and protection of the rights of legal entities and individuals.

The problem lies in the necessity of ensuring an effective mechanism for representing the state's interests in court, which would comply with the principles of legal certainty, proportionality and balance between the protection of state interests and the rights of participants in legal relations. Several scholars have raised concerns similar to those discussed regarding the prosecutor's role in protecting the public interest while balancing constitutional principles. For example, Bibikova (2024) discusses how prosecutorial interventions must be carefully regulated to avoid undermining individual rights and the rule of law. Mallinder (2020) highlights that during transitional periods, this regulation is as crucial as essential.[38]

Specifically for Ukraine, Tamozhnia (2020) notes that while reforms have aimed to enhance prosecutorial independence and protect public interest, in practice, challenges remain in ensuring consistency with legal certainty and proportionality.[39] Turlova (2018) has emphasized that prosecutors' broad powers in representing state interests must be balanced against the need to avoid arbitrary interference in private and business activities, warning of risks to legal certainty and fair trial rights. She also stressed the necessity to unify the approach to understanding the concept of 'state interests'.[40] Thus, the concerns raised are reflected in broader academic discourse, emphasizing the ongoing tension between state interest protection and the safeguarding of fundamental rights.

How can we avoid arbitrary interference of the prosecutor's office, ensure proper justification of its actions and simultaneously guarantee the effectiveness of institutional protection of the state interest? What is the 'public interest' or 'interest of the state' in interpreting the prosecution service's functions? What criteria should be considered when determining 'exceptional cases' for prosecutorial intervention?

These issues require in-depth analysis, as they relate not only to law enforcement practice but also to the basic principles of the constitutional order of Ukraine. For this part of the chapter, we will focus on the following duties of the prosecutor's office: 1) maintaining public prosecution in court and 2) representing the interests of a citizen or the state in court.

Maintaining public prosecution in court

This function of the prosecution service is significant because of its increased responsibility, complexity and importance for the entire criminal process. As depicted above, the Constitution of Ukraine and Law No. 1697-VII use somewhat different terms to describe the prosecutor's role. For the public interest analysis in this paper, it is worth examining whether this is the same concept or whether the constitutional provision imposes increased responsibility on the prosecution service.

The prosecutor maintains the public prosecution in court proceedings concerning criminal offences, exercising the rights and performing the duties[41] provided by the Criminal Procedure Code of Ukraine[42] (hereinafter CPC of Ukraine).

Public prosecution is the prosecutor's procedural activity, which consists of bringing the charge before the court to ensure the criminal liability of the person who committed the criminal offence.[43] The legislator defines the accusation as an allegation that a particular person has committed an act under the law of Ukraine on criminal liability, brought by the procedure established by the law.[44]

The Order of the Prosecutor General No. 489 'On Approval of the Prosecution Service Development Strategy for 2021–2023' of 16 October 2020 declares the main visions, missions and values of the prosecution service, among which the priorities are ensuring a high level of quality and efficiency in the implementation of the constitutional functions of the prosecutor's office; effective coordination of activities in the field of combating crime and the functioning of the criminal justice system in general; development of professional competences of prosecutors; increasing the level of openness and public trust in the prosecution service; ethics, integrity of prosecutors and disciplinary responsibility; ensuring the independence of prosecutors and prosecutorial self-government, social security of prosecutors.[45]

A comprehensive analysis of the criminal procedural legislation of Ukraine shows that the essence of prosecution is the way to identify a person guilty of a criminal offence and, in addition, to prove and support the charges brought against him/her in court, which is implemented in stages and depending on the implementation of their activities by the participants in the criminal process. Given that the prosecutor's office is a state body, there is an opinion that the concept of 'state prosecution' is a form of 'public prosecution' and does not fully disclose the essence of the prosecution.[46]

The Supreme Court in its 2019 Decision noted that the terminological conflict in terms of the constitutional, legal and sectoral definition of the prosecution function could be explained by harmonizing the constitutional and legal regulation of the functioning of the prosecution authorities with the relevant international standards. Performing their duties, prosecutors must protect the public interest, act objectively, take due account of the situation of the suspect and the victim and pay attention to all circumstances relevant to the case, regardless of whether they are favourable or unfavourable to the suspect. Therefore, according to the Supreme Court, the state interests, considering the concept of the general interest, human rights and freedoms, are identical to the public interest.[47]

The function of supporting state prosecution has gradually transformed into the function of supporting public prosecution. The activities of the prosecution authorities are open and aimed at achieving increased public confidence in the prosecution authorities. This role is a public one and means that its implementation obliges the prosecutor to adhere to the principles of legality, fairness and objectivity.[48] According to the Committee of Ministers of the Council of Europe, 'public prosecutors' are a public authority that acts on behalf of society and in the public interest. They ensure law enforcement when a breach of the law results in criminal punishment, taking into account at the same time the human rights and the necessary efficiency of the criminal justice system at the same time.[49]

Representing the interests of a citizen or the state in court

In 2014, Law No. 1697-VII significantly changed the prosecutor's powers, including representing the state's interests or a person in court. The function of the prosecutor's office regarding general supervision of compliance with and application of laws was abolished. This was previously considered a vestige of the Soviet system and did not meet European standards. The specification of the prosecutor's powers regarding the representation of the interests of the state in court, and their limitation to an exhaustive list of grounds, led to compliance with the principles of legal certainty and proportionality.[50] Simultaneously, practice so far shows that the prosecutor's office wishes to retain the powers of supervision and control and continues to try to 'interfere' in the activities of local self-government under false pretences.

The prosecutor's representation of the state in court consists of performing procedural and other actions to protect the state's interests in cases, in the manner prescribed by law.[51] The prosecutor shall represent the legitimate interests of the state in court in case of violation or threat of a breach of interests of the state if (1) these interests are not protected or (2) are improperly protected by a state authority, local self-government body or other subjects of power, whose competence includes the relevant powers, as well as (3) in the absence of such a body. The prosecutor must justify the existence of grounds for representation in court. The prosecutor shall represent the interests of a citizen or the state in court only after the court confirms the grounds for representation. The prosecutor must notify the citizen and his/her legal representative or the relevant authority before applying to the court. If the court confirms the grounds for representation, the prosecutor shall use the procedural powers of the respective party to the proceedings. A citizen may challenge the grounds for representation, their legal representative or an authority.[52] If the signs of an administrative or criminal offence are established, the prosecutor must take the law's actions to initiate the relevant proceedings.

A logical interpretation of these legislative provisions in systemic connection with the provisions of Article 53 of the CPC of Ukraine[53] allows us to conclude that the prosecutor represents the legitimate interests of the state in court in case of violation or threat of a breach of the state's interests in two cases: 1) if the protection of these interests is not carried out or is improperly carried out by a public authority, local self-government body or another subject of power, whose competence includes the authority to carry out such protection in disputed legal relations; 2) if there is no public authority, local self-government body or another subject of power, whose competence includes the authority to protect the legitimate interests of the state in disputed legal relations.[54] Consequently, the prosecutor may only represent the interests of the state in court when those interests are violated or threatened to be violated. The concept of 'state interest' is crucial for applying this provision.

In 2014, the Ukrainian prosecution service endured a substantial transformation, which reflects a conceptual evolution aimed at aligning prosecutorial functions with international standards and increasing public confidence in the prosecution authorities. In essence, when determining whether a case should be prosecuted in the public interest prosecutors follow key criteria: (1) they operate within a framework identified by the Constitution of Ukraine and Law No. 1697-VII, with their actions constrained by the Criminal Procedure Code; (2) they may intervene when state interests are not protected or are improperly protected by other state authorities, or when no relevant authority exists; (3) prosecutors must act accurately taking into account the situation of the suspect and the victim and pay attention to all circumstances relevant to the case; (4) prosecutors must impartially consider all circumstances regardless of whether they are favourable or unfavourable to the suspect; (5) they should safeguard the wider public interest, including human rights and freedoms as an element of the public interest; (6) prosecutors are obliged to justify the existence of grounds for representation in court.

In the face of persistent institutional resistance to new limitations on prosecutorial authority, judicial parameters define how prosecutors can operate. Firstly, they can only use the procedural powers of the respective party to the proceedings after confirmation by the court. This results in guaranteeing the balance between prosecutorial discretion and judicial oversight of prosecutors. Secondly, to ensure transparency, prosecutors must inform the citizen and his/her legal representative or the relevant authority before applying to the court. However, to keep an equipoise to prosecutorial authority, individuals have a right to challenge the grounds for representation. For example, victims, according to the Ukrainian legal formula, have the right to apply to the court with a request to review the prosecutor's decision to close or refuse to initiate criminal proceedings. According to Article 303 of the CPC of Ukraine, such decisions, actions and omissions of the prosecutor may be challenged. This mechanism serves as an important guarantee. The legislation establishes a ten-day deadline[55] for such an appeal, which ensures a speedy response to violations of procedural law. This regulation, moreover, allows victims to challenge decisions to refuse to initiate criminal prosecution, which, in their opinion, undermine their right to access to justice or violate public interests. In practice, this is a kind of balancing force, in that the prosecutor's discretion remains a subject of legal responsibility and corresponds to the broader principle of fairness in criminal proceedings. Finally, the prosecutor's representation is circumscribed to specific scenarios where state interests are violated or threatened to be violated, which helps to prevent overly broad intervention.

Public interest through the constitutional oversight

The Constitutional Court of Ukraine (hereinafter CCU) is the only body of constitutional jurisdiction of Ukraine, which operates based on the Constitution of Ukraine[56] and the Law of Ukraine 'On the Constitutional Court of Ukraine'[57] 13 July 2017 No 2136-VIII (hereinafter CCU Law). The CCU, along with other constitutional control functions, provides an official interpretation of the Constitution of Ukraine and binding legal opinions, as the CCU's decisions are final and cannot be appealed.[58] Exploring the terminology of the state interest, the CCU summarizes and utilizes the provisions of the Constitution of Ukraine and other legal acts.

The state's interests differ from the interests of other participants in social relations. The former is always based on the need to implement national (political, economic, social and other) actions and programmes aimed at protecting the sovereignty, territorial integrity and state border of Ukraine, guaranteeing its state, economic, information and environmental security, protecting land as a national treasure, protecting the rights of all subjects of property and business rights, etc. The state's interests may coincide fully, partially or not at all with the interests of state bodies, state-owned enterprises and organizations or with the interests of business entities with a share of state property in the authorized capital. However, the state may see its interests not only in its activities but also in the activities of private enterprises and companies.[59] Prosecutors and their deputies file claims to the court in the state's interests, not in the interests of enterprises, institutions and organizations, regardless of their subordination and form of ownership. Simultaneously, given that the interests of the state are an evaluative concept, the prosecutor or his deputy independently determines and justifies in the statement of claim the violation of the state's interests or the threat to the state's interests.

The understanding of the concept of 'interests of the state' provided by the CCU has an independent meaning. It can interpret the same concept used in Articles 131–1 of the Constitution of Ukraine and Article 23 of Law No 1697-VII.

Accordingly, the 'state's interests' cover a broad and not clearly defined range of legitimate interests that cannot be classified precisely, and therefore, their existence should be subject to independent assessment by the court in each particular case of the prosecutor's claim. Excessive formalization of the 'interests of the state', especially in public legal relations, may lead to unreasonable restriction of the prosecutor's powers to protect socially significant interests where necessary (a similar position is set out in the resolutions of the Supreme Court).[60] In court proceedings, the state is the actual party to the dispute, even if the plaintiff names a particular state body as a party to the case.

Additionally, exercising constitutional control over the legislation of Ukraine on the exercise of functions by the prosecutor's office, the CCU noted that the Constitution of Ukraine establishes an exhaustive list of powers of the prosecutor's office, defines the nature of its activities and thus ensures its existence and stability. This guarantees that the primary purpose of the said body cannot be changed, and other state bodies cannot duplicate its powers/functions, as the opposite may lead to a change in the constitutionally defined mechanism of exercising state power by its bodies or affect the scope of their constitutional powers.

Simultaneously, the CCU emphasized that the legislature determines the organization and procedure of the prosecutor's office. Therefore, the powers of the prosecutor's office, including representing the state's interests in court, established by the Fundamental Law of Ukraine, cannot be transferred by law to any other state bodies.[61]

Regarding the powers of the prosecutor's office to represent the state's interests in court, the Fundamental Law of Ukraine contains a stipulation 'in exceptional cases and following the procedure established by law'. According to the CCU, this is due to the prevention of arbitrary interference by the prosecutor's office in the economic and statutory activities of legal entities, achievement of the objectives of the functioning of a party to the relevant legal relationship, fulfilment of contractual obligations, etc. Simultaneously, the prosecutor's office is obliged to justify the need for such interference and the basis for the prosecutor's representing the state's interests – the existence of violations or threats of violations of these interests.

As noted by the CCU,[62] the concept of 'legally protected interest', used in part one of Article 4 of the Civil Procedure Code of Ukraine and other laws of

Ukraine in logical and semantic connection with the concept of 'rights', should be understood as a desire to use a specific material and/or non-material benefit, as simple legitimate permission, conditioned by the general content of objective law and not directly mediated in subjective law, which is an independent object of judicial protection and other legal remedies to meet individual and collective needs that do not contradict the Constitution and laws of Ukraine, public interests, justice, good faith, reasonableness and other general legal principles.

Furthermore, the public interest as an exclusive condition for imposing restrictions on human rights and freedoms is explained as follows:

1. Constitutional rights and freedoms of a person and a citizen may not be restricted except in cases provided by the Constitution of Ukraine.[63] The CCU emphasizes that restrictions on human and civil rights and freedoms are permissible only if they are proportionate and socially necessary.[64]
2. Restrictions on exercising constitutional rights and freedoms may not be arbitrary and unfair. They must be established exclusively by the Constitution and laws of Ukraine, pursue a legitimate aim, be conditioned by the social need to achieve this aim, and be proportionate and justified. In case of restriction of a constitutional right or freedom, the CCU pointed out that the legislator is obliged to introduce such legal regulation that will allow optimal achievement of the legitimate goal with minimal interference with the exercise of this right or freedom and not violate the essential content of such right.[65]
3. Within another case, the CCU assumes that the law was adopted 'to prevent the repetition of crimes of the communist and national socialist (Nazi) totalitarian regimes, any discrimination on national, social, class, ethnic, racial or other grounds in the future, restore historical and social justice, eliminate threats to the independence, sovereignty, territorial integrity and national security of Ukraine'.[66] This is a demonstrative example of the meaning of public interest.
4. Concerning the understanding of the public interest and its impact on the administration of justice under martial law, CCU stressed that the provisions of the Law of Ukraine 'On Amendments to the Law of Ukraine "On Perpetuation of the Victory in the Great Patriotic War of 1941–1945" on the procedure for the official use of copies of the Victory Flag of 21 April 2011 should be understood in such a way that the Constitution of Ukraine defines an exhaustive list of state symbols of Ukraine, which are the State

Flag of Ukraine, the State Emblem of Ukraine and the State Anthem of Ukraine'.[67] Such an example of implementing the public interest concept reveals a link between constitutional review and criminal law.

5. On 31 March 2023, the CCU received a constitutional petition from forty-nine MPs of Ukraine regarding the compliance with the Constitution of Ukraine (constitutionality) of the Agreement between Ukraine and the Russian Federation on the Presence of the Black Sea Fleet of the Russian Federation on the Territory of Ukraine of 21 April 2010, ratified by the Law of Ukraine No. 2153-VI of 27 April 2010 'On Ratification of the Agreement between Ukraine and the Russian Federation on the Presence of the Fleet of the Russian Federation on the Territory of Ukraine'. The grounds of this petition are that the Agreement contradicts national security principles.[68] Although there is no decision, accepting this application for proceedings indicates public interest in these legal relations. It requires a detailed explanation for practical use in criminal law enforcement.

The CCU activities illustrate that the criminal legal understanding of the public/state interest concept is often inadequate for its purpose in specific criminal cases. If it is applied in a manner that does not comply with the Constitution of Ukraine, the CCU, operating the constitutional control, may emphasize this. Consequently, previous court decisions will be subject to review. Therefore, the application of criminal law to maintain public prosecution and protect the state's interest must be consistent with the official interpretation and legal positions of the constitutional control body.

Public interest reflected in supreme court decisions

The Supreme Court is the highest in the judicial system of Ukraine, which ensures the consistency and unity of judicial practice and carries out its analysis and generalization. Ensuring the consistency and unity of judicial practice is a fundamental function of the Supreme Court,[69] which another body of state power cannot perform. There are several examples of public/state interest ideas recognized.

1. By the first Supreme Court's opinion,[70] the claim in cassation proceedings on applying a sanction provided for in paragraph 11 of part 1 of Article 4 of the Law of Ukraine 'On Sanctions' was denied.[71]

In assessing the relevance of the cassation appeal and its admissibility for consideration, the Court noted that Ukraine has the sovereign right to protect its sovereignty and territorial integrity, which is enshrined, in particular, in the Constitution of Ukraine, the Declaration of State Sovereignty of Ukraine and generally recognized international norms and rules. Simultaneously, the provisions of Article 1 of the Law of Ukraine 'On Sanctions' allow the state to apply special economic and other restrictive measures (sanctions) to protect the national interests, national security, sovereignty and territorial integrity of Ukraine, counteract terrorist activities and prevent violations and restore violated rights, freedoms and legitimate interests of Ukrainian citizens, society and the state.

The Court considered that national security is a complex concept encompassing the peaceful and stable existence of the state and its institutions and the absence of real existential threats in the social, administrative and interstate relations. A threat to national security means, in particular, the existence of risks to state sovereignty, constitutional order and territorial integrity of the country, which may lead to the termination of the country's existence or its part.

This decision illustrates the state's approach to ensuring the uniform application of the concept of 'state interest'. It demonstrates that, in cases determined by law, decisions taken by the state in response to real threats to national security may constitute a legal basis for interference with and/or restriction of certain rights, in particular property rights, the right to privacy, the right to access information and freedom of speech. The existence of real threats to national security may serve as a justified criterion for the legitimacy of certain deviations of the state from the general rules (approaches) relating to the operation of the law in time, observance of the principle of legality, the principles of competition and equality of participants in the judicial process, the binding nature of the court decision and may also limit the freedom of judicial discretion.

In conclusion, the main criteria for determining the legitimacy of applying the principle of state interest for decision-making by public authorities are justice (morality), humanity, proportionality, legitimate purpose and no alternative.

2. A second extremely paramount example is when the Supreme Court noted that the phrase 'significant public interest' used by the legislator should be understood as a serious, well-founded interest that is of great importance

for the whole society, certain groups of people, territorial communities, associations of citizens, etc. in a particular case in the context of the possible impact of the court decision on the rights, freedoms and interests of individuals, the rights and interests of legal entities.[72]

This concept covers those needs of society or its groups related to the preservation, enhancement and protection of existing values, as well as the devaluation and/or loss of which would have a significant negative impact on the development of civil society. The existence of a significant public interest can also occur when the subject of the dispute affects the national importance, such as the definition and changes in the constitutional order in Ukraine, the electoral process (referendum), the state's defence capability, its sovereignty, the highest social values defined by the Constitution of Ukraine, etc.

The extraordinary significance of understanding the public interest concept can only be assessed by considering the idea of national interest, which the Constitution of Ukraine provides.

3. The Supreme Court reviewed in cassation an administrative case brought by the head of the local prosecutor's office in the state's interests, a third illustrative example. In upholding the cassation appeal and cancelling the court decisions of the courts of previous instances, the Supreme Court concluded that society is a separate subject of public law relations, which may have its own (public) interests, which are different from the interests of a particular (private) person and the interests of the state.[73]

The Fundamental Law of Ukraine stipulates that public (societal) interests are subject to independent protection and must be considered when making significant decisions at the level of the state or the relevant territorial community.

Public interest is an evaluative concept that covers a broad and not defined range of legal and moral interests that constitute a particular set of private interests or needs essential for a significant number of individuals and legal entities and are ensured by public authorities (public administration entities) following the legislatively established competence.

This concept is not subject to unambiguous qualification (definition), and therefore, the existence of public (societal) interests should be subject to independent assessment by the court in each case. The interests of the state in the field of protection of the right to education of children by creating appropriate and safe conditions for education, which are violated by the unlawful inaction of the defendants, are subject to protection. According to the court, this justification is compatible with understanding 'state interests'. The Supreme Court was guided by the provisions of the Law of Ukraine 'On Protection of Childhood',[74] ensuring the best interests of the child – actions and decisions aimed at meeting the individual needs of the child by their age, gender, health, developmental features, life experience, family, cultural and ethnic affiliation and taking into account the child's opinion if they have reached the age and level of development that can express it.

Child protection is a system of state and public measures aimed at ensuring a whole life, comprehensive upbringing and development of a child and protection of their rights. According to the provisions of the Law of Ukraine 'On Education',[75] the right to free education is ensured for students of pre-school and complete general secondary education – through the development of a network of educational institutions of all forms of ownership and their financial support under the procedure established by law and in an amount sufficient to ensure the right to education of all citizens of Ukraine, foreign citizens and stateless persons permanently or temporarily residing in Ukraine.

Therefore, state authorities and local self-government bodies must create conditions within the limits of their powers defined by law for children to receive education, ensuring its accessibility through, in particular, the proper functioning of an extensive network of educational institutions. This practice is common in Ukraine, so the Supreme Court has repeatedly pointed out the need to study disputed legal relations to understand the concept of 'state interests' correctly.[76]

In sum, the Supreme Court's decisions determine that fairness, proportionality, legitimate aim and humanity are fundamental to applying the 'state interest' concept in Ukraine. The Court also has clarified the idea of 'public interest' as a well-founded state interest of national or societal significance and needs a balanced judicial evaluation.

European Court of Human Rights jurisprudence: Shaping Ukrainian prosecutorial standards

Guaranteeing compliance with the principles of the rule of law and legality in the conduct of criminal proceedings, criminal procedural legislation clearly identifies that the criminal procedural legislation of Ukraine must be applied with due regard to the case law of the European Court for Human Rights (hereinafter also ECHR). This provides standards against which Ukraine's evolving prosecutorial framework can be measured.

In cases such as *Guja v. Moldova*[77] and *Kolevi v. Bulgaria*,[78] the ECHR established that the independence of prosecutors must be balanced with appropriate accountability instruments to prevent subjective decision-making. Although prosecutors require sufficient discretion to effectively perform their function, this discretion cannot be boundless or unrestrained. Ukraine's constitutional reform, which integrates the prosecutor's office within the system of justice rather than maintaining its separate status, appears to ally with this European standard by creating structural safeguards against prosecutorial overreach.

Furthermore, in cases like *Kart v. Turkey*[79] and *Ramos Nunes de Carvalho e Sá v. Portugal*,[80] the ECHR repeatedly stressed transparency and effectiveness of prosecutorial decisions. These match the principles that correspond with the requirement that prosecutors in Ukraine (1) must justify the existence of grounds for representation in court and can represent interests (2) only after the court confirms the grounds for representation. The Court also indicates that prosecutors must respect the principle of equality in legal proceedings, which resonates with Ukraine's constitutional mandate that prosecutors should (1) act objectively and (2) consider all relevant circumstances (3) regardless of whether they are favourable or unfavourable to the suspect. These parallels suggest Ukraine's reformed prosecutorial order generally aligns with European legal standards, though implementation challenges likely remain as the system continues to evolve from its post-Soviet origins towards full integration with European judicial norms.

Additionally, the ECHR case of *Goryaynova v. Ukraine*[81] provides insight into the expectations regarding the conduct of prosecutors in the Ukrainian context. In this case, the ECHR studied its role in protecting human rights while pursuing public interest purposes. The decision underscored that prosecutors must maintain objectivity and procedural fairness even when representing state interests. These principles align with Ukraine's constitutional requirement that prosecutorial activities be open and aimed at achieving increased public confidence. This case illustrates the ECHR position that prosecutorial discretion is necessary and must be exercised through the respect of both individual rights and broader public interest considerations. The requirement in Ukraine's reformed system that prosecutors justify their grounds for representation and obtain court confirmation before proceeding reflects this balanced approach, suggesting progressive alignment with European legal standards despite ongoing transformation from its post-Soviet origins.

Conclusions

By declaring the concept of public interest for application in Criminal Law, Ukraine has been attempting to use the instruments of constitutional control to harmonize the practice of its application in all cases. The public interest should be perceived as an objectively existing set of interrelated interests of society and the state, which ensures the satisfaction of ordinary citizens' dominant needs and corresponds to society's development.

Its content is determined on a case-by-case basis, considering all unique situations. However, such an interest is always associated with the need to guarantee human security in all its dimensions, including preserving human life and health and preserving state and interstate entities that are called upon to provide these guarantees using appropriate civilized legal and other mechanisms. Simultaneously, state policy in protecting the public interest is guided by the principles of a reasonable balance of public and private interests and the perception of human life and dignity as the fundamental priorities of state institutions.

The public interest reflects the aspirations of the whole society or its majority. It is directly related to morality and moral principles that can and should coincide with the national interests and/or cover the local interests of a particular territorial community or social group. The public interest outstandingly replicates the interests of the state itself and all social groups to achieve justice in society as the highest good.

Public interest, both as a factor in criminal prosecution and as a key criterion for opening constitutional proceedings, highlights the complex balance between protecting state/societal interests and ensuring individual rights, as well as the balance that is being played out in the context of the intersection of Ukrainian constitutional and criminal law.

The prosecution system of Ukraine balances effective public interest advocacy with necessary constraints on state power. Regardless of integrating prosecutors within the justice system, human dignity remains the central position in the national security framework. Ukraine has aligned with ECHR standards requiring court approval for prosecutorial representation. Prosecutorial discretion is clearly bounded – protect individual rights while preserving the state's ability to address legitimate public interest concerns. This balanced method assists both justice and democracy by making prosecutorial authority simultaneously operational and accountable.

Notes

1 Constitution of Ukraine, preamble.

2 Constitution of Ukraine 1996 No 254к/96-ВР [Vidomosti Verkhovnoi Rady (VVR) 1996, No 30, art 141].

3 Constitution of Ukraine, art 34(3): 'The exercise of these rights may be restricted by law in the interest of national security, territorial integrity or public order, for the prevention of disorder or crime, for the protection of public health, for the protection of the reputation or rights of others, for the prevention of the disclosure of information received in confidence, or for the maintenance of the authority and impartiality of the judiciary'.

4 Constitution of Ukraine, art 35: '1. Everyone has the right to freedom of thought and religion. This right includes the freedom to profess any religion or not to profess any, to perform religious cults and rituals, individually or collectively freely, and to conduct religious activities. 2. The exercise of this right may be restricted by law only in the interest of protecting public order, health and morality of the population or protecting the rights and freedoms of others'.

5 Constitution of Ukraine, art 36: '1. Citizens of Ukraine shall have the right to freedom of association in political parties and public organizations for the exercise and defence of their rights and freedoms and for the satisfaction of political, economic, social, cultural and other interests, except for restrictions established by law in the interests of national security and public order, protection of public health or protection of rights and freedoms of other people'. 2. Political parties in Ukraine contribute to the formation and expression of the political will of citizens and participate in elections. Only citizens of Ukraine may be members of political parties. Restrictions on membership in political parties are established exclusively by this Constitution and the laws of Ukraine. 3. Citizens shall have the right to participate in trade unions to protect their labour and socio-economic rights and interests. Trade unions are public organizations that unite citizens who are bound by common interests by the nature of their professional activity. Trade unions are formed without prior permission based on the free choice of their members. All trade unions have equal rights. Restrictions on membership in trade unions are established exclusively by this Constitution and the laws of Ukraine'.

6 Constitution of Ukraine, art 44: 'Those who work shall have the right to strike in defence of their economic and social interests'.

7 Constitution of Ukraine, art 4(7): 'The use of property may not harm the rights, freedoms and dignity of citizens, the interests of society, or worsen the environmental situation and natural qualities of the land'.

8 Constitution of Ukraine, art 54: 'Citizens shall be guaranteed freedom of literary, artistic, scientific and technical creativity, protection of intellectual property, their copyrights, moral and material interests arising in connection with various types of intellectual activity'.

9 Constitution of Ukraine, art 125: '1. The judicial system in Ukraine is based on the principles of territoriality and specialization and is determined by law. 5. To protect the rights, freedoms and interests of persons in the field of public law relations, administrative courts shall operate'.

10 Constitution of Ukraine, art 130–1: 'To protect the professional interests of judges and resolve issues of internal operation of courts, judicial self-government is established by law'.

11 Constitution of Ukraine, art 140(3): 'The local self-government bodies representing the common interests of and territorial communities of villages, towns and cities are rayon and oblast councils'.

12 Constitution of Ukraine, art 32: '1. No one shall be subjected to interference with his or her private and family life, except in cases provided for by the Constitution of Ukraine. 2. It is not allowed to collect, store, use and disseminate confidential information about a person without his/her consent, except in cases determined by law, and only in the interest of national security, economic well-being and human rights'.

13 Constitution of Ukraine, art 36. and Constitution of Ukraine, art 39: '1. Citizens shall have the right to assemble peacefully, unarmed, and to hold meetings, rallies, marches and demonstrations, the holding of which shall be notified in advance to the executive authorities or local self-government bodies. 2. Restrictions on exercising this right may be imposed by a court in accordance with the law and only in the interest of national security and public order – to prevent riots or crimes, to protect public health or the rights and freedoms of others'.

14 Constitution of Ukraine, art 39: '1. Citizens shall have the right to assemble peacefully, unarmed, and to hold meetings, rallies, marches and demonstrations, the holding of which shall be notified to the executive authorities or local self-government bodies. 2. Restrictions on exercising this right may be imposed by a court by the law and only in the interest of national security and public order – to prevent riots or crimes, to protect public health or the rights and freedoms of others'.

15 Constitution of Ukraine, art 79, art 104:
– Art 79: Before taking office, the People's Deputies of Ukraine shall take the following oath before the Verkhovna Rada of Ukraine: 'I pledge allegiance to Ukraine … to perform my duties in the interest of all my compatriots'.
– Art 104: 'The newly elected President of Ukraine takes office not later than thirty days after the official announcement of the election results, from the moment of taking the oath of office to the people at a solemn session of the Verkhovna Rada of Ukraine. The President of Ukraine takes the following oath: "I, (name and surname), elected President of Ukraine by the will of the people, solemnly swear allegiance to Ukraine upon assuming this high office. I undertake … to perform my duties in the interest of all my compatriots and to raise the authority of Ukraine in the world"'.

16 Constitution of Ukraine, art 89(3): 'The Verkhovna Rada of Ukraine shall form temporary investigative commissions to conduct investigations into matters of public interest if at least one-third of the constitutional composition of the Verkhovna Rada of Ukraine votes for it'.

17 Constitution of Ukraine, art. 131–1(3): 'In Ukraine, there is a public prosecutor's office, which carries out: 3) representation of interests of the state in court in exceptional cases and in accordance with the procedure established by law'.

18 Law of Ukraine 'On National Security of Ukraine' 2018 No 2469-VIII [VVR 2018, No 31].

19 Law No 2469-VIII, art 3(9)(10).

20 Law No 2469-VIII, art 1(1) para 6.

21 Law No 2469-VIII, art 3(3).

22 Law No 2469-VIII, art 3.

23 Constitution of Ukraine, art 3, art 5, art 6.

24 Criminal Procedural Code of Ukraine 2012 No 4651-VI [VVR 2013, No 9–10, No 11–12, No 13], art 50: '2)The punishment shall be aimed not only at penalizing but also reformation of sentenced persons and prevention of further offences by both the sentenced and other persons. 3) The punishment shall not mean to cause physical sufferings or humiliate human dignity'.

25 'Mechanism for Implementing Restorative Justice Programs' https://www.uaa.org.ua/pub/uploads/articles/about-komitety-presa-mechanizm_v05.pdf accessed 9 March 2025. Restorative Justice https://imip.org.ua/ accessed 9 March 2025.

26 Order on the Implementation of the Pilot Project 'Restorative Justice Program for Juveniles Suspected or Accused of Criminal Offenses' 2024 No 2176/5/501/176 https://zakon.rada.gov.ua/laws/show/z1116-24#Text accessed 9 January 2025.

27 Law of Ukraine 'On Amendments to the Constitution of Ukraine (regarding justice)' 2016 No 1401-VIII [VVR 2016, No 28].

28 Venice Commission, 'Report on European Standards as regards the Independence of the Judiciary: Part II – the Prosecution Service' (CDL-AD(2010)040-e, 17–18 December 2010) para 19 https://www.venice.coe.int/webforms/documents/CDL-AD(2010)040.aspx accessed 9 January 2025.

29 Constitution of Ukraine, art 131(10).

30 Decision of the Constitutional Court of Ukraine (hereinafter CCU) (Second Senate) of 18 June 2020, No 5-p(II)/2020, para 1–2.

31 Law of Ukraine 'On the Prosecutor's Office' 2014 No 1697-VII [VVR 2015, No 2-3, p 12].

32 Law No 1697-VII, preamble.

33 Law No 1697-VII, art 2(1) para 1.

34 Not public, as stated in the Constitution of Ukraine.

35 Civil Procedural Code of Ukraine 2004 No 1618-IV [VVR 2004, No 40–41, 42, art 492].

36 Criminal Procedural Code of Ukraine 2012 No 4651-VI [VVR 2013, No 9–10, No 11–12, No 13].

37 Law No 1697-VII, art 22, 23.

38 Margaryta Bibikova (Бібікова М. О.), 'Роль прокурора у забезпеченні швидкого, всебічного та об'єктивного досудового розслідування через процесуальне керівництво' [The Prosecutor's Role in Ensuring a Quick, Comprehensive, and Objective Pre-Trial Investigation Through Procedural Guidance] (2024) 33 *Академічні візії* https://academy-vision.org/index.php/av/article/view/1364 accessed 29 April 2025.

39 Oleksandra Tamozhnia, 'Представництво інтересів держави в адміністративному судочинстві: особливості та проблеми нормативно-правового регулювання' [Representation of State Interests in Administrative Proceedings: Features and Problems of Legal Regulation] (2020) 4 Підприємництво, господарство і право: адміністративне право і процес 172, 178.

40 Yuliia Turlova, 'Implementation by Prosecutor of the Representation Function in the Context of Legislative Changes' (2018) Науковий вісник Ужгородського національного університету 157, 160.

41 Law No 1697-VII, art 22(1).

42 Criminal Procedural Code of Ukraine 2012 No 4651-VI [VVR 2013, No 9–10, No 11–12, No 13], art 88.

43 CPC of Ukraine, art 3(1)(3).

44 CPC of Ukraine, art 3(1)(13).

45 Prosecution Development Strategy for 2021–2023, approved by the Order of the Prosecutor General on 16 October 2020, No 489 https://zakon.rada.gov.ua/laws/

show/v0489905-20#Text accessed 9 January 2025.

46 O Krajnikova, 'Суб'єкти реалізації функції підтримання обвинувачення в суді' [Subjects of the Implementation of the Function of Supporting Prosecution in Court] (2016) 6 Pravo i Suspil'stvo 193.

47 Resolution of the Supreme Court, 26 June 2019 https://reyestr.court.gov.ua/Review/82885531 accessed 9 January 2025.

48 A Plyuskva, 'Розмежування поняття підтримання "публічного" чи "державного" обвинувачення' [Distinguishing the Concept of 'Public' or 'State' Prosecution] (2023) 7 Юридичний науковий електронний журнал 430, 432.

49 Recommendation REC (2000) 19 of the Committee of Ministers of the Council of Europe to Member States on the Role of the Public Prosecution Service in the Criminal Justice System (6 October 2000) https://rm.coe.int/16804be55a accessed 9 January 2025.

50 N Naulik, 'Прокуратура україни як інститут системи захисту прав і свобод людини, інтересів суспільства та держави: історія розвитку' [Prosecutor's Office of Ukraine as an Institution of the System of Protection of Human Rights and Freedoms, Interests of Society and the State: History of Development] (2016) 1 Актуальні проблеми правознавства 166, 169.

51 Law No 1697-VII, art 23(1).

52 Law No 1697-VII, art 23(2)(3).

53 CPC of Ukraine, art 53.

54 Resolution of the Supreme Court, 31 October 2019, Case No 923/35/19; Resolution of the Supreme Court, 23 July 2020, Case No 925/383/18 https://court.gov.ua/archive/1514873/ accessed 9 January 2025.

55 CPC of Ukraine, art 303.

56 Constitution of Ukraine, Section XII.

57 Law of Ukraine 'On the Constitutional Court of Ukraine' 2017 No 2136-VIII [VVR 2017, No 35, p 376].

58 CCU Law, art 7, art 92. Constitution of Ukraine, art 151–2.

59 Decision of the CCU of 8 April 1999, No. 3-рп/1999.

60 Resolution of the Supreme Court, 25 April 2018, Case No 806/1000/17 https://verdictum.ligazakon.net/document/73763984 accessed 9 January 2025; Resolution of the Supreme Court, 26 July 2018, Case No 926/1111/15 https://protocol.ua/ua/postanova_kgs_vp_vid_26_07_2018_roku_u_spravi_926_1111_15/ accessed 9 January 2025; Resolution of the Supreme Court, 8 February 2019, Case No 915/20/18 https://verdictum.ligazakon.net/document/79687771 accessed 9 January 2025.

61 Decision of the CCU (Second Senate) of 5 June 2019, No. 4-p(II)/2019.

62 Decision of the CCU of 1 December 2004, No. 18-рп/2004.

63 Constitution of Ukraine, art 64(1).
64 Decision of the CCU of 19 October 2009, No. 26-рп/2009.
65 Decision of the CCU of 1 June 2016, No. 2-рп/2016.
66 Decision of the CCU of 16 July 2019, No. 9-r/2019.
67 Decision of the CCU of 16 June 2011, No. 6-rp/2011.
68 Constitutional Petition regarding the Compliance with the Constitution of Ukraine https://ccu.gov.ua/sites/default/files/3_125_2023_utochnennya.pdf accessed 9 January 2025.
69 Law of Ukraine 'On the Judiciary and the Status of Judges' 2016 No 1402-VIII [VVR 2016, No 31, art 545], art 36(1).
70 Ruling of the Supreme Court, 5 January 2023, Case No 991/5572/22 https://reyestr.court.gov.ua/Review/108273593 accessed 9 January 2025.
71 Law of Ukraine 'On Sanctions' 2014 No 1644-VII [VVR 2014, No 40, art 2018].
72 Ruling of the Supreme Court, 5 April 2021, Case No 420/8512/20 https://reyestr.court.gov.ua/Review/96015770 accessed 9 March 2025.
73 Resolution of the Supreme Court, 2 December 2021, Case No 320/10736/20 (Administrative Proceedings No K/9901/37572/21) https://reyestr.court.gov.ua/Review/101608812 accessed 9 March 2025.
74 Law of Ukraine 'On Protection of Childhood' 2001 No 2402-III [VVR 2001, No 30, p 142], art 1.
75 Law of Ukraine 'On Education' 2017 No 2145-VIII [VVR 2017, No 38–39, p 380], art 4(2).
76 Resolution of the Supreme Court, 18 October 2018, Case No 822/3692/17 http://www.reyestr.court.gov.ua/Review/77248378 accessed 9 January 2025; Resolution of the Supreme Court, 5 November 2019, Case No 804/4585/18 https://zakononline.com.ua/court-decisions/show/85493166 accessed 9 March 2025.
77 *Guja v Moldova*, App no 14277/04 (ECHR, 12 February 2008).
78 *Kolevi v Bulgaria*, App no 1108/02 (ECHR, 5 November 2009).
79 *Özkan Kart v Turkey*, App no 24241/09 (ECHR, 31 May 2016).
80 *Ramos Nunes de Carvalho e Sá v Portugal*, Apps nos 55391/13, 57728/13 and 74041/13 (ECHR, 6 November 2018).
81 *Goryaynova v Ukraine*, App no 41752/09 (ECHR, 8 October 2020, final 8 January 2021).

References

Civil Procedural Code of Ukraine (2004) No 1618-IV [VVR 2004, No 40–41, 42, art 492].
Constitution of Ukraine (1996) No 254к/96-ВР [VVR 1996, No 30, art 141].

Criminal Procedural Code of Ukraine (2012) No 4651-VI [VVR 2013, No 9–10, No 11–12, No 13].
Decision of the CCU of 1 June 2016, No. 2-рп/2016.
Decision of the CCU of 1 December 2004, No. 18-рп/2004.
Decision of the CCU (Second Senate) of 5 June 2019, No. 4-р(II)/2019.
Decision of the CCU of 8 April 1999, No. 3-рп/1999.
Decision of the CCU of 16 June 2011, No. 6-рп/2011.
Decision of the CCU of 16 July 2019, No. 9-р/2019.
Decision of the Constitutional Court of Ukraine (CCU) (Second Senate) of 18 June 2020, No. 5-р(II)/2020.
Decision of the CCU of 19 October 2009, No. 26-рп/2009.
Goryaynova v Ukraine, App no 41752/09 (ECHR, 8 October 2020, final 8 January 2021).
Guja v Moldova, App no 14277/04 (ECHR, 12 February 2008).
Kolevi v Bulgaria, App no 1108/02 (ECHR, 5 November 2009).
Krajnikova O, 'Суб'єкти реалізації функції підтримання обвинувачення в суді' [Subjects of the Implementation of the Function of Supporting Prosecution in Court] (2016) 6 *Pravo i Suspil'stvo* 193.
Law of Ukraine, 'On Amendments to the Constitution of Ukraine (regarding justice)' (2016) No 1401-VIII [VVR 2016, No 28].
Law of Ukraine, 'On National Security of Ukraine' (2018) No 2469-VIII [VVR 2018, No 31].
Law of Ukraine, 'On Protection of Childhood' (2001) No 2402-III [VVR 2001, No 30, p 142].
Law of Ukraine, 'On Sanctions' (2014) No 1644-VII [VVR 2014, No 40, art 2018].
Law of Ukraine, 'On the Constitutional Court of Ukraine' (2017) No 2136-VIII [VVR 2017, No 35, p 376].
Law of Ukraine, 'On the Judiciary and the Status of Judges' (2016) No 1402-VIII [VVR 2016, No 31, art 545].
Law of Ukraine, 'On the Prosecutor's Office' (2014) No 1697-VII [VVR 2015, No 2–3, p 12].
'Mechanism for Implementing Restorative Justice Programs' https://www.uaa.org.ua/pub/uploads/articles/about-komitety-presa-mechanizm_v05.pdf accessed 9 March 2025.
Naulik N, 'Прокуратура України як інститут системи захисту прав і свобод людини, інтересів суспільства та держави: історія розвитку' [Prosecutor's Office of Ukraine as an Institution of the System of Protection of Human Rights and Freedoms, Interests of Society and the State: History of Development] (2016) 1 *Aktual'ni Problemy Pravoznavstva* 166.
Özkan Kart v Turkey, App no 24241/09 (ECHR, 31 May 2016).
Plyuskva A, 'Розмежування поняття підтримання "публічного" чи "державного" обвинувачення' [Distinguishing the Concept of 'Public' or 'State' Prosecution] (2023) 7 *Yuridychnyi Naukovyi Elektronnyi Zhurnal* 430.

Prosecution Development Strategy for 2021–2023, approved by the Order of the Prosecutor General on 16 October 2020, No 489 https://zakon.rada.gov.ua/laws/show/v0489905-20#Text accessed 9 January 2025.

Ramos Nunes de Carvalho e Sá v Portugal, Apps nos 55391/13, 57728/13 and 74041/13 (ECHR, 6 November 2018).

Recommendation REC (2000) 19 of the Committee of Ministers of the Council of Europe on the Role of the Public Prosecution in the Criminal Justice System (6 October 2000) https://rm.coe.int/16804be55a accessed 9 January 2025.

Resolution of the Supreme Court, 18 October 2018, Case No 822/3692/17 http://www.reyestr.court.gov.ua/Review/77248378 accessed 9 January 2025.

Resolution of the Supreme Court, 23 July 2020, Case No 925/383/18.

Resolution of the Supreme Court, 25 April 2018, Case No 806/1000/17 https://verdictum.ligazakon.net/document/73763984 accessed 9 January 2025.

Resolution of the Supreme Court, 26 June 2019 https://reyestr.court.gov.ua/Review/82885531 accessed 9 January 2025.

Resolution of the Supreme Court, 26 July 2018, Case No 926/1111/15 https://protocol.ua/ua/postanova_kgs_vp_vid_26_07_2018_roku_u_spravi_926_1111_15/ accessed 9 January 2025.

Resolution of the Supreme Court, 31 October 2019, Case No 923/35/19.

'Restorative Justice' https://imip.org.ua/accessed9 March 2025.

Ruling of the Supreme Court, 5 January 2023, Case No 991/5572/22 https://reyestr.court.gov.ua/Review/108273593 accessed 9 January 2025.

Ruling of the Supreme Court, 5 April 2021, Case No 420/8512/20 https://reyestr.court.gov.ua/Review/96015770 accessed 9 March 2025.

Tamozhnia O, 'Представництво інтересів держави в адміністративному судочинстві: особливості та проблеми нормативно-правового регулювання' [Representation of State Interests in Administrative Proceedings: Features and Problems of Legal Regulation] (2020) 4 *Pidpryiemnytstvo, Hospodarstvo i Pravo: Administratyvne Pravo i Protses* 172.

Turlova Y, 'Implementation by Prosecutor of the Representation Function in the Context of Legislative Changes' (2018) 51 (2) *Naukovyi Visnyk Uzhhorodskoho Natsionalnoho Universytetu* 157–60.

Venice Commission, 'Report on European Standards as Regards the Independence of the Judiciary: Part II - the Prosecution Service' (CDL-AD(2010)040, 17–18 December 2010) https://www.venice.coe.int/webforms/documents/CDL-AD(2010)040.aspx accessed 9 January 2025.

10

The public interest balancing theory in prosecution

An analysis based on Chinese prosecutorial practice

Tang Lanchi

Introduction

Since July 2024, Chinese judicial authorities have fully suspended all practices allowing procuratorial organs to conduct public interest balancing in criminal proceedings. In July 2024, an Article titled 'Building a Just, Efficient, and Authoritative Socialist Criminal Procedure System with Chinese Characteristics', written by staff members of the national legislative body, was published in Legal Application, Issue 7 of 2024.[1] In the conclusion of this Article, it was clearly stated that there is a need to 'study and improve systems such as relative non-prosecution and conditional non-prosecution, and summarize and reflect on the pilot cases of criminal compliance systems for the involved enterprises'.[2] Subsequently, although no publicly issued documents explicitly prohibited the discretionary prosecution through public interest balancing, the judicial authorities, through internal communications, comprehensively prohibited the reform led by the Supreme People's Procuratorate regarding the non-prosecution of involved enterprises based on compliance. Following this, the practice of expanding the scope of relative non-prosecution in the governance of minor offences was gradually halted. Even though China did not completely stop the application of 'private prosecution to public prosecution'[3] in cases of defamation and insult due to the provisions of Article 246, Paragraph 2 of the Criminal Law, in practice, such cases have rarely been seen.[4]

These phenomena seem to indicate that China intends to fully prohibit the use of public interest balancing in the prosecution system, opposing decisions of relative non-prosecution or conditional non-prosecution based on public interest, and not particularly encouraging the use of public interest balancing as a standard for initiating public prosecutions.

However, from a global perspective, public interest balancing is indeed a factor commonly considered in criminal prosecutions in various countries. Looking specifically at the East Asian region, it is common practice in criminal proceedings to use public interest balancing as a standard for deciding whether or not to prosecute. For example, Article 248 of Japan's Criminal Procedure Law stipulates that after considering various circumstances, prosecutors may decide not to bring charges against a suspect. In such cases, the consideration of necessity should inevitably include an evaluation of public interest. In judicial practice, it is very common to exercise prosecutorial discretion based on public interest.[5] Similarly, in South Korea, according to Article 247 of the Korean Criminal Procedure Law, prosecutors can decide not to initiate a public prosecution after comprehensively considering the circumstances of the crime, including post-crime situations. If prosecution is deemed not to align with public interest, the prosecutor may, at their discretion, decide not to prosecute.[6] In Western countries, whether in common law countries like the UK and the United States, or in traditional civil law countries like Germany and France, public interest is considered before deciding whether to proceed with a prosecution.[7] Therefore, given the global trend in the rule of law, which allows for the consideration of public interest in criminal prosecutions, Chinese judicial authorities have no reason to terminate the use of public interest balancing in criminal prosecutions.

Therefore, the reasonable interpretation of the previously mentioned 'suspension' should be: in practice, the public interest balancing approach in prosecutions that had been promoted by Chinese judicial authorities encountered deviations, and it is necessary to temporarily pause, reflect on the underlying issues and then scientifically move forward with its implementation after addressing those issues.

Considering that most readers of this chapter are scholars from outside China, and given the significant differences between China's prosecutorial system and those of common law countries, this chapter will first provide an overview of China's prosecutorial system, focusing on its unique characteristics. In the formal discussion, starting from the scientific application of public interest balancing in criminal proceedings, the chapter will first establish, in theoretical terms, the rationale for considering public interest in criminal prosecution. Next, based on the fundamental theories of public interest balancing, it will analyse the deviations that occurred when Chinese procuratorial organs, in practice, promoted two systems involving public interest balancing: the compliance-based non-prosecution of involved enterprises and the 'private prosecution to public prosecution' system. Finally, on the basis of clarifying the concept of 'public interest', the chapter will discuss the limitations to be placed on the scope of criminal compliance non-prosecution and 'private prosecution to public prosecution' when further advancing the reform of public interest balancing in the future.

An overview of China's procuratorial system

As mentioned in the previous paragraph, considering the intended audience of this chapter, it is necessary to first provide an overview of the operation of China's procuratorial system. In common law countries, since the establishment of government agencies follows the principle of the separation of powers, the procuratorate has been viewed as a representative of the state's prosecutorial interests, similar to police agencies, thus functioning as a broadly defined prosecuting body.[8] Under this system, the procuratorial organ is considered a 'special administrative agency with quasi-judicial powers'.[9] However, in China, procuratorates at all levels are neither purely prosecutorial bodies nor judicial bodies, but rather entities that both check and cooperate with the aforementioned two types of institutions. This institutional arrangement is quite different from how prosecutorial organs and prosecutorial power are defined in Western countries such as the UK and the United States. Without an introduction to the context of China's prosecutorial practice, it may be difficult to understand the approaches Chinese procuratorial organs might take regarding public interest balancing, as discussed later in this chapter.

Following the establishment of the People's Republic of China in 1949, the country moved away from the practice adopted during the revolutionary war period, in which the procuratorial organ was placed within the judiciary. In line with the basic spirit of the Constitution of the People's Republic of China (adopted in 1954), under the framework of the National People's Congress as the national authority, the procuratorial organ was established as an independent specialized agency.[10] Article 134 of the current Chinese Constitution,[11] adopted in 1982, states that the procuratorial organ is 'the state's legal supervisory agency'. Furthermore, Article 136[12] of the current Constitution explicitly stipulates that the procuratorial organ independently exercises its prosecutorial powers, free from interference by any administrative agency, group or individual. These constitutional provisions form the legal basis for the constitutional status of China's procuratorial organs, which have had a systematic and foundational impact on the prosecutorial system.[13]

According to this basic framework, a series of supporting laws, such as the Organization Law of the People's Procuratorates of the People's Republic of China (hereinafter referred to as the 'Procuratorate Organization Law'), have established the position of the procuratorial organ and the scope of prosecutorial authority, thereby facilitating the extensive practice of prosecutorial work. In the study of China's prosecutorial system, the legal nature of the procuratorial organ and the scope of its prosecutorial powers have always been key issues.[14] To understand the reasonable scope of public interest balancing, it is necessary to answer these two questions.

The legal nature of the procuratorial organ in China

As mentioned earlier, according to Article 134 of the current Chinese Constitution, the nature of the procuratorial organ is defined as a specialized legal supervisory body.[15] Whether it is performing its criminal prosecution function or other functions beyond prosecution, it embodies a supervisory role. In carrying out its prosecutorial function, the procuratorial organ, in accordance with the division of responsibilities outlined in Article 3[16] of the Criminal Procedure Law, performs duties such as 'prosecution, approval of arrests, investigation of cases directly handled by the procuratorial organ, and initiating public prosecutions'. This allows the procuratorial organ to fully supervise the actions of the investigation and trial bodies in criminal proceedings.[17] In non-criminal prosecution activities, the procuratorial organ can also supervise the application of legal issues in civil and administrative cases.[18] In recent years, the procuratorial organ has further expanded its supervisory function by directly intervening in litigation as a plaintiff, exploring the initiation of public interest litigation against actions that harm national interests or public interests.[19] According to legal provisions and the aforementioned practices, the legal nature of the procuratorial organ cannot simply be summarized as a prosecuting body or a public prosecution agency; rather, it should be defined as a broader legal supervisory body.

Moreover, this legal supervisory nature is distinct from the legal supervisory powers enjoyed by prosecutorial organs in Western countries. In both common law countries and civil law countries in the West, although procuratorial organs also possess some supervisory functions over specific matters and civil or administrative cases, their organizational systems are generally more decentralized compared to China, and there is no clear hierarchical relationship between higher and lower levels.[20] In contrast, China adopts a system of the National People's Congress, where the legislative and executive powers are integrated, explicitly opposing the division of state powers based on the principle of 'separation of powers'. The legal supervision by the procuratorial organ is carried out as a whole to monitor potential legal violations by other agencies.[21] According to Articles 24–26[22] of the Organization Law of the People's Procuratorates, there is a hierarchical relationship between higher and lower levels within the procuratorial system. Higher organs can issue written orders on matters such as case jurisdiction, substantive handling and personnel assignments, and lower organs are required to execute them.

The basic connotation of prosecutorial power in China

In earlier years, there was a theoretical debate about the nature of prosecutorial power in China, with some arguing it was judicial power, others asserting it was administrative power, and still others proposing the 'dual nature theory'.[23] In recent years, scholars have gradually come to recognize that prosecutorial power should be an independent state power. It encompasses four collective powers: legal supervision over litigation, investigation of misconduct and abuse of power by judicial personnel in judicial activities, initiation of public prosecution and support for appeals and initiation of public interest litigation.[24] These enumerated powers fully demonstrate the essence of prosecutorial power as a supervisory and review authority. In prosecutorial discretion, prosecutors can only decide not to prosecute in cases where the crime is minor, involves a juvenile or concerns significant national interests. Moreover, the conditions for exercising this discretion are strictly controlled by law.

In terms of the organizational structure of procuratorial organs at all levels, China has established procuratorates in each administrative district above the county level. Within the procuratorates, departments are divided according to the types of cases handled. A Procuratorial Committee, consisting of the Chief Prosecutor, Deputy Chief Prosecutors and several senior prosecutors, is also set up within the procuratorates to decide on major matters related to prosecutorial work.[25]

Compared to traditional civil law and common law countries in the West, the distinctive feature of the Chinese prosecutorial system is its clear rejection of the administrative nature of prosecutorial power. It firmly opposes viewing the procuratorial organ merely as the 'major prosecutor' or a prosecuting body, and avoids a 'prosecution-police integration' in its institutional design. Instead, it clearly defines the procuratorial organ as a state institution, similar to the investigative and judicial organs, generated by the state power organs, responsible to them, and supervised by them.[26] All organs are unified under the coordination of the state power organs, with distinct responsibilities, mutual cooperation and mutual checks and balances. The exercise of prosecutorial power is strictly controlled by rigid legal provisions. According to Article 33 of the Organization Law of the People's Procuratorates, prosecutors must report all major decisions to the Chief Prosecutor or the Procuratorial Committee for approval.

The rationality of integrating public interest balancing into the prosecution standards of Chinese procuratorial organs

As mentioned earlier, China currently still adheres to the principle of prosecutorial legality and the principle of prosecutorial discretion. Therefore, integrating public interest balancing into the prosecution standards requires special justification within the existing legal framework. In China, based on existing research on incorporating public interest balancing into criminal case handling, the prevailing theories either focus solely on the substantive criminal law interpretation and application in criminal cases, proposing a balance of interests in the handling of substantive issues in criminal cases,[27] or concentrate on procedural law, emphasizing the 'ripple effect' that may arise from handling corporate criminal cases and highlighting the necessity of incorporating public interest balancing in corporate crime cases.[28]

However, to justify the necessity of incorporating public interest balancing into criminal prosecutions, it is not enough to merely state the need for purpose-based interest considerations in substantive conclusions or to only explain the utilitarian reasons for introducing public interest balancing. A reasonable justification must simultaneously address both the legitimacy of the means of incorporating public interest balancing into criminal prosecution standards and the practical necessity of its intended effects.

The theoretical legitimacy of the means of justification

From the perspective of the nature of state organs, the reason why the procuratorial organ can decide to initiate a public prosecution through public interest balancing is determined by its theoretical position and role in the state organizational structure. Unlike other countries, according to Article 134 of the Constitution of China and Article 3 of the Criminal Procedure Law, the nature of China's procuratorial organ is not limited to being a public prosecution organ. It is an independent legal supervisory organ, separate from the administrative and judicial organs. It exercises its legal supervisory powers through a combination of means such as initiating public prosecution, supporting appeals and issuing prosecutorial recommendations, all aimed at achieving the justice goals set by laws and regulations.[29]

In other words, in China, the function of the procuratorial organ is not just to serve as a representative of the investigative organs for prosecution, but also to actively uphold public interest. The procuratorial organ not only presents evidence to support prosecution but can also proactively collect evidence that may demonstrate the innocence or lesser guilt of the suspect or defendant.[30]

From this perspective, when initiating a public prosecution, the procuratorial organ can, according to legal provisions, determine whether specific cases of insult or defamation involve national or public interest and decide whether to prosecute. Similarly, when deciding not to prosecute, the procuratorial organ is not necessarily bound by the evidence provided by the public security organs. It should actively assess whether initiating prosecution or not aligns more with the needs of national or public interest. When the public interest harmed by prosecution outweighs the public interest harmed by the criminal act itself, the procuratorial organ can decide to abandon prosecution, thus achieving the greatest public good for the majority.

In addition to finding legitimacy in the theoretical division of powers among state organs, rationality can also be found within the tiered framework of criminal substantive law. Today's concept of criminal responsibility has long moved away from a purely existence-based, deontological system with practical implications. It has been transformed into a responsibility system grounded in functionalism. According to the functionalist concept of criminal responsibility, the necessity for punishment does not solely derive from the perpetrator's past wrongdoings but also from another form of necessity: the necessity of punishment for preventive purposes.[31]

Building further on functionalism, crime is seen as an expression of a normative violation, and the purpose of punishment is to ensure that 'through human actions, the norm can be established and proven'.[32] In other words, unlike scholars advocating for retributive justice, who argue that the punishment the offender deserves is determined by the moral worth of the act, scholars who hold a functionalist view of criminal responsibility believe that whether or not an offender should be prosecuted does not depend solely on the severity of the offence or the offender's subjective malice. It also depends on the necessity for general deterrence and the possibility of resolving social conflicts, both of which are, in essence, considerations of public interest.[33]

If the functionalist concept of criminal responsibility is accepted in criminal substantive law, then theoretically, it is entirely justifiable that the procuratorial organ, as a legal supervisory and prosecutorial body, can possess the power to decide whether to initiate public prosecution based on the standard of public interest. When not initiating a public prosecution does not hinder the resolution of social conflict, or when there is no necessity for general deterrence regarding the perpetrator's actions, even if the crime is objectively present, under the functionalist concept of criminal responsibility, the procuratorial organ can choose not to prosecute. Conversely, even if an offence is, in principle, a private prosecution crime, when private prosecution cannot achieve social conflict resolution or restore citizens' trust in norms, the procuratorial organ, according to legal provisions, can initiate public prosecution to achieve the goals of criminal law's accountability.

The practical necessity of the intended effects

From a practical perspective, the adoption of the public interest balancing theory by Chinese procuratorial organs when deciding whether to initiate a public prosecution holds significant real-world importance. Public interest balancing requires the procuratorial organ to comprehensively consider various factors in a case when exercising its public prosecution powers, in order to ensure judicial fairness and uphold social order and public safety. The practical significance of this can primarily be reflected in the following four aspects:

First, as the representative of public interest, the procuratorial organ bears the responsibility of maintaining social order and public safety.[34] By assessing the public interest in a case, the procuratorial organ can determine whether to initiate a public prosecution to effectively safeguard social order and public safety.

Second, judicial resources are limited,[35] and the procuratorial organ needs to prioritize handling cases that pose significant harm to society. Public interest balancing helps the procuratorial organ identify and prioritize serious criminal cases, avoiding the waste of resources.

Third, public interest balancing requires the procuratorial organ to consider various factors in the case, including the social harm of the crime, the personal circumstances of the defendant and the attitude of the victim. This comprehensive consideration helps ensure fairness and justice in criminal justice.

Fourth, when exercising its public prosecution powers, the procuratorial organ must go beyond the prosecution's position and adhere to the principle of objectivity and impartiality.[36] Public interest balancing reflects the objectivity and independence of the procuratorial organ, ensuring that it is not subject to improper external interference during the case handling process.

In summary, adopting the public interest balancing theory helps the procuratorial organ comprehensively consider various factors in a case when exercising its public prosecution powers, ensuring judicial fairness and maintaining social order and public safety. Since other scholars in China have already thoroughly explained these utilitarian considerations in their works,[37] this article will not delve into these practical necessities in detail. Therefore, incorporating the balancing of public interest into the consideration of criminal case prosecution and the decision to prosecute is both reasonable in terms of means and objectives.

Bias in the use of the public interest measure in prosecutorial practice

Theoretically, the process of considering public interest in the decision of whether to prosecute seems to have an inherent legitimacy and does not appear to raise any issues. However, in China's prosecutorial practice, particularly in the reform of corporate compliance and the operation of the 'private prosecution to public prosecution' system, there have been practical problems that differ from those in other countries. Whether in terms of the basis for public interest balancing or in the actual operation of the specific systems, there have been deviations from the theoretical framework.

The lack of clear standards for public interest balancing

In both the decision to transition a case from private to public prosecution and the handling of compliance-based non-prosecution for enterprises, the applicable criteria remain unclear in practice.

Unlike countries that have directly adopted the cheap prosecution doctrine, China's criminal prosecution model is still based on the legal prosecution doctrine, supplemented by the cheap prosecution doctrine. Of the five types of non-prosecution systems established in China, only the relative non-prosecution provided for in Article 177(2)[38] of the Criminal Procedure Law and the special non-prosecution provided for in Article 182[39] of the Criminal Procedure Law may involve the factor of weighing interests.

However, from the content of these two articles, it seems difficult to provide a clear basis for the full inclusion of the public interest measure on its own. As far as the provision on relative non-prosecution is concerned, the law clearly stipulates that the condition is that 'the offence is minor and does not require the imposition of a penalty'. This in fact shows that, although discretionary weighing of interests is possible in relative non-prosecution, the key factor in deciding not to prosecute a person is still that the offence suspected is minor and does not require the imposition of a penalty in the sense of culpability.

As for the special non-prosecution provided for in Article 182, from the point of view of the provisions of the law, how to determine that the repair of the perpetrator after the offence can involve significant merit in the interests of the state, in theory, it is very difficult to measure the problem. And in practice, since 2018, after the addition of this paragraph of legislation, in fact, there is no basis for this article to measure the public interest, the national interest of the case for the offence, this article was eventually reduced to a 'zombie clause'. Therefore, China's existing non-prosecution system lacks a robust foundation in legal provisions to achieve the same degree of prosecutorial discretion as found in Western countries.

Similarly, regarding the substantive conditions for converting a case from private prosecution to public prosecution, the Criminal Law stipulates two criteria: the act must have 'seriously endangered social order' or harmed 'national interests' (which represent public interests). However, in the prosecution practice of the Chinese procuratorial authorities, there are no criteria for determining public or national interests. In exercising their discretionary power to prosecute, procuratorial organs often rely on a generalized and comprehensive assessment, rather than adhering to a set of well-defined standards that could be systematically summarized from individual cases.

'Prosecution to public prosecution' attaches 'too much' importance to social influence

In the process of 'private prosecution to public prosecution', the procuratorial authorities often equate the social impact of the case with the public interest, which in turn directly results in a huge social impact equal to the damage to the public interest.

In the Supreme People's Procuratorate's Guiding Case No. 137 – Lang Mou, Han Mou defamation case, which has attracted widespread attention, the procuratorate initiated the public prosecution procedure on the basis of the following: online defamation is widely spread, harmful and difficult to eliminate the impact, and once it is carried out, it will jeopardize the social order and the public interest, and the procuratorate can of course initiate public prosecution ex officio in the case of damage to the public interest. When the public interest is damaged, the procuratorial organ can of course initiate public prosecution ex officio.[40] That is to say, as long as the defamation behaviour has great social influence and wide dissemination, the defamatory information is known to the public, the public interest will be lost, and at this time the procuratorial organs are duty-bound to transfer the private prosecution procedure to the public prosecution procedure. The idea of handling this typical case was eventually absorbed by the interpretation issued by the highest judicial authority. In paragraph 2 of Article 12 of the Guiding Opinions on Punishing Cyber Violence and Illegal Crimes in accordance with the Law issued by the Supreme People's Court, the Supreme People's Procuratorate and the Ministry of Public Security, the three state organs jointly stipulated the specific circumstances under which proceedings could be converted to public prosecution. In each of these cases, 'serious social impact' is taken as an important evaluation condition.

It is true that, as a general rule of thumb, cases with wide-ranging social impacts are often likely to involve sensitive personality interests and are of immediate concern to the public. However, the general public concern itself does not mean that public interest is involved. In the case of online defamation and insults, take Guiding Case No. 137 as an example, the reason for public concern is often not that it harms the interests of the majority, but that the topic of the rumour fabricated by the public has an eye-catching effect, which ultimately triggers widespread concern. Even if the rumour attracts wide public attention, it is still the victims of the case who are ultimately harmed, not the public.

As mentioned above, it is not appropriate to equate a social impact directly with an infringement of the public interest in practice.

Ex officio with non-prosecution: One-sided focus on local interests

Non-prosecution compliance is an increasingly popular tool used by prosecutors in cases involving corporate misconduct. Compliance without prosecution has been called off at the moment, but before that, the Supreme People's Procuratorate has provided guidance and established concrete standards for effective compliance, non-prosecution and the application of leniency by releasing four batches of typical cases.

Unlike the United States and other Western countries, where criminal compliance adopts the model of 'sparing the enterprise and severely punishing the natural person', China's reform of compliance for enterprises involved in criminal cases has previously adopted the model of 'sparing both the enterprise and the natural person'.[41] Regardless of the size of the enterprise, as long as the enterprise effectively and efficiently carries out compliance rectification after committing the offence, and passes the compliance inspection and acceptance by the regulatory body, the enterprise and the natural person responsible for the enterprise can be granted substantial leniency in punishment or even the lenient treatment of not prosecuting.[42] According to general logic, if enterprises and natural persons can obtain more favourable treatment in the Chinese context, then the standards for compliance and rectification should be more stringent, and the public interest intended to be protected behind non-prosecution or through effective compliance and rectification should be greater.[43]

However, judging from the four batches of typical cases of corporate compliance released by the Supreme People's Procuratorate, the procuratorial authorities around the world, when deciding to initiate compliance rectification and thus leniency for the enterprises involved in the case, tend to unilaterally emphasize the contribution of the enterprises to the local tax payment, employment and economic development of the regions where they are located before they are suspected of committing the crime. When determining whether an enterprise has formulated a comprehensive compliance plan and whether it has effectively completed compliance rectification, the procuratorial authorities often commission third-party supervisory organizations or other specialized authorities and personnel to carry out inspections within a short period of time, and the conclusions reached are often that compliance rectification has been found to be effective. Moreover, the second case within the Supreme People's Procuratorate's third batch of typical cases addresses crimes committed by private enterprise executives against their own companies. In such instances, the enterprise is mandated to carry out compliance rectification, following which the executives may receive lenient penalties. A critical issue arises as this practice appears to seriously violate the general principles that should govern corporate compliance programmes.[44] The reason for the subsequent hasty rectification, simple leniency or even non-prosecution of the natural persons and enterprises involved in the offence is fundamentally due to the fact that the motivation of the local procuratorial authorities at the beginning of the initiation of compliance is to safeguard the tax revenue and economic growth of the region in which they are located, while ignoring other factors that should be taken into account.

Even if it can be argued that local economic development, employment and tax revenues are an integral part of the public interest, the public interest theory of weighing the benefits of not prosecuting should at least be weighed against the benefits of the offence. Without such a comparison and weighing, it is obviously one-sided to conclude that non-prosecution is more in line with the public interest criterion simply by taking into account the economic and employment benefits originally created by the enterprise.

The limitations on the use of public interest balancing in prosecution decisions

The use of public interest as a guiding principle in criminal justice decision-making has become an increasingly prominent issue. In particular, its application to prosecution decisions – especially in a jurisdiction like China – raises a host of questions that require careful analysis. The chaotic nature of public interest measurement, observed in criminal justice practices, has brought to light the need for a stable and consistent framework for integrating public interest into prosecution decisions. If we are to ensure that the integration of public interest in criminal justice is both stable and effective under the current legal system, we must approach this issue with careful thought, respect for existing legal doctrines and a nuanced understanding of the broader legal context. This includes considering the connotations of public interest, the scope of its application and the practical limitations on its use in the criminal justice system.

Preliminary issues: Delineating the connotation of the concept of 'public interest'

At the heart of this discussion is the concept of 'public interest'. This is a concept that has long eluded a precise and universally accepted definition. It is both a complex and somewhat ambiguous term in legal theory and political science. The question of how to define public interest in the context of criminal law does not have a singular answer, and the definition must be approached from multiple perspectives. While criminal law may provide one lens, the definition of public interest must also be understood in the broader context of legal theory, including civil, economic and administrative law.

The difficulty in defining public interest lies in its abstract nature. In some legal systems, public interest is treated as a general welfare principle, signifying the collective good that transcends individual or private interests. However, this general definition raises further issues when applied to criminal law. If criminal law aims to protect society from harm, then public interest may be interpreted as safeguarding the interests of the community as a whole. But what does this mean in practice, and how does it affect decisions in individual cases?

In the context of Chinese law, and particularly in criminal law, the approach to public interest must also consider the principle of the unity of the legal order. This principle underscores the need for a coherent legal system where the definitions and standards of one branch of law do not contradict or deviate from those in another.[45] Therefore, in situations where criminal law does not offer a distinct provision for public interest, it becomes necessary to refer to other branches of law – such as civil law, commercial law and administrative law – to help define what constitutes the public interest in criminal matters.

Legal scholars have historically debated various theories of public interest, including the justice theory, common interest theory and convergence theory.[46] Despite differences in the terminology and specific expressions used in these theories, a common thread among them is the idea that public interest must cater to the majority's needs, rather than the interests of a minority.[47] In other words, a determination of public interest in a criminal case should prioritize outcomes that benefit the majority of individuals in society over the interests of a smaller group or an individual.[48]

This approach is particularly important when it comes to criminal justice, where determining whether an act is in the public interest can help to decide whether or not prosecution is warranted. For example, if a crime results in damage to the majority's interests, this may provide a stronger justification for prosecution, especially if the crime involves a serious breach of public trust or harm to public safety. The key principle here is that, in cases where public interest is at stake, the criminal justice system must carefully weigh the social consequences of both prosecution and non-prosecution.

In practical terms, when prosecutors are evaluating whether to prosecute a case, they must consider whether pursuing the prosecution will ultimately protect or enhance the public interest. This involves assessing whether prosecution will provide greater benefits than abandoning the case, and whether the criminal act has caused harm to the majority of individuals within the relevant jurisdiction.

Limitations on the scope of 'private prosecution to public prosecution'

One of the most significant developments in the application of public interest in criminal justice is the shift from private to public prosecution. In the Chinese legal system, Article 246 (2) of the Criminal Law addresses the process by which private prosecutions can be converted into public prosecutions, a practice that has raised concerns about the balance between individual rights and societal interests.

The framework for measuring public interest in this context follows a 'two-step' process. In the first step, prosecutors must carefully evaluate the scope of the interests that have been harmed by the crime. This evaluation should be based on concrete evidence of harm, rather than a general assessment of the crime's social influence. For example, in cases involving damage to reputation, prosecutors should gather statistics on how many individuals or entities have been affected by the crime. This helps to clarify whether the harmed parties represent a majority of individuals within the jurisdiction of the procuratorate, which is a crucial factor in determining whether public interest is truly at stake.

The second step involves a comparison of the benefits derived from pursuing a public prosecution versus those that might result from private prosecution. In cases where public prosecution can more effectively protect the interests of the majority – such as upholding an individual's right to honour or safeguarding broader societal interests – the transition from private to public prosecution may be warranted. Prosecutors must assess whether the public interest will be better served by taking over the case, thereby ensuring that the criminal justice system provides equitable protection to society at large.

However, the application of this two-step model raises important questions. In some instances, it may be unclear whether private prosecution should be converted into public prosecution, particularly in cases where the harm caused by the crime is difficult to quantify or where the public interest is ambiguous. Some of the cases previously converted from private to public prosecution by the Supreme People's Procuratorate may not meet the procedural standards required for such a conversion, prompting concerns about the uniformity and fairness of these decisions.

Limitations on the application of non-prosecution compliance

In addition to the private-to-public prosecution transition, another key area where public interest considerations are relevant is the practice of non-prosecution compliance, particularly as it applies to corporate crime. As mentioned above, non-prosecution compliance is an increasingly popular tool used by prosecutors in cases involving corporate misconduct. This tool allows prosecutors to forgo prosecution if a corporation agrees to implement compliance measures designed to rectify the wrongs it committed. While this approach has been effective in encouraging corporate entities to take responsibility for their actions, it also introduces challenges related to the scope and fairness of its application.

In order to ensure that non-prosecution compliance is applied appropriately, the scope of its use must be clearly defined. This includes setting strict limitations on the types of cases in which compliance may be considered. For example, corporate crimes that involve economic offences or property crimes may be more appropriate for non-prosecution compliance than cases involving more severe offences, such as those that harm individuals' lives or health. In cases where a corporation is responsible for a major accident that leads to significant harm to people, the benefits of forgoing prosecution are unlikely to outweigh the harm caused by the crime. Therefore, the non-prosecution compliance approach should not be applied in cases where the interests of individuals or public safety are at risk.

Moreover, the decision to forgo prosecution in favour of compliance must be based on a careful evaluation of whether the corporation's compliance efforts can effectively remedy the harm caused by its actions. This includes assessing whether the corporation has taken sufficient steps to address the economic and social consequences of the crime, as well as whether its compliance measures will prevent future misconduct.

The application of non-prosecution compliance has been a subject of significant debate, particularly in relation to its fairness and the potential for abuse. In some cases, companies may attempt to use compliance measures as a way to avoid criminal liability without making meaningful changes to their operations. Therefore, it is essential that prosecutors rigorously assess the effectiveness of compliance measures before deciding to forgo prosecution.

Concluding remarks

Unlike traditional common law countries, China's procuratorial organs are legally defined as supervisory bodies, and they implement the principle of mandatory prosecution. However, with the development of the times, the application of the public interest balancing theory in China's criminal procedure is both legitimate in terms of procedural means and necessary in terms of its objectives and outcomes. In practice, however, three major issues have emerged within Chinese procuratorial agencies: unclear standards, excessive emphasis on social impact in prosecutions and a one-sided focus on regional economic interests in non-prosecution decisions. It is necessary, based on the principle of the unity of legal order, to clarify the concept of public interest as 'the interests of the majority within a relevant space', in line with its definition in prior laws, and to explicitly define this concept in judicial documents. On this basis, China should restrict the scope of 'private prosecution to public prosecution' and the application of criminal non-prosecution according to this concept. During the fourth revision of the Criminal Procedure Law of the People's Republic of China, it should be clarified that only when an offence threatens the real interests of the majority of citizens in the procuratorial agency's jurisdiction can specific self-prosecuted crimes be transferred to public prosecution. Moreover, only when the crime committed by an enterprise is an economic crime or a simple order-related offence, capable of restoring legal interests and making proportionate economic and social contributions, should it be eligible for direct non-prosecution.

The application of public interest measurement in prosecution decisions is a complex issue that requires careful legal, social and ethical considerations. In the context of China's criminal justice system, this issue has prompted significant debate and calls for reform. While public interest should be a guiding principle in prosecution decisions, its application must be carefully limited to ensure that it is used in a fair, consistent and effective manner. The two most prominent systems of interest – the transition from private to public prosecution and the use of non-prosecution compliance – both present challenges that must be addressed through thoughtful legal frameworks and clear limitations.

In the future, the integration of public interest into criminal justice practice should be adjusted, enriched and improved. By establishing clear criteria for measuring public interest, and by ensuring that these criteria are consistently applied across different types of cases, the criminal justice system can better serve the interests of society at large while safeguarding individual rights. This will require ongoing reflection, adaptation and refinement as new challenges emerge in the evolving landscape of criminal law.

Notes

1 Although this article is academic in nature, in China's judicial practice, articles authored by staff members of the national legislative bodies under their official titles often represent the stance of state authorities themselves on specific issues. Even when presented as scholarly papers, the content addressed in such articles can exert significant influence on judicial practice.

2 Yong Huang, '建设公正高效权威的中国特色社会主义刑事诉讼制度 – – 中国刑事诉讼立法历程回顾和再修改前瞻[Building a Just, Efficient and Authoritative Socialist Criminal Procedure System with Chinese Characteristics: A Retrospective on the Development of China's Criminal Procedure Legislation and Prospects for Further Reforms]' (2024) 7 *Legal Application* 3, 12 (in Chinese).

3 The so-called 'private prosecution converted to public prosecution' is a system stipulated in Article 246(2) of the *Criminal Law of the People's Republic of China* for defamation and insult crimes. While these are generally private prosecution offenses, the provision allows procuratorates to initiate prosecution when such acts seriously harm social order or national interests. This system gained prominence during the 2020 defamation case involving Lang and He, where the Hangzhou procuratorate invoked it, highlighting the role of public interest balancing in prosecutorial decisions.

4 As the aforementioned content has not been publicly reported, the relevant suspension directives were communicated internally within the judicial system and are collectively acknowledged by legal academia and practitioners. Thus, the author

cannot provide formal citations to elaborate on this phenomenon.

5 Yongzhong Gu, Feng Xue and Chaoxia Zhang, '日本近期刑事诉讼法的修改与刑事司法制度的改革 - - 中国政法大学刑事法律中心赴日考察报告 [Recent Amendments to Japan's Criminal Procedure Law and Reforms in the Criminal Justice System - Report on the Criminal Law Center of China University of Political Science and Law's Visit to Japan]' (2005) 2 *Comparative Law Studies* 114, 127–9 (in Chinese).

6 Xiaojian Ge, 大韩民国刑法与刑事诉讼法 [Criminal Law and Criminal Procedure of the Republic of Korea] (China People's Public Security University Press 2019) 113 (in Chinese).

7 Jianjian Qi, '域外检察机关不起诉的公共利益考量 [Public Interest Considerations in Prosecutorial Decisions of Foreign Prosecuting Agencies]' (2022) 21 *People's Procuratorate* 63, 63–6 (in Chinese).

8 Hongwei Zhang, '美国检察制度溯源与发展 The Origins and Development of the American Prosecutorial System' (2009) 11 *Chinese Criminal Law Journal* 123, 123–6 (in Chinese).

9 Hongwei Zhang, '美国检察机关起诉裁量权刍议 A Preliminary Discussion on Prosecutorial Discretion in the United States' (2010) 6 *Chinese Criminal Law Journal* 121 (in Chinese).

10 Shuang Xu and Jian Han, '中国检察制度历史变迁之回顾 A Review of the Historical Changes in China's Procuratorial System' (2008) 3 *Legal Journal* 102, 102–3 (in Chinese).

11 Constitution of the People's Republic of China (2018 Amendment) Article 134 The people's procuratorates of the People's Republic of China are the legal oversight organs of the state.

12 Constitution of the People's Republic of China (2018 Amendment) Article 136 The people's procuratorates shall, in accordance with the provisions of law, independently exercise procuratorial power, and shall not be subject to interference from any administrative organ, social organization or individual.

13 Qinhua He and Jinde Zhang, '中国检察制度三十年 Thirty Years of China's Procuratorial System' (2008) 4 *Journal of the National Prosecutors College* 3, 4 (in Chinese).

14 Xinyi Hou, '中国检察制度史研究现状及相关文献 The Current State of Research on the History of China's Procuratorial System and Relevant Literature' (2016) 4 *Journal of the National Prosecutors College* 154, 156 (in Chinese).

15 It should be noted that while this is legally stipulated, in practice, China's public security organs (police agencies) and prosecutorial organs belong to separate administrative systems. Local public security chiefs often concurrently serve as vice mayors or vice governors, resulting in public security officials holding higher

administrative ranks than their prosecutorial counterparts. Consequently, public security organs often hold a more dominant position in practice, and there remains an investigation-centred approach in China's criminal proceedings. However, this does not preclude prosecutorial organs from exercising comprehensive supervisory authority over cases, provided there is no direct intervention from higher-ranking officials.

16 Criminal Procedure Law of the People's Republic of China (2018 Amendment) Article 3: Public security authorities are responsible for criminal investigation, detention, execution of arrest warrants and interrogation in criminal cases. People's Procuratorates are responsible for procuratorial supervision, approval of arrests, investigation of cases directly accepted by procuratorial authorities and initiation of public prosecution. People's Courts are responsible for trial and sentencing. Except as otherwise provided for by law, no other authority, organization or individual shall exercise such powers.

17 However, in criminal proceedings, whether the procuratorate can supervise and inspect the investigation activities of other agencies and their staff is still a subject of theoretical debate. For related discussions, see Yan Cheng, '监检衔接视角下 "制约型" 监检关系的构建Constructing a "Restrictive" Supervision and Inspection Relationship from the Perspective of the Supervision-Inspection Connection' (2024) 4 *Journal of Nanjing University* (Philosophy, Humanities, and Social Sciences) 147, 147–54 (in Chinese).

18 Xiaoqing Zhu, '中国检察制度的几个问题 Several Issues in China's Procuratorial System' (2007) 2 *Chinese Law Journal* 108, 113–16 (in Chinese).

19 Yi Liu, '检察公益诉讼的司法实践与理论探索 Judicial Practice and Theoretical Exploration of Public Interest Litigation by Procuratorial Agencies' (2017) 2 *Journal of the National Prosecutors College* 3, 5–7 (in Chinese).

20 Honglang Li, '英国检察制度评介 A Review of the British Prosecutorial System' (2000) 1 *Law Review* 139, 139–46 (in Chinese).

21 Jun Wen, '国家权力结构与检察制度关系探析 The Relationship Between National Power Structure and Procuratorial System' (2018) 5 *Guizhou Social Sciences* 10, 14–16 (in Chinese).

22 Organic Law of the People's Procuratorates of the People's Republic of China (2018 Revision)
Article 24 A people's procuratorate at a higher level shall exercise the following functions and powers over a people's procuratorate at a lower level:
(1) Ordering the people's procuratorate at a lower level to make corrections or conducting revocation and alteration according to the law, where it deems that the decision of a people's procuratorate at a lower level is wrong.
(2) It may designate jurisdiction over cases under the jurisdiction of a people's procuratorate at a lower level.

(3) It may handle cases under the jurisdiction of a people's procuratorate at a lower level.
(4) It may transfer the procuratorial personnel within the jurisdiction to handle a case in a unified manner.
A decision of a people's procuratorate at a higher level shall be made in writing.
Article 25: The people's procuratorates at lower levels shall implement the decisions of the people's procuratorates at higher levels; and different opinions, if any, may be reported to the people's procuratorates at higher levels at the time of implementation.
Article 26 The presidents of people's procuratorates or deputy presidents entrusted by presidents may attend the meetings of the judicial committees of the people's courts at the same levels as non-voting delegates.

23 For related debates, see Pengcheng Xie, '论检察权的性质 On the Nature of Prosecutorial Power' (2000) 2 *Legal Studies* 15, 15–18 (in Chinese).

24 Haijun Wang, '中国语境下的 "检察权" 概念考察 An Examination of the Concept of "Prosecutorial Power" in the Chinese Context' (2022) 6 *Chinese Law Journal* 262, 278–80 (in Chinese).

25 Xin Zhou, '检察机关内设机构改革的逻辑与面向 – – 权力属性视角下的实践分析 The Logic and Direction of Internal Institutional Reform in Procuratorial Agencies – A Practical Analysis from the Perspective of Power Attributes' (2020) 2 *Contemporary Jurisprudence* 108, 108–18 (in Chinese).

26 Hanming Xu and Hui Li, '人民检察事业 90 年: 发展历程、制度优势及其效能转化 The 90-Year History of the People's Procuratorial Work: Development, Institutional Advantages, and the Transformation of Effectiveness' (2022) 11 *Journal of South-Central University for Nationalities (Humanities and Social Sciences Edition)* 105, 108–9 (in Chinese).

27 Yanjun Ren, '论利益衡量方法在我国刑事裁判中的运用 On the Application of Interest Balancing Methods in China's Criminal Judgments' (2013) 5 *Law Review* 40, 40–7 (in Chinese).

28 Yixiao Mao, '合规不起诉的公共利益衡量理论 The Theory of Public Interest Balancing in Non-Prosecution of Compliance Cases' (2024) 7 *Law Forum* 43, 44–8 (in Chinese).

29 Yi Wan, '论法律监督效能 On the Effectiveness of Legal Supervision' (2025) 1 *Journal of the National Prosecutors College* 102, 103–6 (in Chinese).

30 From this perspective, the comprehensive suspension of corporate compliance initiatives and public interest balancing mechanisms for involved enterprises highlighted at the beginning of the article may raise questions about potential overcorrection.

31 Klaus Roxin, 刑事政策与刑法体系 *Criminal Policy and the System of Criminal Law* (2nd edn, tr Guisheng Cai, Renmin University of China Press 2011) 79 (in Chinese).

32 Günter Jacobs, 刑法归责体系 *The System of Criminal Responsibility* (tr Shuhong Zhao, Law Press 2024) 6–7 (in Chinese).

33 While this functionalist approach to criminal law theory indeed originated from academic propositions by German and Japanese criminal law scholars, the Chinese criminal law academia has fully embraced this concept in recent years as the influence of German and Japanese legal dogmatics continues to expand in China. Given that functionalism's core tenets – assessing the necessity of general prevention and the appropriateness of punishment for offenders – demonstrate fundamental compatibility with Chinese criminal law principles, there exists no theoretical contradiction in applying functionalist perspectives to analyse China's criminal justice system.

34 Lingyun Yu, 检察行政公益诉讼的理论构造 'Theoretical Construction of Administrative Public Interest Litigation by Procuratorial Agencies' (2023) 5 *Administrative Law Studies* 79, 79–96 (in Chinese).

35 Weiping Zhang, '案多人少' 困境的程序应对之策 'Strategies for Dealing with the 'Case-Overload, Understaffing' Dilemma' (2022) 3 *Legal Research* 91, 91–9 (in Chinese).

36 Zongzhi Long, 中国法语境中的检察官客观义务 'The Objective Duty of Prosecutors in the Chinese Legal Context' (2009) 4 *Legal Studies* 137, 137–56 (in Chinese).

37 Fenfei Li, 涉案企业合规改革中的疑难争议问题 'Difficult and Controversial Issues in Corporate Compliance Reform' (2022) 6 *Journal of East China University of Political Science and Law* 23, 23–37 (in Chinese); Yanhong Liu, 论涉案企业合规改革的公检法一体推进 – – 以穿透式激励理论为中心 'On the Joint Promotion of Public Security, Prosecution, and Court in Corporate Compliance Reform – With a Focus on Penetrative Incentive Theory' (2024) 2 *Journal of East China University of Political Science and Law* 6, 6–21 (in Chinese); Yixiao Mao, 企业刑事合规激励模式 – – 以反腐败专项合规为例' Corporate Criminal Compliance Incentive Model – Taking Anti-Corruption Special Compliance as an Example' (2024) 2 *Comparative Law Studies* 164, 164–75 (in Chinese) etc.

38 Article 177: Where a criminal suspect has no criminal facts or falls under any of the circumstances as set forth in Article 16 of this Law, a people's procuratorate shall make a decision not to initiate a public prosecution.
Where the circumstances of a crime are minor and no criminal punishment is necessary or the criminal suspect is exempted from criminal punishment in accordance with the Criminal Law, a people's procuratorate may decide not to initiate a public prosecution.

Where a people's procuratorate decides not to initiate a public prosecution, it shall, at the same time, terminate the seizure, impoundment, or freeze of the property seized, impounded or frozen during criminal investigation. If it is necessary to impose administrative punishment on or take disciplinary action against a person who is not prosecuted or confiscate the illegal income of the person, the people's procuratorate shall offer a procuratorial opinion, and transfer the case to the appropriate authority for handling. The appropriate authority shall notify the people's procuratorate of the handling result in a timely manner.

39 Article 182: Where a criminal suspect voluntarily and truthfully confesses to the facts of the suspected crime or has any major meritorious act, or the case involves any major national interest, with the approval of the Supreme People's Procuratorate, the public security authority may dismiss the case, and the people's procuratorate may decide not to initiate prosecution or decide not to prosecute one or more crimes in the multiple crimes suspected.

Where prosecution is not initiated or a case is dismissed under the preceding paragraph, the people's procuratorate or the public security authority shall, in a timely manner, handle the seized, impounded or frozen property and any fruits thereof.

40 Guoqing Chen, 利用信息网络侵犯公民人格权行为的刑法规制 – – 最高人民检察院第 34 批指导性案例述评 'Criminal Legal Regulation of Infringements on Citizens' Personality Rights via Information Networks – Comment on the 34th Batch of Guiding Cases by the Supreme People's Procuratorate' (2022) 2 *Chinese Criminal Law Journal* 3, 11 (in Chinese).

41 Li Yuhua, 企业合规本土化中的 '双不起诉' 'The "Dual Non-Prosecution" in the Localization of Corporate Compliance' (2022) 1 *Legal System and Social Development* 25, 25–39.

42 Yunbao Liang, 简式合规: 我国小微企业刑事合规新模式 'Simplified Compliance: A New Model for Criminal Compliance in Small and Micro Enterprises in China' (2024) 3 *Law Forum* 92, 92–103 (in Chinese).

43 Hong Li, 企业合规不起诉: 误解及纠正 'Corporate Compliance and Non-Prosecution: Misunderstandings and Corrections' (2021) 3 *China Legal Review* 177, 177–88 (in Chinese).

44 Hong Li, 我国刑法中的单位犯罪规定与企业合规不起诉改革实践 'Provisions on Corporate Crime in China's Criminal Law and the Practice of Corporate Compliance Non-Prosecution Reform' (2023) 1 *Jiangxi Social Sciences* 40, 46–9 (in Chinese).

45 Guangquan Zhou, 刑法谦抑性的实践展开 'Practical Development of the Repressive Nature of Criminal Law' (2024) 5 *East Law Studies* 131, 131–44 (in Chinese).

46 For related discussions, see Wuyang Zhang, 公共利益界定的实践性思考 'Practical Considerations on the Definition of Public Interest' (2004) 10 *Legal*

Studies 20, 20–2 (in Chinese). Xuexian Huang, 公共利益界定的基本要素及应用 'The Essential Elements and Application of Defining Public Interest' (2004) 10 *Legal Studies* 10, 10–12 (in Chinese). Benhong Wang and Zhihong Gao, 公共利益界定主体研究 'Study on the Subject of Defining Public Interest' (2012) 8 *Academic World* 85, 85–95 (in Chinese).

47 Jingguang Hu and Kai Wang, 论公共利益概念的界定 'On the Definition of the Concept of Public Interest' (2005) 1 *Law Forum* 10, 10–3 (in Chinese).

48 Yilong Wu, 如何界定社会公共利益 – – 以 '电梯劝烟猝死案' 切入 'How to Define Social Public Interest – Starting with the 'Elevator Smoking Sudden Death Case'' (2020) 2 *Nanjing University Law Journal* 73, 81–9 (in Chinese).

References

Benhong Wang and Zhihong Gao, 公共利益界定主体研究 'Study on the Subject of Defining Public Interest' (2012) 8 *Academic World* 85 (in Chinese).

Fenfei Li, 涉案企业合规改革中的疑难争议问题 'Difficult and Controversial Issues in Corporate Compliance Reform' (2022) 6 *Journal of East China University of Political Science and Law* 23 (in Chinese).

Guangquan Zhou, 刑法谦抑性的实践展开 'Practical Development of the Repressive Nature of Criminal Law' (2024) 5 *East Law Studies* 13 (in Chinese).

Günter Jacobs, 刑法归责体系 *The System of Criminal Responsibility* (tr Shuhong Zhao, Law Press 2024) 6–7 (in Chinese).

Guoqing Chen, 利用信息网络侵犯公民人格权行为的刑法规制——最高人民检察院第 34 批指导性案例述评 'Criminal Legal Regulation of Infringements on Citizens' Personality Rights via Information Networks – Comment on the 34th Batch of Guiding Cases by the Supreme People's Procuratorate' (2022) 2 *Chinese Criminal Law Journal* 3 (in Chinese).

Haijun Wang, '中国语境下的 "检察权" 概念考察 An Examination of the Concept of "Prosecutorial Power" in the Chinese Context' (2022) 6 *Chinese Law Journal* 262 (in Chinese).

Hanming Xu and Hui Li, '人民检察事业 90 年: 发展历程、制度优势及其效能转化 The 90-Year History of the People's Procuratorial Work: Development, Institutional Advantages, and the Transformation of Effectiveness' (2022) 11 *Journal of South-Central University for Nationalities (Humanities and Social Sciences Edition)* 105 (in Chinese).

Hong Li, 企业合规不起诉: 误解及纠正 'Corporate Compliance and Non-Prosecution: Misunderstandings and Corrections' (2021) 3 *China Legal Review* 177 (in Chinese).

Hong Li, 我国刑法中的单位犯罪规定与企业合规不起诉改革实践 'Provisions on Corporate Crime in China's Criminal Law and the Practice of Corporate

Compliance Non-Prosecution Reform' (2023) 1 *Jiangxi Social Sciences* 40 (in Chinese).
Honglang Li, '英国检察制度评介 A Review of the British Prosecutorial System' (2000) 1 *Law Review* 139 (in Chinese).
Hongwei Zhang, '美国检察制度溯源与发展 The Origins and Development of the American Prosecutorial System' (2009) 11 *Chinese Criminal Law Journal* 123 (in Chinese).
Hongwei Zhang, '美国检察机关起诉裁量权刍议 A Preliminary Discussion on Prosecutorial Discretion in the United States' (2010) 6 *Chinese Criminal Law Journal* 121 (in Chinese).
Jianjian Qi, '域外检察机关不起诉的公共利益考量 [Public Interest Considerations in Prosecutorial Decisions of Foreign Prosecuting Agencies]' (2022) 21 *People's Procuratorate* 63 (in Chinese).
Jingguang Hu and Kai Wang, 论公共利益概念的界定' On the Definition of the Concept of Public Interest' (2005) 1 *Law Forum* 10 (in Chinese).
Jun Wen, '国家权力结构与检察制度关系探析 The Relationship Between National Power Structure and Procuratorial System' (2018) 5 *Guizhou Social Sciences* 10 (in Chinese).
Klaus Roxin, 刑事政策与刑法体系 *Criminal Policy and the System of Criminal Law* (2nd edn, tr Guisheng Cai, Renmin University of China Press 2011) 79 (in Chinese).
Li Yuhua, 企业合规本土化中的 '双不起诉' 'The "Dual Non-Prosecution" in the Localization of Corporate Compliance ' (2022) 1 *Legal System and Social Development* 25.
Lingyun Yu, 检察行政公益诉讼的理论构造' Theoretical Construction of Administrative Public Interest Litigation by Procuratorial Agencies' (2023) 5 *Administrative Law Studies* 79 (in Chinese).
Pengcheng Xie, '论检察权的性质 On the Nature of Prosecutorial Power' (2000) 2 *Legal Studies* 15 (in Chinese).
Qinhua He and Jinde Zhang, '中国检察制度三十年 Thirty Years of China's Procuratorial System' (2008) 4 *Journal of the National Prosecutors College* 3 (in Chinese).
Shuang Xu and Jian Han, '中国检察制度历史变迁之回顾 A Review of the Historical Changes in China's Procuratorial System' (2008) 3 *Legal Journal* 102 (in Chinese).
Weiping Zhang, '案多人少' 困境的程序应对之策 'Strategies for Dealing with the "Case-Overload, Understaffing" Dilemma' (2022) 3 *Legal Research* 91 (in Chinese).
Wuyang Zhang, 公共利益界定的实践性思考 'Practical Considerations on the Definition of Public Interest' (2004) 10 *Legal Studies* 20 (in Chinese).
Xiaojian Ge (tr), 大韩民国刑法与刑事诉讼法 [Criminal Law and Criminal Procedure of the Republic of Korea] (China People's Public Security University Press 2019) 113 (in Chinese).
Xiaoqing Zhu, '中国检察制度的几个问题 Several Issues in China's Procuratorial System' (2007) 2 *Chinese Law Journal* 108 (in Chinese).

Xin Zhou, '检察机关内设机构改革的逻辑与面向——权力属性视角下的实践分析 The Logic and Direction of Internal Institutional Reform in Procuratorial Agencies – A Practical Analysis from the Perspective of Power Attributes' (2020) 2 *Contemporary Jurisprudence* 108 (in Chinese).

Xinyi Hou, '中国检察制度史研究现状及相关文献 The Current State of Research on the History of China's Procuratorial System and Relevant Literature' (2016) 4 *Journal of the National Prosecutors College* 154 (in Chinese).

Xuexian Huang, 公共利益界定的基本要素及应用 'The Essential Elements and Application of Defining Public Interest' (2004) 10 *Legal Studies* 10 (in Chinese).

Yan Cheng, '监检衔接视角下 "制约型" 监检关系的构建 Constructing a "Restrictive" Supervision and Inspection Relationship from the Perspective of the Supervision-Inspection Connection' (2024) 4 *Journal of Nanjing University* (Philosophy, Humanities, and Social Sciences) 147 (in Chinese).

Yanhong Liu, 论涉案企业合规改革的公检法一体推进——以穿透式激励理论为中心 'On the Joint Promotion of Public Security, Prosecution, and Court in Corporate Compliance Reform – With a Focus on Penetrative Incentive Theory' (2024) 2 *Journal of East China University of Political Science and Law* 6 (in Chinese).

Yanjun Ren, '论利益衡量方法在我国刑事裁判中的运用 On the Application of Interest Balancing Methods in China's Criminal Judgments' (2013) 5 *Law Review* 40 (in Chinese).

Yi Liu, '检察公益诉讼的司法实践与理论探索 Judicial Practice and Theoretical Exploration of Public Interest Litigation by Procuratorial Agencies' (2017) 2 *Journal of the National Prosecutors College* 3 (in Chinese).

Yi Wan, '论法律监督效能 On the Effectiveness of Legal Supervision' (2025) 1 *Journal of the National Prosecutors College* 102 (in Chinese).

Yilong Wu, 如何界定社会公共利益——以 '电梯劝烟猝死案' 切入 'How to Define Social Public Interest – Starting with the "Elevator Smoking Sudden Death Case"' (2020) 2 *Nanjing University Law Journal* 73 (in Chinese).

Yixiao Mao, 企业刑事合规激励模式——以反腐败专项合规为例' Corporate Criminal Compliance Incentive Model – Taking Anti-Corruption Special Compliance as an Example' (2024) 2 *Comparative Law Studies* 164 (in Chinese) etc.

Yixiao Mao, '合规不起诉的公共利益衡量理论 The Theory of Public Interest Balancing in Non-Prosecution of Compliance Cases' (2024) 7 *Law Forum* 43 (in Chinese).

Yong Huang, '建设公正高效权威的中国特色社会主义刑事诉讼制度——中国刑事诉讼立法历程回顾和再修改前瞻 [Building a Just, Efficient, and Authoritative Socialist Criminal Procedure System with Chinese Characteristics: A Retrospective on the Development of China's Criminal Procedure Legislation and Prospects for Further Reforms]' (2024) 7 *Legal Application* 3 (in Chinese).

Yongzhong Gu, Feng Xue and Chaoxia Zhang, '日本近期刑事诉讼法的修改与刑事司法制度的改革——中国政法大学刑事法律中心赴日考察报告 [Recent

Amendments to Japan's Criminal Procedure Law and Reforms in the Criminal Justice System – Report on the Criminal Law Center of China University of Political Science and Law's Visit to Japan]' (2005) 2 *Comparative Law Studies* 114 (in Chinese).

Yunbao Liang, 简式合规: 我国小微企业刑事合规新模式' Simplified Compliance: A New Model for Criminal Compliance in Small and Micro Enterprises in China' (2024) 3 *Law Forum* 92 (in Chinese).

Zongzhi Long, 中国法语境中的检察官客观义务' The Objective Duty of Prosecutors in the Chinese Legal Context' (2009) 4 *Legal Studies* 137 (in Chinese).

Conclusion

Public interest in prosecution – from rhetoric to normative frameworks

Rahime Erbaş

The public interest, arguably one of the most elusive yet profoundly consequential concepts in criminal justice, stands as a defining benchmark for the administration of criminal justice in a democratic society. This is a theme underscored throughout the chapters of this edited volume. It provides a normative anchor for the exercise of prosecutorial discretion, helping to ensure that decisions to prosecute or not to prosecute are grounded in broader principles of fairness, proportionality and societal need. In this sense, the public interest test is not merely an abstract ideal but a practical evaluative tool.

Considering the widespread application of the public interest test as a flaw risks overlooking the core issue: it is not the presence of discretion that is problematic, but the absence of clear structure and normative justification. In a wide range of jurisdictions, the criminal process advances through a series of prosecutorial assessments, evaluations and exercises of discretion long before a case ever reaches trial as a public action. This includes, for example, determinations about which evidence to gather and by what means, the timing and content of questions posed to suspects, and the choice of expert witnesses, among other procedural decisions.[1] As such, the authority responsible for assessing the public interest becomes a key architect of the criminal justice process; being the public prosecutor in many jurisdictions. Therefore, understanding the public interest test, constructing clear and legitimate boundaries for its application, and reinforcing its normative foundations are essential for ensuring that discretion operates within a transparent and principled framework.

In 1987, the Council of Europe drew attention to the structural factors impeding the efficiency of criminal justice systems. In Recommendation

No. R (87) 18, it emphasized that delays in justice could not be addressed solely through increased resources. Instead, a more coherent definition of priorities, particularly through the use of discretionary prosecution based on the public interest, was deemed necessary. The 1987 Recommendation complemented this framework by setting out key criteria to guide the exercise of prosecutorial discretion. In line with domestic law, decisions should reflect equality before the law and the individualization of justice, taking into account factors such as the seriousness of the offence, the offender's personality, the likely sentence, the impact of conviction and the victim's position. These elements help ensure that discretion serves not only efficiency, but also fairness and legitimacy within the criminal justice process. As such, the Recommendation underscored the importance of grounding prosecutorial discretion in general principles, most notably the public interest, which serve not only to enhance efficiency but also to reflect evolving societal values and expectations. It is precisely this objective that the present volume has sought to address, by exploring how the concept of public interest informs and constrains prosecutorial discretion in diverse legal systems.

The comparative design of this volume has moved geographically and conceptually from Western Europe to Eastern Europe and then to East Asia. This is because the concept of public interest is deeply shaped by cultural, political and historical contexts, meaning that what counts as 'in the public interest' can vary significantly from one jurisdiction to another. Cultural values, such as the emphasis on individual rights versus collective welfare, attitudes towards authority, trust in institutions and the role of the state, inevitably influence how prosecutors, judges and lawmakers interpret and apply the notion of the public interest. For example, in some legal cultures, public interest may be closely associated with national security or social stability, whereas in others it may prioritize transparency, individual autonomy or minority rights. This cultural embeddedness helps explain why the public interest cannot be reduced to a universal legal formula – it is not only a legal principle, but also a reflection of societal norms, political expectations and historical experiences. Therefore, in a comparative context, recognizing the cultural dimension of the public interest is crucial. It shows why attempts to transplant legal standards or prosecutorial practices from one system to another without regard for underlying cultural and institutional differences often leads to inconsistency or even failure.

Yet, despite these cultural and institutional differences, the book identifies a shared pattern across systems. A striking observation from the book is that, despite deep differences between common law and civil law traditions, as well as between adversarial and inquisitorial systems, prosecutorial discretion in relation to public interest tends to suffer from similar deficits. These include a lack of transparency, limited public accountability and the absence of a principled framework. The extent of discretion varies considerably across jurisdictions. For example, prosecutorial authorities enjoy broad autonomy in Scotland and in England and Wales, whereas their mandates are more tightly constrained in countries such as North Macedonia, Romania and Türkiye. Nevertheless, the core challenge remains the same: ensuring that prosecutorial power, when exercised in the name of the public, truly reflects the values of justice, fairness and legitimacy. As a matter of fact, in some jurisdictions, prosecutors are not entrusted with any meaningful discretion to weigh cases through the lens of public interest at all, as the legal framework either excludes such considerations or severely limits their application. This absence raises further questions about whether procedural rigidity can itself undermine the pursuit of public justice.

This book set out to examine how the notion of the public interest functions within prosecutorial discretion across various jurisdictions, including China, England and Wales, North Macedonia, Poland, Romania, Scotland, Spain, Türkiye and Ukraine. As the chapters have shown, public interest is invoked both as a justification and as a limitation. However, it remains legally underdefined, operationally inconsistent and often normatively underdeveloped.

Chapter 1 by Dinesson asserts that prosecutors are more than mere safeguards against police power, and have a more robust role than narrowly protecting human rights. The emphasis of this function lies in the fact that prosecutors do not only protect human rights from the perspective of criminal law, but they also have important roles when looking at criminal law from a human rights perspective, particularly from the ECHR and International Criminal Court. Former ECtHR Judge Françoise Tulkens notes this as two-way relationship between criminal law and human rights.[2] Still, some also argue that the role of prosecutors (in some jurisdictions, referred to as: 'judge of instructor') as safeguard for human rights in criminal proceedings in continental European jurisdictions may be itself a myth.[3] In view of these discussions, therefore, Dinesson's argument in Chapter 1 is especially noteworthy: prosecutors function as key intermediaries between lawmakers, the judiciary and the public. Although the role of the prosecutor in democratic criminal justice systems is subject to ongoing transformation, the concept of the public interest persists as a foundational reference point in this evolving landscape.

Chapter 1 shows that institutional reforms – such as the creation of independent prosecution services – have not necessarily resulted in greater conceptual clarity or normative coherence across jurisdictions. Instead, it may have a persistent gap between bureaucratic organization and principled prosecutorial discretion in the example of England and Wales. By contrast, Chapter 2 presents Scotland as a jurisdiction with a long-standing yet unchecked tradition of prosecutorial autonomy, not only for decision not to prosecute but also for diverse direct (alternative) measures. Unlike in England and Wales, Scotland has a long-established and deeply rooted public prosecutions system in which prosecutors wield significant authority, with the public interest serving as a key guiding principle in their decision-making. The Scottish example illustrates how a robust discretionary system can be rooted in history yet responsive to contemporary demands for efficiency, fairness, and legitimacy. As Chapters 1 and 2 compellingly illustrate, even under the shared umbrella of the UK, the role of the public interest in decisions to prosecute is approached in markedly different ways in English and in Scots law, reflecting divergences both in normative conception and institutional structure.

In terms of its normative coherence, Chapter 3 presents a typical example of a continental European model of criminal process by illustrating how the principle of the rule of law functions in a democratic state, specifically within the Polish context. It offers a bird's-eye view of the rule of law, its reflection in criminal law, and how it shapes the role of the prosecutor and the concept of public interest in criminal proceedings. As such, Chapter 3 presents the public interest as a key motivator for prosecutorial actions, particularly for the prosecutors. Because the prosecutor's role as an advocate of the rule of law becomes especially vital in situations where a disparity in competencies between public authorities and individuals exists. As such, it is the prosecutor who strives to achieve public objectives while simultaneously addressing the individual goals of the affected person.

In Spain, as discussed in Chapters 4 and 5, reforms intended to promote efficiency and address systemic delays have led to a selective application of opportunity principles, often raising concerns about the dilution of victim rights and the marginalization of public oversight. Efficiency-oriented reforms and the expansion of alternative dispute resolution mechanisms signal a broader recalibration of legal priorities under the opportunity principle. In Türkiye, as examined in Chapter 6, the highly formalized and restrictive approach to prosecutorial discretion, although possibly intended to prevent arbitrariness, ultimately suppresses the possibility of engaging with the public interest as a dynamic legal principle. It reduces the public interest to a matter of procedural formality or to bypass mechanisms such as serial process and prepayment. By contrast, in Scots law, the Procurator Fiscal enjoys extensive discretion in assessing the public interest, shown in Chapter 2 – an authority almost entirely absent for the Republic Prosecutor in Türkiye. Turkish law and Scots law stand at opposing poles of the spectrum in relation to prosecutorial authority over the public interest.

Chapter 7 on Romania and Chapter 8 on North Macedonia offer intriguing examples of legal systems in transition. While both attempt to balance legality with opportunity, their efforts reveal the fragility of such equilibrium. Romania's cautious implementation of public interest as a filtering tool reflects a systemic ambivalence – caught between managing caseloads and preserving legality. North Macedonia, meanwhile, demonstrates the tension between legislative intent and judicial interpretation, where penal policy reflects a mismatch between statutory aims and real-world outcomes. Similar to Chapter 8, Chapter 9 adopts a notably expansive view of the concept of public interest, situating it within broader legal, constitutional and societal contexts. As such, Chapter 9 offers a broader and more nuanced perspective on the concept of public interest by situating it within the framework of international law and the jurisprudence of the European Court of Human Rights. It explores the complex and often contested relationship between public interest and state sovereignty, with particular attention to the Ukrainian context. Chapter 10 illustrates that in China, despite its highly centralized system displays a cyclical relationship with public interest balancing: initially embracing experimental reforms, only to suspend them in the face of perceived excesses in China. This oscillation underscores the instability of the concept when it lacks doctrinal anchoring or institutional safeguards.

The comparative design of this volume moving geographically and conceptually from Western Europe to Eastern Europe and then to East Asia reinforces a critical insight: there is no jurisdiction in which the application of public interest is fully principled, transparent and normatively grounded. Some jurisdictions suffer from excess discretion; others from its near-total absence. Yet both extremes pose risks – to fairness, to equality before the law, and to public trust in prosecution as a legitimate arm of justice. What becomes evident across all chapters is that the language of public interest often serves as a rhetorical veil, masking discretionary decisions that are shaped as much by systemic constraints such as caseload pressure, political expectations or resource scarcity as by legal reasoning.

The volume thus calls not merely for better doctrinal definitions, but for a rethinking of prosecutorial legitimacy itself. If the public interest is to serve as more than a procedural fig leaf, it must be underpinned by clear normative values, institutional transparency and mechanisms of accountability. Future research and policy must focus on developing frameworks that not only limit arbitrariness but affirmatively articulate the values that should guide prosecutorial decisions in a democratic society.

It should be emphasized that this book does not claim to offer a unified model for the use of public interest in prosecution – indeed, its central contribution lies in showing why such a model may be impossible. But it strongly asserts that discretion without principle is not discretion – it is power without direction. By exposing the legal, institutional and cultural logics that shape how public interest is deployed in prosecution, this volume provides a critical foundation for what must come next: a global conversation about how to make public interest truly public.

This edited book rather contributes to filling that gap by drawing on comparative experiences from Europe and beyond. By examining how public interest is invoked in criminal procedure, penal policy and institutional design, the volume challenges both the over-reliance on formal legality and the uncritical trust in unreviewed discretion. In doing so, it calls for a reimagining of public interest as a legally, ethically and democratically grounded concept – one that balances individual rights, social harm, institutional capacity and the rule of law. Future avenues of research and reform might build on this book's insights to further harmonize, clarify and promote the responsible application of the public interest in criminal prosecution across jurisdictions – not only enriching academic and policy debates, but also guiding practical improvements in legal systems worldwide.

Notes

1 See Victoria Colvin, 'The Riddle of Prosecutorial Discretion', in Victoria Colvin and Philip Stenning (eds), *The Evolving Role of the Public Prosecutor: Challenges and Innovations* (Routledge 2019) 146.

2 Françoise Tulkens, 'The Paradoxical Relationship between Criminal Law and Human Rights' (2011) 9 *Journal of International Criminal Justice* 577, 584. For further discussion, see Rahime Erbaş, 'Effective Criminal Investigations in

Combating Domestic Violence and the ECtHR: Prima Ratio v. Ultima Ratio?' in Elettra Stradella (eds) *Gender Based Approaches to the Law and Juris Dictio in Europe* (Pisa University Press 2020) 221 ff.

3 Abraham S Goldstein and Martin Marcus, 'The Myth of Judicial Supervision in Three "Inquisitorial" Systems: France, Italy, and Germany' (1977) 87 *Yale Law Journal* 240 ff.

Index

Page numbers followed by n denote endnotes and page numbers in italics refer to figures and tables.

About the Editor

Dr. Rahime Erbaş is an Associate Professor of Criminal Law at Istanbul University. She has conducted extensive international research in the field of criminal law. Between 2023 and 2024, she was a postdoctoral fellow at Glasgow Law School in Scotland, where she carried out research in Criminal Law and Criminal Justice with the support of the Scientific and Technological Research Council of Türkiye (TÜBİTAK). Previously, she was a visiting scholar at the Max Planck Institute for the Study of Crime, Security and Law in Freiburg (2019), the University of Zurich (2020) and Alma Mater Studiorum – University of Bologna (2023). She also spent a year (2016–17) at Osnabrück University in Germany as part of her doctoral research. Dr Erbaş completed her PhD in 2019 at Istanbul University with a dissertation titled 'Legal Duty to Act in Crimes of Omission' (*delicta commissionis per omissionem*) in the Turkish Penal Code. She earned her law degree from Selçuk University and completed a master's in public law at Istanbul University, writing her thesis on 'The Mandatory Reporting Duty of Healthcare Providers from a Comparative Law Perspective'. During her master's studies, she participated in the Erasmus Exchange Programme at Justus Liebig University Giessen in Germany (2012). She has also taken part in specialized workshops on intervention programmes for sexual offenders, organized by the Department of Probation under the Ministry of Justice in Türkiye.

Dr. Erbaş has contributed significantly to the literature in her field. Her edited volumes include *A Comparative Analysis of Pre-Trial Procedure in Europe: The Search for an Ideal Model* (Istanbul University Press, 2020, with E. Johnston and D. Jasinski), *The 10th Anniversary of the Istanbul Convention* (Pisa University Press, 2022, with V. Bonini) and *Dangerousness and Criminal Justice: Dialogue between Italy and Türkiye* (Pisa University Press, 2023, with V. Bonini and S. Türkoğlu). Further, *Global Problems in Sexual Offenses* (Lexington, 2022), *Combatting Violence against Women from a Criminal Law Perspective* (Volumes I–III, Adalet, 2022–4), *Sexual Offenses from Legal and Criminological Perspectives* (Adalet, 2023, with S. Çakırhan), *European Perspectives on Attrition in Sexual Offenses* (Lexington, 2023), *Restorative Justice Conversations with the Experts* (Adalet, 2024) and *Criminal Prosecution of Domestic Violence: A Comparative*

Analysis (Springer, Ius Gentium: Comparative Perspectives on Law and Justice, 2025).

She currently serves as Section Editor of the *Journal of Penal Law and Criminology* and sits on the Editorial Board of *Women's Studies International Forum*, an Elsevier journal.

About the Contributors

Dr **Aleksandra Deanoska Trendafilova** is Full Professor in Criminal Law at the Iustinianus Primus Faculty of Law in Skopje, N. Macedonia. She holds an MSc and a PhD in Criminal law. She has been a member of the working groups on drafting the Criminal Code, Law on Classified Information, Law on Public Prosecution, etc. She is also a lecturer at the Academy for Judges and Public Prosecutors, a coordinator at the National Convention on the EU, a member of many associations, editorial boards of scientific journals and an expert in many research projects. She is the author of many articles, scientific papers, monographs, books of commentaries, etc. in the area of criminal law, justice system, bioethics, security, etc.

Dr **Kajsa Dinesson** is Lecturer in Law at the University of York. Her primary area of research is criminal law and criminalization broadly conceived, drawing on empirical, doctrinal and theoretical work. Her research to date includes anti-terror legislation and policy, prosecutions and prosecutorial discretion, and questions around criminalization and criminal responsibility.

Çiğdem Dönmez graduated from the Istanbul University Faculty of Law in 2021. She has been a member of the Istanbul Bar Association since 2022, following the completion of her mandatory legal internship. She is pursuing a master's degree in Public Law at the Istanbul University Institute of Social Sciences.

Professor **Pamela R. Ferguson** has held the Chair in Scots Law at the University of Dundee for twenty-five years. She qualified as a solicitor and practised as a lawyer with the Crown Office and Procurator Fiscal Service (the Scottish prosecution service) before becoming an academic. Her research offers a normative dimension, considering not only how the law operates, but why it does so and how it may be improved. This is exemplified by her monograph on *Breach of the Peace* (2013), and her work as one of the authors of the *Draft Criminal Code for Scotland* (2003). Her most recent book is *The Law of Criminal Procedure in Scotland* (2024). She co-authors (with Claire McDiarmid) *Scots*

Criminal Law: A Critical Analysis, the third edition of which was published in 2025.

Dr **Aleksandra Gruevska Drakulevski** is Professor of Criminology, Penology and Criminal Law at the Ss Cyril and Methodius University, Iustinianus Primus Law Faculty in Skopje (North Macedonia). She holds an MPhil in Criminology from the University of Cambridge, Faculty of Law, Institute of Criminology, UK, and a PhD in Criminal Law from the Ss Cyril and Methodius University, Iustinianus Primus Law Faculty. Her research interests include criminology, penology, victimology, criminal law and juvenile justice. She is an author of textbooks, manuals, more than 100 articles, and policy papers. Aleksandra is involved in many research in national and international projects.

Adán Carrizo González-Castell is Senior Lecturer in the Procedural Law Area at Universidad de Salamanca (Spain), where he obtained the BA in Law and the PhD degree with Extraordinary Prize. He teaches on the BA in Law and Criminology, and on the MA in Anti-Corruption Strategies and Integrity Policies, and in Interdisciplinary Gender Studies. He currently holds the position of Academic Secretary of the Centre for Human Rights and Public Policies Research at Universidad de Salamanca. He is the author of more than fifty publications, has given numerous lectures and has carried out several international research stays.

Tang Lanchi is a PhD Candidate in Law at Tsinghua University (commencing 2025), building upon an academic foundation that includes a Bachelor of Law degree from Zhongnan University of Economics and Law and a Master of Law from Tsinghua University, China. His research specializes in Criminal Law Dogmatics, China's Procuratorial System, Duty-Related Crimes and Economic Crimes. He has authored two peer-reviewed journal articles, one of which is indexed in the prestigious PKU Core Journals List.

Cristian Dumitru Miheș is an Associate Professor at Faculty of Law – University of Oradea, Romania, presently – Dean of the Faculty. His teaching subjects are Criminal and Forensic Sciences, Criminal Law (BA Level); the Influence of New Technologies on Administration of Justice (BA Level), European Criminal Law; AI and Criminal Sciences (LLM level).

Dr Miheş attended specialization courses on topics of International and European Criminal Law organized by The International Institute of Higher Studies in Criminal Science (ISISC) & University of Palermo – Faculty of Law – Siracusa, Italy, (2005–2007) and, respectively on topics of *'The life cycle of e-evidence: handling e-evidence in child sex abuse material' (2108), Artificial Intelligence and Criminal Justice (2019)* and *'Computer Forensics in Legal Proceedings'* (2020) organized by The Academy of European Law, Trier, Germany.

He was involved in several projects, among them: ALPhA – *'Auswirkungen der Liberalisierung des Internethandels in Europa auf den Phänomenbereich der Arzneimittelkriminalität'* University of Osnabrück (Germany) (2014–16); Compliance Assessment of Framework Decision 2008/947/JHA; HUUNIMISKOLCPFI (2018–19) and EUINVESTIGUNIMISKOLC (2021–2022) – University of Miskolc (Hungary); 'European challenges, Central-Eastern European responses in the Criminal science of the 21st century', Universitatea din Miskolc, Ungaria, Expert – Romania, 2021–2022;'Comparative Research Platform 2023' – '*Efficency of Justice – Research team Group*' beneficiar Institute of Justice (Instytut Wymiaru Sprawiedliwości) Varşovia, Polonia, Expert – Romania, 2023; 'The rights of the child in public law – Central European comparative perspective', Beneficiar: Central European Academy, Budapest, Hungary, Expert – Romania, 2023–2024; Further, he is Attorney at Law since 2007.

Bartłomiej Oręziak is an Assistant Professor at the Faculty of Law and Administration of the Cardinal Stefan Wyszyński University in Warsaw, PhD in legal sciences, former Council of Europe expert (TJENI), Coordinator of the Center for Strategic Analysis of Institute of Justice in Warsaw (2019–2024), member of the Management Team of the Polish-Hungarian Professors Network, former researcher in the Central European Professors' Network 2021, 2022 and 2023, researcher in the Central European Professors' Network 2024, laureate of the Minister of Science and Higher Education Scholarship for outstanding achievements in science for the academic year 2017/18, winner of the DOCUP 2020 competition, member of the Artificial Intelligence Working Group at the Chancellery of the President Council of Ministers, reviewer of project proposal in Maynooth University (Innovation Value Institute), author of over fifty scientific texts. He is or was a head and member of international and national research projects, as well as a speaker and organizer of international and national scientific conferences. He won third place (PolOn team) in Hackathon 'Pioneering Digital

Solutions for Human Rights in Justice' organized by the Council of Europe in Paris. Main interests: new technologies law, human rights protection, intellectual property law, public international law, EU law and criminal law and trial.

Dr **Hüseyin Şık** is a jurist who graduated from Marmara University Faculty of Law, earning his master's and doctorate degrees. He completed his PhD thesis on 'Public Prosecution Service within Turkish Judiciary System'. He began his career as a public prosecutor in 2007 and was appointed as judge to the General Directorate of Prisons and Detention Houses/MoJ/Türkiye in 2015. He played a key role in international penal projects within the Foreign Relations Department. In 2021, he was appointed Head of Rehabilitation and Reintegration, and in 2024, Head of the Probation Department. Dr Şık has presented on radicalization and terrorism at international conferences and has authored books and peer-reviewed articles on criminal law.

Selena Tierno Barrios is a Postdoctoral Researcher (POP) within the Procedural Law Area at Universidad de Salamanca (Spain), where she obtained the PhD Degree with international mention and Extraordinary Prize in 2024, through a contract obtained through the Spanish Ministry of Universities' FPU (training for university teachers) programme. She holds a BA in Law from Universidad de Salamanca in 2018, and an MA in Access to the Legal Profession from Universidad Nacional de Educación a Distancia (Spain) in 2020, with an award for the best Master's Thesis in 2022. She is the author of multiple publications in publishers and journals of impact, participating in several research projects.

Mihail Udroiu is an Associate Professor at Faculty of Law – University of Oradea, Romania. His teaching subjects are Criminal Procedure Law (BA Level); Criminal Procedure Law. Current issues of theory and practice (LLM Level), Influence of ECHR decisions in criminal matters (LLM level). He is also a Judge in the Criminal Division of the High Court of Cassation and Justice, Bucharest, Romania. He has been involved in several large-scale drafting projects in criminal matters. Thus, Dr Udroiu was Member of the Commission for the preparation of the draft Law for the implementation of the Criminal Procedure Code and for the amendment and completion of some normative acts containing criminal procedural provisions; Member of the Commission for the elaboration of the draft Law for the implementation of the Criminal Code and for the modification and completion of some normative acts containing penal provisions; member of the Commission for the drafting of the new Penal Code and member of the Commission for the drafting of the new Code of Criminal Procedure.

Marcin Wielec is a Professor at the Cardinal Wyszyński University in Warsaw. Currently, at this Faculty, he is also Vice-Dean for Student Affairs in the field of 'Law', as well as 'Man in Cyberspace' and the Head of the Department of Criminal Procedure of the Faculty of Law and Administration of the Cardinal Stefan Wyszyński University in Warsaw. Head of the Institute of Justice in Warsaw (2019– 2024). Member of many programme bodies of scientific journals in Poland and abroad. Member of the Central European Professor Network, co-founder of an international research project called the Polish-Hungarian Research Platform conducted by the Institute of Justice in Warsaw, President of the Polish Association of Comparative Law and Vice-President of the Central European Association of Comparative Law based in Miskolc (Hungary). Promoter at an international doctoral school. Author of many scientific studies in the field of criminal law and procedure, disciplinary law and proceedings, executive criminal law, axiology of law, etc. He was TJENI (Foster Transparency of Judicial Decisions and Enhancing the National Implementation of the ECHR – Project within Council of Europe) expert. He was awarded by Hungarian President with the Hungarian Order of Merit.

Dr **Larysa Zhdankina** is an Associate Professor at the Interregional Academy of Personnel Management (Ukraine) and a Research Fellow at the Scottish Council on Global Affairs (UK). She is currently a Visiting Academic at the School of Law, University of Glasgow, where she collaborates on interdisciplinary projects in constitutional law, international law, and transitional justice. Dr Zhdankina is also a guest lecturer at the University of Strathclyde and the University of Liverpool, contributing to comparative public law and European legal studies. Her current research explores the role of judicial review and constitutional oversight in Ukraine's dual transformation process – simultaneously pursuing EU integration and post-war legal reconstruction. Dr Zhdankina is a Ukrainian-qualified attorney and a member of the Ukrainian National Bar Association. She serves as an expert to the Constitutional Court of Ukraine and formerly held a research position at the Institute of Legislation of the Verkhovna Rada (Parliament) of Ukraine, contributing to constitutional development and legal reform in Ukraine. She has received the Honorary Award of the Constitutional Court of Ukraine (2021) and the 3rd Degree Honorary Award of the National

Association of Advocates of Ukraine (2023), and was nominated for the Inspirational UK Women in Law Awards as Humanitarian Lawyer of the Year (2023).

www.ingramcontent.com/pod-product-compliance
Ingram Content Group UK Ltd.
Pitfield, Milton Keynes, MK11 3LW, UK
UKHW020217290926
15470UKWH00001B/244

9 798216 380542